ROADMAP B1

STUDENTS' BOOK
with digital resources and mobile app

Heather Jones, Monica Berlis

Contents

FAST-TRACK ROUTE

MAIN LESSON		GRAMMAR/FUNCTION	VOCABULARY	PRONUNCIATION	SPEAKING GOAL
UNIT 1	**page 6**				
1A	Profiles page 6	present simple and present continuous	personal details	*do you*	get to know someone
1B	Life maps page 8	*be going to* and present continuous	personal characteristics	*-ing*	describe future plans and arrangements
1C	What next? page 10	*will* for prediction	describing change	*will/won't*	make predictions about the future
1D	English in action page 12	make and respond to suggestions			make and respond to suggestions
Check and reflect page 13 — Go online for the Roadmap video.					
UNIT 2	**page 14**				
2A	What happened? page 14	past simple and past continuous	describing feelings and events	weak forms	describe past experiences
2B	Memories page 16	*used to*	memories	*used to*	talk about memories
2C	Culture shock page 18	*so/such ... that; too ... to; not ... enough to*	feelings and reactions	*so/such*	describe a new experience
2D	English in action page 20	show interest in a conversation			show interest in a conversation
Check and reflect page 21 — Go online for the Roadmap video.					
Communication game: First to finish! (Units 1-2) page 146					
UNIT 3	**page 22**				
3A	Bucket lists page 22	present perfect and past simple	experiences	contractions	talk about experiences
3B	Catching up page 24	present perfect continuous and present perfect simple	keeping in touch/ catching up	weak forms	talk about what you've been doing recently
3C	My kind of town page 26	articles	features of a town	articles	talk about a favourite town, city or neighbourhood
3D	English in action page 28	ask for, follow and give directions			ask for, follow and give directions
Check and reflect page 29 — Go online for the Roadmap video.					
UNIT 4	**page 30**				
4A	The internet generation page 30	comparatives	lifestyles	weak forms	discuss and compare lifestyles
4B	Popular brands page 32	superlatives	products and services	stressed syllables; *most*	express preferences about brands
4C	Favourite films page 34	defining relative clauses	types of film	stressed syllables; *which/that*	describe the plot of a film
4D	English in action page 36	ask for and give opinions			ask for and give opinions
Check and reflect page 37 — Go online for the Roadmap video.					
Communication game: True or False (Units 3-4 review) page 147					
UNIT 5	**page 38**				
5A	How does it look? page 38	modal verbs: possibility and deduction	describing clothes and appearance	contractions	make guesses about people
5B	Living space page 40	zero and first conditional	places to live	contractions	discuss advantages and disadvantages
5C	Eating well page 42	quantifiers	describing food	weak forms	plan a special occasion
5D	English in action page 44	give instructions and ask for information			give instructions and ask for information
Check and reflect page 45 — Go online for the Roadmap video.					

EXTENDED ROUTE

DEVELOP YOUR SKILLS LESSON	GOAL	FOCUS
1A Develop your reading page 86	understand an article	reading for general understanding
1B Develop your writing page 87	write a job application	using paragraphs in a job application
1C Develop your listening page 88	understand a podcast	recognising positive and negative attitudes
2A Develop your reading page 89	understand a news story	reading for specific information
2B Develop your writing page 90	write an essay	writing paragraphs
2C Develop your listening page 91	understand an interview	understanding linkers
3A Develop your reading page 92	understand adverts	recognising similar ideas
3B Develop your listening page 93	understand a conversation	understanding discourse markers
3C Develop your writing page 94	write a guide	planning a piece of writing
4A Develop your listening page 95	understand a radio programme	predicting information
4B Develop your writing page 96	write a biography	using linkers
4C Develop your reading page 97	understand a magazine article	understanding paragraph structure
5A Develop your writing page 98	write a personal email	using informal words and expressions
5B Develop your reading page 99	understand a factual article	guessing unknown words
5C Develop your listening page 100	understand announcements	listening for specific information

Contents

FAST-TRACK ROUTE

MAIN LESSON	GRAMMAR/FUNCTION	VOCABULARY	PRONUNCIATION	SPEAKING GOAL
UNIT 6 page 46				
6A Life without … page 46	second conditional	everyday activities	contractions	discuss hypothetical situations
6B A difficult choice page 48	structures for giving advice	describing bad behaviour and crime	connected speech	ask for and give advice
6C Take action! page 50	question tags	environmental issues	intonation in question tags	plan a campaign
6D English in action page 52	make and respond to requests			make and respond to requests
Check and reflect page 53 Go online for the Roadmap video.				
Communication game: Cross the lake (Units 5–6 review) page 148				
UNIT 7 page 54				
7A New skills page 54	modal verbs: ability	skills and abilities	weak forms	discuss study options
7B Life events page 56	past perfect	milestones	contractions	talk about life events
7C Trip of a lifetime page 58	expressing purpose	outdoor equipment	weak forms	decide what to take on a trip
7D English in action page 60	ask for information			ask for information
Check and reflect page 61 Go online for the Roadmap video.				
UNIT 8 page 62				
8A Changing rules page 62	modal verbs: obligation and necessity	multi-word verbs	contractions	talk about rules
8B Who says I can't? page 64	passives: present and past	comment adverbs	weak forms	talk about someone's life
8C Natural world page 66	non-defining relative clauses	geographical features	*wh-*	describe and recommend places
8D English in action page 68	make excuses and apologise			make excuses and apologise
Check and reflect page 69 Go online for the Roadmap video.				
Communication game: Roadmap race (Units 7–8 review) page 149				
UNIT 9 page 70				
9A Shopping page 70	the passive: all tenses	shopping	word stress	discuss and suggest improvements
9B What if …? page 72	third conditional	strong and weak adjectives	contractions	tell a story
9C Is it art? page 74	short responses with *so, neither/nor, too/either*	describing art	connected speech	express agreement and disagreement
9D English in action page 76	make complaints			make complaints
Check and reflect page 77 Go online for the Roadmap video.				
UNIT 10 page 78				
10A Education page 78	reported statements	education	contractions	report opinions
10B Green cities page 80	verb patterns	suggestions and improvements	weak forms	talk about improving your town or city
10C What's in a job? page 82	reported questions	work activities	intonation in direct and reported questions	report the results of a survey
10D English in action page 84	ask and answer interview questions			ask and answer interview questions
Check and reflect page 85 Go online for the Roadmap video.				
Communication game: Keep talking (Units 9–10 review) page 150				

Grammar bank page 116   Vocabulary bank page 136   Communication bank page 151   Irregular verbs page 160

EXTENDED ROUTE

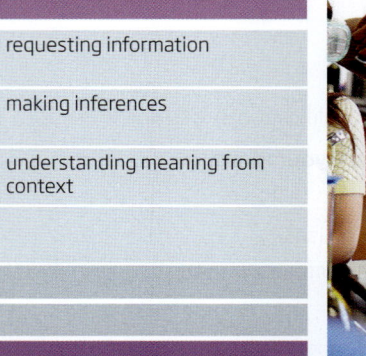

DEVELOP YOUR SKILLS LESSON	GOAL	FOCUS
6A Develop your listening page 101	understand a short talk	identifying the stages of a talk
6B Develop your reading page 102	understand a magazine article	understanding linkers
6C Develop your writing page 103	write a for and against essay	organising ideas
7A Develop your writing page 104	write short notices	engaging a reader
7B Develop your reading page 105	understand a magazine article	understanding the sequence of events
7C Develop your listening page 106	understand a presentation	listening for specific information
8A Develop your writing page 107	write a short email	adding and contrasting ideas
8B Develop your listening page 108	understand a radio phone-in programme	guessing the meaning of unknown words
8C Develop your reading page 109	understand a brochure	understanding reference
9A Develop your reading page 110	understand a short article	recognising degrees of certainty
9B Develop your writing page 111	write a story	making comparisons
9C Develop your listening page 112	understand a radio discussion	recognising a speaker's opinions
10A Develop your writing page 113	write an email asking for information	requesting information
10B Develop your reading page 114	understand an article	making inferences
10C Develop your listening page 115	understand short conversations	understanding meaning from context

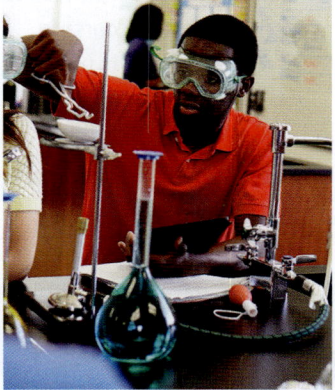

5

1A Profiles

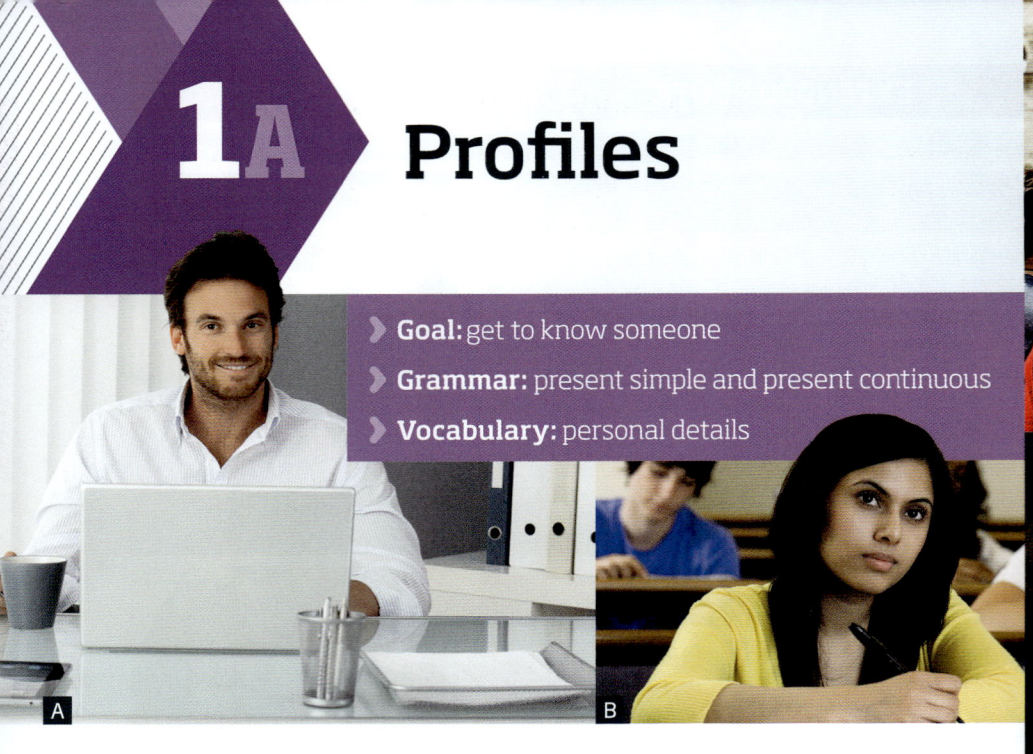

> **Goal:** get to know someone
> **Grammar:** present simple and present continuous
> **Vocabulary:** personal details

Reading and vocabulary

1 **Look at the photos. What do you think the people do? What are they doing in the photos?**

2 a **Read the profiles. Match them with photos A–D.**

  b **Read the profiles again and answer the questions.**
   1 What does each person do?
   2 Where do they come from?
   3 What do they like doing in their free time?
   4 Why are they learning English?

3 a **Match the verbs in the box with phrases 1–8. There may be more than one possible answer.**

do   get   have   pass   run   study   take   train   work

   1 *do/take* a course in   5 your own company
   2 a degree/qualification in 6 for a company/myself
   3 an exam   7 for a degree/qualification
   4 as a tour guide   8 part time/full time

  b **Correct the information in each sentence.**
   1 Sofia is a qualified tour guide.
   2 She's taking a course in Spanish.
   3 Xavier works part time.
   4 Rafael is doing a degree in engineering.
   5 Esma is training to be a scientist.
   6 She's studying English for her job.

4 a **Complete the sentences with your own ideas.**
   1 I'd like to do a course in …
   2 It was difficult to pass …
   3 I'd like to train …
   4 Someone I know has a qualification in …

  b **Work in pairs and compare your ideas.**

5 **Discuss the questions.**
   1 Why are you studying English?
   2 Do you have anything in common with the people in the profiles?

Go to page 136 or your app for more vocabulary and practice.

Name: *Sofia Bianchi*
Occupation: I'm training as a tour guide here in Rome. I want to get a qualification in tourism.
About: In my free time, I love eating out with my boyfriend. I'm taking this course in English because I want to improve my speaking skills.

Name: *Xavier Lopez*
Occupation: I'm a qualified accountant and I run my own company. I work full time and I enjoy working for myself.
About: I come from Bilbao, but right now I'm living in Madrid. My wife is doing a degree in economics here. In my spare time, I volunteer for a local charity. I like helping people. I am studying English because I need it for my job.

Name: *Rafael Silva*
Occupation: I have a degree in civil engineering and I work for a multi-national company.
About: I'm from Macae in Brazil. I usually listen to music in my spare time. I'm a big fan of rock music. I'm studying English because I often have to travel abroad for work. My wife works full time teaching English and she's helping me. I have to take my exam soon! I hope I pass it.

Name: *Esma Sadik*
Occupation: At the moment I'm studying for a degree in environmental science.
About: I'm from Ankara in Turkey. I like reading in my free time and I'm trying to read books in English. I'm studying English because I need to pass an exam before I can graduate from university. I work part time to help pay for my studies.

Listening

6 a 🔊 **1.1** Sonya and Pierre are starting an English class at a language school. Listen to their conversation. Which question don't they ask?
1 Where are you from?
2 What do you do?
3 Do you enjoy your job?
4 Why are you studying English?
5 Do you like travelling?
6 What do you usually do in your free time?

b Listen again and complete the sentences. Who says each sentence, Sonya (S) or Pierre (P)?
1 I usually _____ from home, but right now I _____ on site for a local company.
2 I _____ my job most of the time ... but I _____ it at the moment!
3 At the moment, I _____ for a teaching qualification ... I really _____ children.
4 Right now, I _____ part time in a local school.
5 And after I graduate, I _____ to get a job abroad.
6 I often _____ for foreign companies.
7 I _____ to play the guitar at the moment.
8 I _____ tennis every weekend.
9 I _____ much sport. I _____ watching it on TV!

Grammar

7 Read the grammar box and choose the correct alternatives.

Present simple and present continuous

Use the ¹*present simple/present continuous*:
- to talk about habits and routines or repeated actions, often with adverbs of frequency like *usually*, *often* and *sometimes*.
  I **usually listen** to music.
- for permanent situations.
  I **come from** (Bilbao).
  I **run** my own company.

Use the ²*present simple/present continuous* to talk about actions at the present moment, happening around now and temporary situations, often with *at the moment* and *right now*.
I'm studying for a degree.
My wife **is doing** a degree **at the moment**.

Some verbs almost always use ³*simple/continuous* forms, for example, *have/have got, like, love, hate, prefer, hear, see, know, want*.
He**'s got/has** a degree in civil engineering.
She **wants** to get a job abroad.

8 a 🔊 **1.2** Listen and notice the pronunciation of *do you*.
1 Where do you live?
2 What do you do?
3 What university do you go to?
4 Do you like sport?

b Listen again and repeat.

9 Choose the correct alternatives.

A I'm in my first year at university and I ¹*like/am liking* it very much. I ²*share/am sharing* a flat with another student this term. Xavier ³*comes/is coming* from Spain and he ⁴*learns/is learning* English like me. He ⁵*wants/is wanting* to be a tour guide.

B I can't find a job so I ⁶*don't work/am not working* right now. I ⁷*live/am living* with my parents because I can't afford my own flat. They ⁸*live/are living* in the country and there's not much to do! My father ⁹*tries/is trying* to get me a work experience job in his office.

10 a Make questions using the prompts.
1 where / you / come / from?
  Where do you come from?
2 what / you / do / at work (or university) / at the moment?
3 you / usually / enjoy / your work (or studies)?
4 you / take / any other courses / at the moment?
5 you / study / for any exams?
6 where / you / usually / go / on holiday?

b Work in pairs. Ask and answer the questions.

📱 Go to page 116 or your app for more information and practice.

Speaking

PREPARE

11 You're going to introduce a classmate you don't know well to the rest of the class. First, write some questions to ask your partner. Think about these topics:
- work and study
- family
- travel
- interests and hobbies
- reasons for learning English
- home (city/area)

SPEAK

12 a Work in pairs. Ask and answer questions to find out about each other. Use the Useful phrases to help you.

Useful phrases
What/How about you?
And you?
That's interesting.
Me too!

b Introduce your partner to the class. What are their reasons for learning English?

Develop your reading page 86

1B Life maps

> **Goal:** describe future plans and arrangements
> **Grammar:** *be going to* and present continuous
> **Vocabulary:** personal characteristics

Vocabulary and reading

1 a Look at the photos and discuss the question. What jobs do you think the people do?

b Match photos A–E with comments 1–5.
1 'I think I'm a **caring** person. I like helping people. I'm **reliable** and people trust me to take care of them.'
2 'I work from home so I need to be **organised**, but sometimes I feel a bit **lazy** and I don't want to work at all!'
3 'I'm **ambitious** and I want to get to the top! I'm not **shy**. I'm very **confident** when I speak. I always keep **calm** when things go wrong.'
4 'I have to be **patient** when I coach players as people are very **sensitive**, but I still need to be **open** and **honest** and say what I think.'
5 'I'm pretty **hard-working**. I practise ten hours a day. I'm **creative** and I love performing.'

2 a Choose the correct alternatives.
1 Jacky always has exciting new ideas. She's very *creative/reliable*.
2 Antonio never does anything to help us. He's very *hard-working/lazy*.
3 Grace doesn't tell lies. She's completely *ambitious/honest*.
4 Miguel says he's waiting in a very long queue. It's a good thing he's so *shy/patient*.
5 Azra never tries to hide what she feels about something. She's a very *open/calm* person.

b Work in pairs and describe yourself using adjectives in Exercise 1b.

📱 Go to page 136 or your app for more vocabulary and practice.

3 Read the article on page 9. What is a life map? How can it help you?

4 Match statements 1–4 with questions A–D in the article.
1 'I'm happy with my family life and I enjoy my hobbies, but my work life is very stressful.'
2 'I'm meeting her next week to discuss my ideas.'
3 'I'm going to ask my boss if I can apply for a new role in the company.'
4 'I really want to have a job where I can have more fun and get to know the people I work with.'

Grammar

5 Read the grammar box and choose the correct alternatives.

be going to and present continuous

Use *be going to* and the present continuous to talk about plans, intentions and arrangements for the ¹*present/future*.

Use the present continuous for future arrangements, often with other people and giving a time/place.
I'm meeting an old friend **next month**.

Use *be going to* to talk about your intentions. In this situation, you might not know all the details of your plan.
What **are** you **going to** do? **I'm going to** ask for advice.

6 a 🔊 1.3 Listen and notice the pronunciation of *-ing*.
1 When are you going to take that holiday?
2 I'm seeing my boss tomorrow.
3 I'm going to ask for advice.

b Listen again and repeat.

Where is your life going?

When you make a life map, you write down important details about your journey through life. By answering questions like the ones below, a life map can help you to decide what you'd like to do in the future.

A What's your life like at the moment?
What do you like about it? What don't you like? What things do you enjoy? What would you like to change? Think about your job, friends and family, studies, money, the way you live, etc.

B What are your goals?
Set yourself some goals. How ambitious are you? Do you want a better job and more money or do you want to spend more time with friends and family? How creative are you? Do you want to learn a new skill or try a new sport or hobby? Decide what you really want and make a list of goals for each area of your life.

C How are you going to achieve them?
Now you need to decide what actions you can take to achieve your goals. What can you do now and what are you going to do in the future? Make a list of all the things – big or small – that you can do to achieve your goals. Here are some examples:
I'm going to ask my boss if I can work part time.
I'm going to stop staying late at the office.

D When are you going to achieve them?
When are you going to look for a new job or join the gym? When are you going to ask your boss for more money? When are you going to take that holiday? Decide on a date for each action. And finally, be patient … you can't do everything at once, but remember your goals, start working to achieve them and you really will change your life!

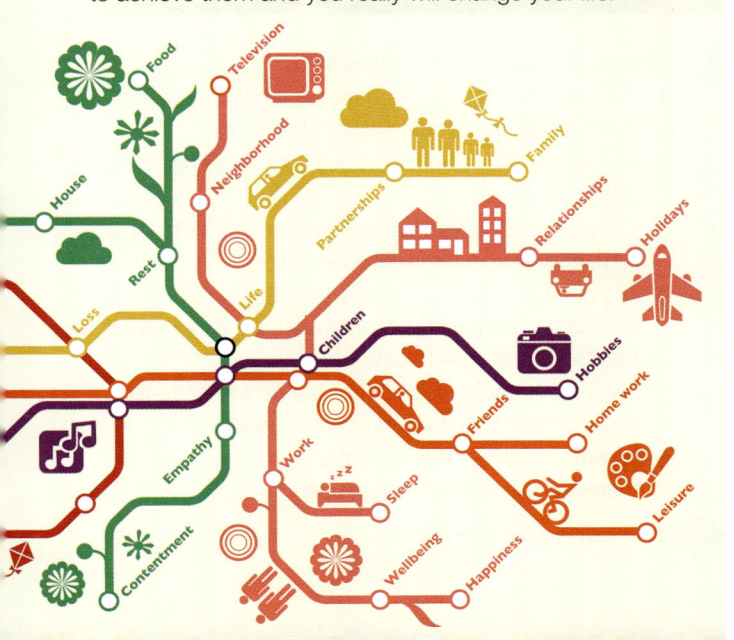

7 Complete the sentences with the verbs in the box. Use *be going to* or the present continuous. Sometimes both forms are possible.

| be | do | find | go | play | relax | talk |

1 I _____ to Matthew this afternoon at 3 p.m. about the new role.
2 She _____ a job when she finishes her degree.
3 What _____ you _____ when the course finishes?
4 I _____ to an interview tomorrow for a job in sales.
5 I think we _____ busier when the new baby arrives.
6 She _____ tennis this evening at 7 p.m.
7 When I'm older, I _____ more and work less!

8 a Complete the sentences with your own ideas. Use *be going to* or the present continuous.
1 Tomorrow, I'm …
2 Later this evening, …
3 After this lesson, …
4 At the weekend, …
5 Next week, …
6 Next year, …

b Work in pairs and compare your ideas.

Go to page 116 or your app for more information and practice.

Speaking

PREPARE

9 a 1.4 You're going to plan and discuss your own life map. First, listen to a life coach talking to a client. Which topics below does the client want to talk about?
- money and success
- a job
- family
- friends and relationships
- learning something new
- a way of life

b Listen again and make notes about Ben's likes, dislikes, goals and plans.

c Think about your likes, dislikes, goals and plans. Look at the topics in Exercise 9a and make notes.

SPEAK

10 a Work in pairs. Tell your partner about your life map. Use your notes and the Useful phrases to help you.

Useful phrases
One of my life goals is to …
I really enjoy …
I'm a very … person, so I want to …
That's a nice plan!
When are you going to …?

b Were your life maps the same or different? Did anything in your partner's life map surprise you?

Develop your writing page 87

1c What next?

> **Goal:** make predictions about the future
> **Grammar:** *will* for prediction
> **Vocabulary:** describing change

Vocabulary and reading

1 Look at the photos. What can you see?

2 a Match sentences 1–6 with photos A–F.
1. The number of online dating sites is **increasing**. Finding a date is **becoming easier**.
2. The number of young people buying houses has **decreased** this year. The number of new home owners **went down** last year, too.
3. Driverless cars could **reduce** the number of accidents. Driving in big cities should **improve**.
4. The population of cities **is rising** as more young people move to big cities. The population of London **went up** again this year.
5. In some countries, power from wind farms and the sun is replacing energy from oil. Air pollution in towns **is falling** as a result.
6. The weather is not likely to **improve**. In fact, it is **getting worse**, not **getting better**. Experts say it is **becoming harder** to fight events like forest fires.

b Match the words and phrases in box A with their opposites in box B. Use Exercise 2a to help you.

A

decreasing/falling/going down
getting harder   getting worse

B

getting easier   improving/getting better
increasing/rising/going up

3 Choose the correct alternatives.
1. It is fantastic that it's becoming *easier/harder* to get electricity from the sun and the wind.
2. People can't buy a house because the prices are going *up/down* all the time.
3. The number of driverless cars needs to *get better/go up* to make the roads in big cities safer.
4. The number of people experiencing bad weather is *increasing/decreasing* and scientists are very worried that this situation will continue.
5. Everyone is happy when things *get better/decrease* and worried when they *improve/get worse*.
6. In some countries, the population is *rising/falling* so there aren't enough young people.

Go to your app for more practice.

4 Read the comments about changes in the future. How many people talk about changes at work?

1. A lot of people already use dating sites, but I think in the future the number of people who use them will rise even more. Dating sites will improve, so they will get better at finding you the perfect person. In the future, they will be the only way that couples meet.

2. These days, some people work at home one or two days a week instead of going to an office every day. I think in the future lots more people will work from home all the time, and the number of offices will decrease. It's sad, because people won't be as sociable.

3. I think the number of people on the planet will continue to increase. There'll be less space, so we'll need to change the way we live. Maybe we'll live underground, or maybe lots of people will live together in a single house. Life will definitely get worse!

4. Driverless cars are a new thing at the moment, but I think in the future it will be normal to have one. I think it'll be a good thing, because we won't have so many accidents. Maybe we'll stop using petrol, too. That would be good!

5. The weather will change a lot in the future. It will become more extreme. There'll be big changes in temperature, too. It won't be good!

5 Match comments 1–5 in Exercise 4 with replies a–e.

a 'I agree. There won't be enough houses for everyone because the population will rise.'

b 'That won't happen. I think we will be able to control the weather and everything will get better.'

c 'I think meeting partners online is a terrible idea! Will it become easier to meet people? I don't think so!'

d 'You're right. In the future, it's possible that everyone will work from their homes.'

e 'At last things will improve! Goodbye to dirty air in our cities. I can't wait!'

Grammar

6 Read the grammar box and choose the correct alternative.

will for prediction

Use *will* or *won't* to talk about [1] *future/past* actions.
*A big change **will** be how people meet each other.*
*They **won't** meet through work or family any more.*
Use phrases like *next year*, *in the future* or *in a (few/ten/twenty,* etc.*) year's time* when we predict the future.
*In the future, everyone **will** meet their partners on online dating sites.*
Use verbs like *think*, *believe*, *expect* and *hope*, to introduce predictions.
*I think we **will** live in a different way.*
When you feel very confident about a prediction, use phrases like *I'm sure* or *I'm certain*.
*I'm sure there **will** be temperature changes.*

7 a 🔊 1.5 Listen and notice the pronunciation of *will* and *won't*.

1 Will there be a change?
2 We don't know what will happen.
3 He won't come to the party.

b Listen again and repeat.

8 Make sentences with *will* using the prompts.

1 I / sure / Harry / get / a new job / next year.
   I'm sure Harry will get a new job next year.
2 I / not / think / the weather / get / worse here.
3 We / not / have / driverless cars / for a long time.
4 There / be / more work / for everyone in future.
5 The population / in our country / rise.
6 We / not / have / enough new houses / for everyone.
7 People / have to / live together.
8 I / think / people / still / want / to get married.
9 I / not / think / everyone / meet / online.

9 What will change in your life in the next five years? Write six predictions about your life. Think about these topics:

- home
- work
- hobbies

I will move to a new house next year.

📱 Go to page 116 or your app for more information and practice.

Speaking

PREPARE

10 a 🔊 1.6 You're going to make predictions about your country. First, listen to Daniel and Sofia talking about the future and choose the correct alternatives.

1 Daniel predicts that there won't be any *doctors/robots* in the future.
2 He thinks people *will/won't* get sick in the future.
3 Daniel says there will be *no/more* offices in the future.
4 He says people will work from *big offices/cafés*.
5 Sofia and Daniel think people will meet each other *at home/online*.

b Which of the predictions do you agree with?

11 Make notes about how you think the things below will change in your country.

- education
- fashion
- work
- free time
- health
- technology

SPEAK

12 a Work in pairs and discuss your predictions.

b Decide which predictions are more likely to come true. Rate them from 1 (not likely) to 5 (very likely). Report back to the class.

Develop your listening page 88

1D English in action

Goal: make and respond to suggestions

1 Look at the photo and discuss the questions.
1. How is the man feeling?
2. What activities do you think would make him feel better?

2 a 🔊 1.9 Listen to two friends, Katy and Pete, talking on the phone and answer the questions.
1. What is Pete's problem?
2. What does Katy recommend?
3. What three suggestions does she make?
4. What does Pete decide to do?
5. Why doesn't he like the other suggestions?

b Listen again and match suggestions 1–4 with reasons a–g. Some suggestions match with more than one reason.
1. I really recommend doing regular exercise.
2. What about running?
3. How about going hiking in the countryside?
4. Or why not try volleyball?

a. You'll meet interesting people and have fun.
b. It makes you feel better and it helps you sleep.
c. Being in nature makes you feel happy.
d. It's good for your health.
e. Your social life will improve.
f. You'll have more energy.
g. You can do it on your own.

c Work in pairs and compare your answers. Then listen again and check.

3 a Complete the sentences. Use the Useful phrases to help you.
1. **A:** What _____ drinking green tea? It _____ you to relax.
   B: I'm not keen _____ green tea, I don't like the taste.
2. **A:** I _____ taking regular breaks. You'll _____ better.
   B: That's a great _____ ! I'll do it.
3. **A:** Why _____ try online dating?
   B: I _____ fancy it. I prefer to meet people in real life!
4. **A:** How _____ joining a dance class? Dancing is very _____ for your heart.
   B: _____ sounds fun.

Useful phrases

Making suggestions and recommendations
What/How about (trying/taking up yoga)?
Why not try (hiking)?
Here's another idea.
I recommend (doing some exercise).
I think you'll enjoy (swimming).

Giving reasons
It's very good for (your health).
It helps you to (relax/sleep).
It makes you feel (better/happier).
You'll feel (much better/great).

Rejecting
I'm not sure (hiking) is a good idea because …
I'm not keen on (swimming).
I'm not really into that kind of thing, I'm afraid.
I don't fancy (dancing) because …

Agreeing and expressing enthusiasm
That's a (great/brilliant) idea.
That sounds (interesting/fun).

b 🔊 1.10 Listen to suggestions 1–4 in Exercise 2b. Does the speaker's voice rise or fall at the end?

c Listen again and repeat.

4 a Look at the problems below and think of suggestions you could make.
- I can't sleep at night.
- My neighbours are very noisy.
- I never have enough free time.
- My English is not getting better.
- It's difficult for me to make new friends.

b Work in groups. Choose one of the problems in Exercise 4a. Ask other students for advice.

c Work in pairs. Discuss who gave you the best advice.

Go online for the Roadmap video.

Check and reflect

1 a Choose the correct alternatives.
   1 I *have/passed* a degree in economics from Oxford.
   2 I'd like to *get/take* a course in education, *get/study* a qualification and maybe *run/train* to be a teacher.
   3 I recently *got/took* some important exams. I *finished/passed* them all!
   4 I *have/work* part-time in a café and I also *study/train* biology and chemistry at college.
   5 I'd like to *run/work* my own company one day.
   6 I'm working *as/like* an accountant.
   7 I want to do a course *at/in* ancient history.

  b Work in pairs and discuss which sentences are true for you. Say why or why not.

2 a Complete the questions with *you* and the correct form of the verb in brackets.
   1 What _____ (do) in your free time? _____ (have) any hobbies?
   2 _____ (read) a book at the moment?
   3 Why _____ (learn) English? _____ (enjoy) it?
   4 How many languages _____ (know)? _____ (learn) any other languages at the moment?
   5 _____ (have) a job at the moment or _____ (study) full time?
   6 In the future, what _____ (want) to do for a job?
   7 _____ (go) to the gym much at the moment?
   8 _____ (have) a lot of work to do this week?

  b Work in pairs. Ask and answer the questions in Exercise 2a. Find out more information.

3 a Write three sentences about things you plan or intend to do and three sentences about things which are arranged. Use the phrases in the box.

   | at the weekend | in the next few years |
   | later this year | later today | next week | tomorrow |

   I'm going to the cinema this evening.

  b Work in pairs. Discuss your future plans and arrangements. Give more information.

4 a Complete the sentences with the words in the box.

   ambitious   calm   creative   hard-working
   honest   lazy   reliable   shy

   1 She finds it difficult to speak to people she doesn't know. She's actually quite _____ .
   2 He never does any work or makes much effort. To be honest, he's really _____ .
   3 He's a(n) _____ person. He always tells the truth.
   4 She has lots of interesting ideas. She's very _____ .
   5 She's very _____ . She'll be successful in her career.
   6 She's a very _____ person. She never gets angry or loses her temper.
   7 She always does what she says she will do, she's really _____ .
   8 He's very _____ , he always finishes work later than the others.

  b Work in pairs. Choose the three adjectives that best describe you and three that least describe you. Explain why you chose your adjectives.

5 a Complete the predictions with *will* and the verbs in the box.

   be able to   become   be delivered   go   learn
   live   not go   order

   1 People _____ to be 150 years old.
   2 Humans _____ to the Moon again.
   3 English _____ less important as a language.
   4 We _____ to 'talk' with animals.
   5 We _____ fly from the UK to Australia in just two hours.
   6 We _____ to shops. We _____ everything online and it _____ immediately.

  b Work in pairs and discuss the predictions in Exercise 5a. Do you think they will happen? When?

6 a Replace the word or phrase in bold with the correct form of a word or phrase in the box. Sometimes more than one answer is possible.

   decrease   easier   fall   harder   get better
   increase   rise   worse

   1 Standards of living are **improving** in most countries.
   2 It's getting **more difficult** to buy your own house.
   3 Thanks to social media, staying is touch has become much **less difficult**.
   4 Some people think life will be **less good** for the next generation.
   5 Unemployment is **going down** in many places.
   6 The cost of petrol is **going up** all the time.

  b Work in pairs. Do you agree with the sentences in Exercise 6a? Discuss other things that are:
   • going up/down
   • improving
   • becoming easier/more difficult, etc.

Reflect

How confident do you feel about the statements below? Write 1–5 (1 = not very confident, 5 = very confident).
• I can get to know someone.
• I can describe future plans and arrangements.
• I can make predictions about the future.
• I can make and respond to suggestions.

Want more practice?
Go to your Workbook or app.

2A What happened?

> **Goal:** describe past experiences
> **Grammar:** past simple and past continuous
> **Vocabulary:** describing feelings and events

Vocabulary

1 Look at the photos and discuss the questions.
  1 What do you think is happening in each photo?
  2 How do you think the people are feeling? Which of the adjectives in the box would you use to describe them?

| amazed | annoyed | disappointed | embarrassed |
| frightened | relaxed | surprised | tired | worried |

2 a Read the comments below and match them with three of the photos.
  1 'The other day I met an old friend for the first time in years. It was such a **surprising** meeting! We were **amazed** and excited to see each other again.'
  2 'Yesterday was a really **annoying** day. I borrowed my wife's car and got a parking ticket. She was very **annoyed** with me.'
  3 'I love cooking. I find it very **relaxing** after a long and stressful day at work. I don't like shopping for food though. It's so **tiring**.'

b Look at the words in bold in Exercise 2a. When do we use adjectives ending in *-ed* or *-ing*, e.g. *tired/tiring, amazed/amazing*?

3 Choose the correct alternatives.
  1 I get very *annoyed/annoying* when people are late for meetings.
  2 Last year I spent three months travelling round South America. What an *amazed/amazing* experience!
  3 My parents get very *worried/worrying* when I don't come home on time.
  4 The first time I met my boyfriend's parents, I dropped my tea on the floor! It was so *embarrassed/embarrassing*!
  5 I don't like watching horror films on my own. They're too *frightened/frightening*.
  6 My sister was so *disappointed/disappointing* when she didn't pass her driving test.
  7 My brother is travelling abroad and we haven't heard from him for weeks. It's very *worried/worrying*.
  8 After a few days on holiday, I feel so *relaxed/relaxing*.
  9 I hate getting up early every day. It's very *tired/tiring*.

4 Work in pairs. Answer the questions using adjectives in Exercises 1 and 2.
  1 How do you feel when you miss a bus or train?
  2 What do you think about people who talk very loudly on the train?
  3 How do you feel when you're on holiday?
  4 How would you describe a recent film you saw?
  5 How do you feel when you go to an interview?
  6 How would you describe the problem of extreme weather?
  7 How do you feel when you receive a terrible gift?
  8 Why wouldn't you ask someone how old they are?

Go to your app for more practice.

Listening

5 a 🔊 **2.1** Listen to three stories. Match speakers 1–3 with topics a–c.
   a a funny incident
   b an annoying day
   c a surprising meeting

b Listen again. Are the sentences true (T) or false (F)? Correct the false sentences.
   1 Speaker 1 was visiting his old university.
   2 He was going into a café when he met his old friend.
   3 While Speaker 2 was walking to the station, she remembered she didn't have her phone.
   4 When she got to the station, her train was just arriving.
   5 Speaker 3 was leaving the office when she heard a noise.
   6 While she was waiting for the security guard, she saw a cat.

Grammar

6 Read the grammar box and choose the correct alternatives.

> ### Past simple and past continuous
>
> Use the ¹*past simple/past continuous* to talk about completed actions and events in the past.
> *Last year I **had** an interview for a new job.*
> Use the ²*past simple/past continuous*
> • to talk about an action or situation in progress around a time in the past.
>   *One afternoon, I **was walking** along the street …*
> • to describe the background to a story.
>   *I **was working** late at the office one night …*
> Use the past continuous and past simple with *when* and *while* to talk about interrupted actions. Use *while* or *while/when* + past continuous and *when* + past simple.
> *While I **was walking** through the old town, I suddenly **realised** I was late.*
> *She **was just leaving** when she **heard** a noise.*

7 a 🔊 **2.2** Listen and notice the pronunciation of *was*. Is it strong or weak?
   1 While he was visiting his home town, he met an old friend.
   2 While he was walking to the station, it started to rain.
   3 While she was waiting, she saw a cat.

b Listen again and repeat.

8 Complete the story with the correct form of the verbs in brackets.

> While I ¹_____ (study) at university, I ²_____ (join) the Drama Society. I love the theatre and I really ³_____ (want) to act in a play. In my first year, I only had a small part but I ⁴_____ (practise) for weeks! However, the day of my first performance was a disaster! While I ⁵_____ (wait) to go on stage, I ⁶_____ (start) to get nervous. When I finally ⁷_____ (go) on stage, I ⁸_____ (forget) my words. Can you imagine? I ⁹_____ (stand) on stage in front of a big audience. Everyone ¹⁰_____ (wait) for me to speak, but I couldn't say a thing. I was so embarrassed!

9 Complete the sentences with your own ideas.
   1 Recently, I was sitting in the park/the garden/a café when …
   2 While I was walking/driving home the other night, …
   3 My phone/The doorbell rang while I was …
   4 I was having a cup of tea/coffee with my mum/a friend when …
   5 My car/My friend's car broke down while …
   6 My friends/dinner guests arrived at my house while I was still …

📱 Go to page 118 or your app for more information and practice.

Speaking

PREPARE

10 You're going to tell a story about a time when you felt frightened, annoyed, embarrassed, surprised, pleased or disappointed. Think about these questions and make notes.
   • When/Where did it happen?
   • What were you doing at the time?
   • What happened?
   • How did you feel?
   • Why was it annoying/embarrassing etc.?

SPEAK

11 a Work in pairs. Tell your partner your story. Listen to your partner's story and respond. Use the Useful phrases to help you.

> **Useful phrases**
> What happened?
> How amazing!
> Really!
> How did you feel?
> I was surprised/excited.

b What adjectives would you use to describe your partner's story?

Develop your reading — page 89

2B Memories

> **Goal:** talk about memories
> **Grammar:** used to
> **Vocabulary:** memories

Vocabulary

1 a Look at the things in box A and match them with the senses in box B. There may be more than one answer.

A

| a baby's skin   a cup of coffee   freshly baked bread |
| a sunrise   a train arriving at a station |

B

| feel   sight   smell   sound   taste |

b When you think about the past, which of the senses are the most important to you?

2 Read the comments. Match them with photos A–E.
1 The sound of sea birds always **reminds me of** summer and holidays at the beach.
2 The smell of paella **makes me think of** home. I have **happy memories of** eating outside with my family.
3 The sight of city lights from a plane at night **makes me feel** excited.
4 **I'll never forget** the sight of the sun coming up over the mountains and watching it rise into the sky.
5 **I'll always remember** the taste of my mother's homemade apple pie. It was so good!

3 a Which of the phrases in bold in Exercise 2 can be used with …
  a a verb + *-ing*?
  b an adjective?
  c a noun, e.g. a person or a place?

b Choose two correct alternatives.
1 I'll always remember *him/ meeting her/ she*.
2 Looking at the sea always makes me *feel calm/ feeling calm/ calm*.
3 This place reminds me of *being young/ my old friends/ happy*.
4 I'll never forget *the first time I saw it/ travel to that place/ entering that place for the first time*.
5 I have happy memories of *school/ visiting the seaside/ go to my grandmother's house*.

c Complete the sentences with your own ideas.
1 Tasting <u>oysters</u> always reminds me of … <u>visiting the seaside</u>
2 The sound of _____ always makes me think of …
3 The smell of _____ reminds me of …
4 The taste of _____ makes me think of my …
5 Seeing _____ makes me feel …
6 Visiting _____ always reminds me of my …

d Work in pairs and compare your ideas.

📱 Go to page 137 or your app for more vocabulary and practice.

Reading

4 a Read the post and comments below it. Which of the senses do the comments mention?

> Sight, sound, taste, smell, feel – our senses often remind us of important events from our childhood and family life. What are your happiest memories? What helps you remember them?
>
> **Comments**
>
> The smell of chips always reminds me of swimming lessons when I was at school. We used to pass a chip shop when we were walking to the pool every Friday and if we had money, we'd get some. Whenever I eat chips, I remember those Friday swimming lessons. **Ed**
>
> The sound of rain on the windows always makes me think of my childhood. I grew up in Malaysia and it rained a lot from October to March. My sister and I used to love going out and running around in the rain. My mother didn't use to mind! **Tony**
>
> When I hear the old song *Bohemian Rhapsody*, I have happy memories of long car journeys on our holidays. Every summer my father used to drive us to the seaside. During the journey we used to play all kinds of music, but this song was our favourite. It always reminds me of that time. **Tess**
>
> The smell and taste of roast chicken always makes me think of my grandmother. We used to go to her house every Sunday. She used to cook lunch for the whole family. I'll never forget her roast chicken. It tasted so good. **Sara**

b Read the post and comments again and answer the questions.
1. Why does the taste of chips remind Ed of school swimming lessons?
2. Why does Tony remember his childhood when he hears the sound of rain?
3. Why does Tess love that old song?
4. Why does roast chicken make Sara think of her grandmother?

Grammar

5 Read the grammar box. Find more examples of *used to* in the comments in Exercise 4.

used to

Use *used to* to talk about actions that happened regularly in the past, but don't happen now.
*Every summer we **used to** go to the seaside.*
*My mother **didn't use to** mind!*
*What did she and her sister **use to** do?*

Don't use *used to* for actions or events that only happened once in the past. Use the past simple.
*My mum **made** a cake last week.*
NOT: *My mum used to make a cake last week.*

6 a 2.3 Listen and notice the pronunciation of *used to*. Which is pronounced more strongly, *used* or *to*?
1. We used to go every Friday.
2. My mother didn't use to mind!
3. What did they use to do?

b Listen again and repeat.

7 a Complete the sentences with *used to* or *didn't use to*.
When I was a child, …
1. I _____ ride my bike to school.
2. I _____ fight with my brother a lot.
3. I _____ play volleyball with my friends after school.

When I was a teenager, …
4. I _____ go on holiday with my friends.
5. I _____ study hard.
6. I _____ play in the school orchestra.

b Work in pairs and ask your partner the questions.
Did you use to ride your bike to school?
No, I didn't. I used to take the bus.

c Ask and answer more questions about your childhood. Use the prompts and your own ideas.
- play video games
- go to your grandparents' home on Sundays
- be afraid of the dark
- do a lot of sport

Go to page 118 or your app for more information and practice.

Speaking

PREPARE

8 a 2.4 You're going to talk about your childhood memories. First, listen to two friends talking about their memories. Which senses do they mention?

b Listen again and answer the questions.
1. Does Adam like the song? Why/Why not?
2. What smell does Jane love? Why?
3. Why does Adam love the smell of coffee and fresh bread?

9 Think about the questions and make notes.
- What are your happiest memories of childhood? What makes you remember them?
- Does a particular song have a special meaning for you? Does it make you think of a special time in your life?
- Does a particular smell/sight remind you of something or someone special?
- Do you have a favourite food that reminds you of home?
- Do you have a photo that reminds you of happy times?

SPEAK

10 a Work in pairs. Ask and answer the questions in Exercise 9. Use the Useful phrases to help you.

Useful phrases
So, do you have a favourite (food)?
Oh really, why?
Yes, it makes me think of (home/my mum), too.

b Share your memories with another pair. Did you all choose the same sense?

Develop your writing page 90

2c Culture shock

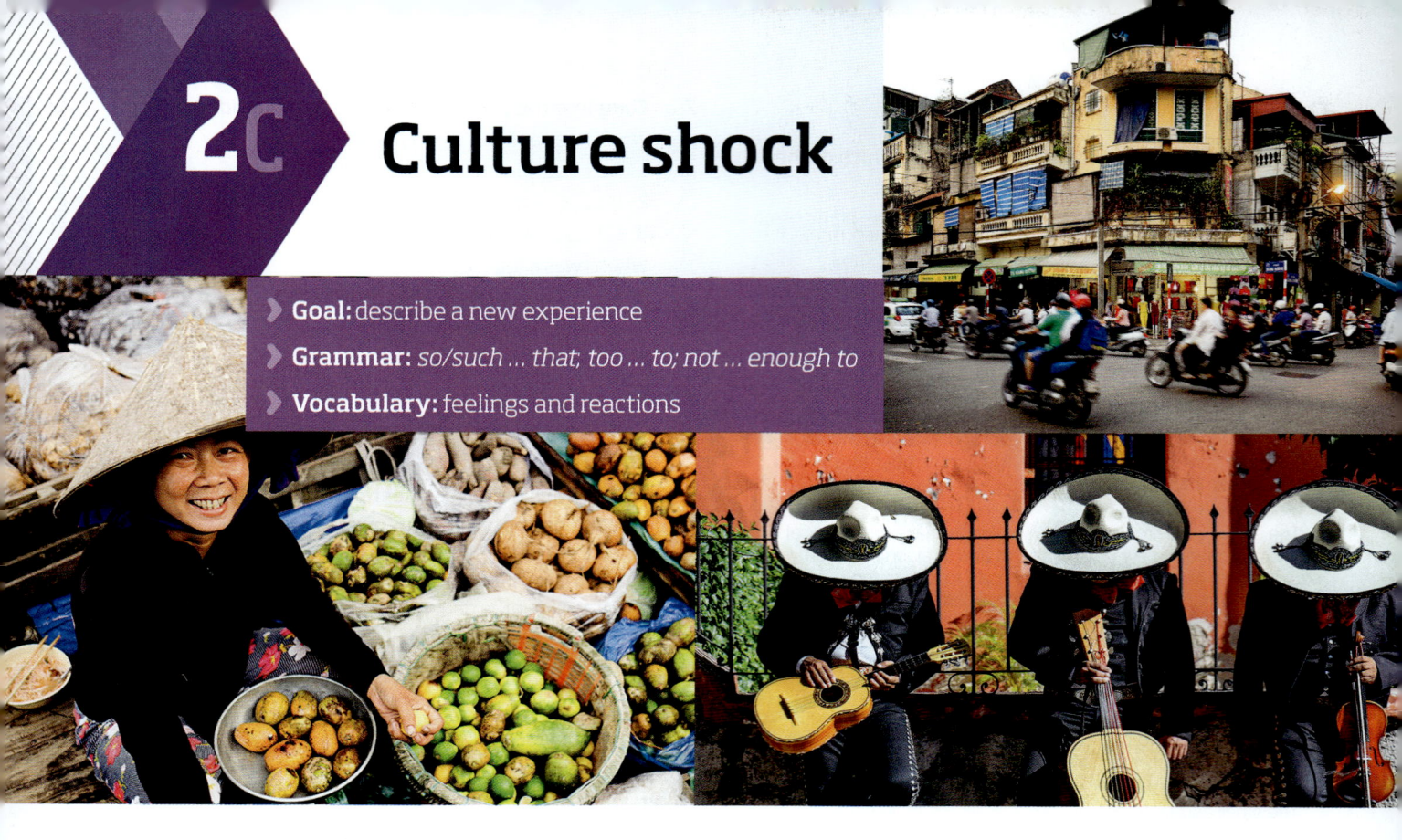

> **Goal:** describe a new experience
> **Grammar:** so/such ... that; too ... to; not ... enough to
> **Vocabulary:** feelings and reactions

Reading and vocabulary

1 Look at the photos and discuss the questions.
1. Where do you think the photos were taken?
2. Would you like to live in these places? Why/Why not?

2 Read the article. Where did Sue and Mike live?

Going to live somewhere new is exciting. You won't be bored because whatever happens it won't be dull. However, will it be too strange for you to enjoy it? It's normal to feel a bit nervous and you may even experience a bit of culture shock, but there's no reason to feel anxious. Here are some tips from two people who have lived abroad.

Remember it will be stressful in the beginning. When I moved to Mexico there were so many new things that I didn't know where to start. Understanding how to pay bills was such a problem that I gave up! I was lucky because friends helped me. Then suddenly everything becomes fun and enjoyable. The towns and cities in Mexico are so lively that you never feel bored. And the historical sites are extraordinary. My best tip is ... learn the language. At first, I didn't feel confident enough to speak. That's the best way to understand the local culture and make friends. – *Sue*

At first, you feel optimistic – you think everything is going to be wonderful, but remember, you will feel homesick. There will be days when you are having such an unpleasant time that you just want to go home! I came to Vietnam. In the beginning, everything was strange. The streets were full of people, cars and bicycles. It was so dangerous, you couldn't cross the road! However, then I started to enjoy life here. The people are so cheerful and friendly that I felt at home very quickly. It's such a beautiful country. The countryside is so peaceful and quiet. In fact, I'm so happy here now that I don't want to go home. So, remember, stay positive! Everything really will be wonderful in the end. – *Mike*

3 Look at the adjectives in the box and answer the questions. Use the article to help you.

| anxious cheerful dull enjoyable extraordinary |
| homesick lively nervous optimistic peaceful |
| positive strange stressful unpleasant |

1. Are the adjectives negative or positive?
2. Which describe how people feel?
3. Which describe what an experience was like?

4 Choose the correct alternatives.
1. It was an *enjoyable/unpleasant* trip. I loved it.
2. I'm really glad I went there. It was a *positive/stressful* experience and I learned a lot.
3. I felt tired and *cheerful/anxious* by the time we arrived.
4. We were lucky to see some *extraordinary/dull* places.
5. I thought it was a *peaceful/lively* place. There were a lot of different things happening all the time.
6. I like going to new places and I never feel *nervous/optimistic* about going somewhere new.
7. I was travelling alone. I went home in the end because I was sad and *cheerful/homesick* all the time.

5 a Complete the sentences with your own ideas.
1. Going to _the dentist_ is always really stressful.
2. Some people think that _____ is really enjoyable, but I find it really dull.
3. _____ is a really pleasant and peaceful place.
4. The first time I tried _____ , I thought it was a bit strange.
5. I'm always cheerful after watching _____ . It makes me laugh so much!
6. _____ is really lively, there's a lot to do.

b Work in pairs and compare your sentences.

📱 Go to page 137 or your app for more vocabulary and practice.

Grammar

6 Read the grammar box and choose the correct alternatives.

so/such ... (that)

Use *so ... that* and *such ... that* to link a cause to a result.
*I'm **so** happy **that** I don't want to go home.*
*Understanding how to pay bills was **such** a problem **that** I gave up!*
Use *so* before a(n) ¹*noun/adjective*.
*And the people are **so** friendly and cheerful ...*
Use ³*so/such* with an adjective and a noun together.
*It's **such** a beautiful **country**!*
Use ⁴*so/such* before *many* and *much*.
*... there were **so many** new things that I didn't know where to start.*

too ... to and (not) enough ... to

Use *too ... to* to say something is more than you want. Use *(not) enough ... to* to say you have or don't have as much as you want.
Use ⁵*too/enough* before an adjective and ⁶*too/enough* after an adjective.
*Will it be **too** strange for you to enjoy it?*
*I didn't feel confident **enough** to cross the road.*
To say you have what you need, use *enough* before a noun.
*There's **enough time** to become perfect.*

7 a 🔊 2.5 Listen and notice the pronunciation of *so* and *such*. In which sentences are they more strongly pronounced? Why?
1 It's such a nice day.
2 He's so quiet today.
3 I was so busy yesterday afternoon.
4 She's such a bad liar.

b Listen again and repeat.

8 Choose the correct alternatives.

My dad had ¹*so/such* a wonderful time living abroad ²*that/than* he didn't want to go home. However, my mum thought this kind of life was ³*too/so* hard to do forever. There wasn't ⁴*enough/too* time to feel at home in one place. It was ⁵*too/enough* stressful for her ⁶*to/that* keep moving all the time, but staying in one place wasn't exciting ⁷*so/enough* for us kids. Mum complained that we went to ⁸*so/such* many different schools ⁹*that/to* we couldn't get a good education. I think we were fine, though!

9 a Complete the sentences with your own ideas.
1 When I was at school, I sometimes felt so ...
2 I'm not old enough ...
3 People are too busy ...
4 My friend got so angry ...
5 I'm not brave enough ...

b Work in pairs and compare your ideas.

📱 Go to page 118 or your app for more information and practice.

Speaking

PREPARE

10 a 🔊 2.6 You're going to talk about a time you experienced something new. First, listen to Nick and Maria. Which of the things do they talk about?
- a new country
- a new school
- a new job
- a new town

b Listen again and answer the questions.
1 What did Nick find strange when he moved?
2 How has the experience changed him?
3 What did Maria's mum find strange when she moved?
4 What did she do?
5 What was different in Nick's second example?
6 How did Nick feel?

c Make notes about a new experience you had. Use the ideas in Exercise 10a to help you.

SPEAK

11 a Work in pairs. Ask and answer questions about your experiences. Use the Useful phrases to help you.

Useful phrases
I remember ...
No one used to ...
I thought everyone/no one ...
It felt/didn't feel strange/stressful.

b Choose one experience and tell the class.

Develop your listening page 91

2D English in action

> **Goal:** show interest in a conversation

A

B

C

1   Look at the pictures. What do you think is happening in each one?

2 a   🔊 2.10 Listen and match conversations 1–3 with pictures A–C. Were your ideas in Exercise 1 correct?

  b   Listen to the conversations again. How does the person listening help the person telling the story?

  c   Listen again. Tick the phrases in the Useful phrases box that you hear.

Useful phrases

Encouraging someone to continue
Uh huh.
Right.
What happened?
What did you do?
And what happened next?
What happened in the end?

Reacting and showing interest
Wow!
That's so cool!
That's awful!
That's amazing!
Great!
Really?
Oh no!

3 a   🔊 2.11 Listen to the phrases below. Which of the people sound interested?
   1   And what happened next?
   2   That's amazing!
   3   Oh no.
   4   So what did you do?

  b   🔊 2.12 Listen and repeat.

4   Work in pairs. Take turns to read this story to each other. Each time you see (…), react to what your partner says and help them to continue talking.

> I had an interesting day yesterday … I was at work, and my boss told me he wanted to speak to me … He told me that he was leaving the company … And that I would be the new boss of the department! … I didn't know what to say. I was so surprised!

> A: I had an interesting day yesterday …
> B: Really? What happened?

5 a   You're going to tell your partner about an experience you've had. First, choose a topic below or think of your own idea.
   • a bad day
   • somewhere new you visited
   • someone famous you saw or met
   • an amazing day you had
   • something surprising that happened

  b   Make some notes. Think about the following:
   • when and where it happened
   • the most important things that happened
   • how you felt

  c   Work in pairs. Ask and answer questions about your experiences. Use the Useful phrases to help you.

Go online for the Roadmap video.

Check and reflect

1 a Complete the words with the correct endings, *-ed* or *-ing*.
   1 The news was surpris____. I was really surpris____ when I heard it.
   2 I was quite disappoint____ with the film. The story was really disappoint____.
   3 I had a really tir____ day. I was so tir____ when I finally got to bed.
   4 I was so embarrass____. It was a really embarrass____ situation.

b Work in pairs. Talk about times when you experienced the things in Exercise 1a.

2 a Complete the sentences with the correct form of the verbs in brackets.
   1 I ____ (meet) my husband while I ____ (study) at university. We ____ (be) at the same party one night.
   2 I ____ (break) my leg while I ____ (ski). I ____ (go) down a difficult route and I ____ (fall) over.
   3 I ____ (meet) my best friend at primary school. We ____ (paint) a picture together and we just ____ (not / stop) talking. We're still best friends today.
   4 While I ____ (travel) around South America just after I ____ (finish) university, I ____ (start) to learn Spanish. I then ____ (become) a Spanish teacher.

b Write sentences about three significant events in your life. Work in pairs and discuss them.

3 a Complete the sentences with the verbs in the box.

| forget | have | reminds | smile | think |

   1 Saturday evening TV always ____ me of my childhood.
   2 The smell of chocolate always makes me ____ of my grandparents.
   3 I ____ very happy memories of my primary school. I loved every second.
   4 I'll never ____ the first time I rode a bike by myself. I felt so happy.
   5 The song *Perfect Day* always makes me ____. It's such a great song.

b Make the sentences in Exercise 3a true for you.

4 a Complete the sentences with the correct form of *used to* and the verbs in the box.

| be | be able | not be | play |

   1 There ____ a big shopping centre. It opened just a few months ago, actually.
   2 There ____ more small independent shops, but many of them have now closed.
   3 We ____ football in the park, but they built offices there.
   4 You ____ to drive in the city centre. Now cars are not allowed there.

b Think about a place you know well. Write three sentences about how it used to be different.

5 a Complete the sentences with the words in the box.

| cheerful | dull | enjoyable | extraordinary |
| homesick | optimistic | peaceful | stressful |

   1 I never feel ____, unless I'm away from home for a long time and then I sometimes do.
   2 To be honest, I find reality TV quite ____ and boring, but I love watching action films and documentaries.
   3 There are some lovely, ____, quiet places near where I live. I go walking there quite often.
   4 I usually get nervous before an exam. I find them quite ____, to be honest.
   5 I think there are some amazing buildings where I live. Some of them are quite ____.
   6 I find cooking very ____. If I've got time, I really like preparing nice meals for my friends and family.
   7 I love spending time with Denise, she's always really ____.
   8 The exam was really difficult but I feel ____ and think I'll pass!

b Work in pairs. Decide if the sentences in Exercise 5a are true or false for your partner. Then check and find out more information.

6 a Choose the correct alternatives.
   1 It's *a such / such a* great city.
   2 It was *so / such* boring!
   3 I spent *so / such* much money.
   4 We were having *so / such* a good time that we didn't want it to end.
   5 I'm *too / enough* young to remember it.
   6 I'm not *enough good / good enough* yet. I need to improve at it.
   7 It was *too / such* expensive. I didn't have *enough money / money enough* to buy it.

b Replace *it* in the sentences in Exercise 6a to make true sentences. Work in pairs and compare your ideas.

Reflect

How confident do you feel about the statements below? Write 1–5 (1 = not very confident, 5 = very confident).
- I can describe past experiences.
- I can talk about memories.
- I can describe a new experience.
- I can show interest in a conversation.

Want more practice? Go to your Workbook or app.

3A Bucket lists

› **Goal:** talk about experiences
› **Grammar:** present perfect and past simple
› **Vocabulary:** experiences

Reading and vocabulary

1 a Read the definition of a bucket list and discuss the questions.

A **bucket list** is a list of all the experiences you want to have during your life.

1 Do you have a bucket list? Why/Why not?
2 What kind of things do you think people put on them?

b Read the bucket list ideas. Which can you see in the photos?
- **take part in** a marathon
- **perform** in a play
- **raise money** for charity
- **take up** a new sport
- **go** backpacking
- **explore** the ancient ruins of Egypt
- **experience** a new culture
- **apply** to be a film extra
- **try** hot-air ballooning

2 a Match the verbs in bold in Exercise 1b with phrases a–i.
a _____ in a band/in a show/on stage
b _____ travelling/hiking/ice skating
c _try_ a new cuisine/scuba diving/learning a new language
d _____ a new cuisine/something new/living abroad
e _____ to appear on a TV programme
f _____ a hobby/golf
g _____ to help animals/for your local school
h _____ the jungle/the coast of Canada
i _____ a singing competition/a race

b Work in pairs and discuss the questions.
1 Which activities have you done?
2 Which would you like to do?

Have you ever felt that time is passing and you haven't achieved very much? I used to feel like that all the time, until I created my bucket list. Here are some ideas of things you could try!

• **Take up a new sport**
Sports are a great way to keep fit and they can be exciting, too. For example, have you tried water sports? I've been diving several times and it's an amazing experience. I'm going to take up skiing too when I find the time!

• **Experience new cultures**
Travelling helps us experience new cultures. This year I've already been to three different continents and I've learned a lot from each place I've been to. My favourite place was Canada. I went to Toronto for two weeks in January. There are some places I haven't been to yet, like South Africa, but it's on my bucket list.

• **Raise money for charity**
Raising money for charity is a great way to help people and it can be fun, too. A friend of mine is going to climb Kilimanjaro for a children's charity next year and she's already raised £1,000 since she started training.

• **Take up a hobby or interest**
I've always enjoyed games of skill like chess. They make you think really hard and help to improve your memory. Doing something creative is fun, too. A friend of mine has just joined a band. He loves performing and he's having a great time.

3 Read the blog and answer the questions.
1 What activities and experiences does the writer recommend? Why?
2 Which activities has the writer already done? Does he say exactly when?
3 Which hasn't he done yet?

📱 Go to page 138 or your app for more vocabulary and practice.

Grammar

4 Read the grammar box and choose the correct alternatives.

Present perfect and past simple

Use the [1] *present perfect/past simple* for:
- experiences in our lives up to now; often with *ever* and *never*.
- events that happened in the past when the exact time is not important.
  I've been diving
- recently completed actions.
  A friend of mine has joined a band recently.

Use the [2] *present perfect/past simple* for:
- completed actions/events in the past at a particular time.
- an action/a situation covering a period of time that started and finished in the past.
  I went to Toronto for two weeks in January.

Other time expressions you can use with the present perfect include:
- *already*, which means 'before now'
  I've already tried scuba diving.
- *yet* with negative verbs and questions, which means 'up to now'.
  I haven't tried sushi yet.

5 a 🔊 3.1 Listen and notice the pronunciation of *you've*, *I've* and *she's*.
1 Write down the things you've always wanted to do.
2 I've travelled to many different countries.
3 She's already raised £1,000.

b Listen again and repeat.

6 a Choose the correct alternatives.
1 **A:** *Have you ever visited/Did you ever visit* New York?
   B: Yes, I *have/did*. I *went/'ve been* there several times.
   A: When *have you last been/did you last go*?
   B: I *'ve been/went* there two years ago.
2 **A:** *Did you/Have you* ever performed in a play?
   B: No, I *haven't/didn't*. I'd like to do it sometime.
3 **A:** Have you ever been to Scotland?
   B: No, I *haven't been/didn't go* yet, but I'd like to go one day. How about you?
   A: I *'ve already been/already went* there – it's great.

b Work in pairs. Ask and answer questions about these topics. Use the present perfect and past simple.
- travel
- languages
- sports
- interests/hobbies

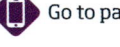

📱 Go to page 120 or your app for more information and practice.

Speaking

PREPARE

7 a 🔊 3.2 You're going to make a bucket list. First, read the ideas below and listen to Paula and her friend John. Which ideas does John suggest?
- go on a hot-air balloon ride
- apply to appear on a TV programme
- go to the next Olympic Games
- join a drama club and perform in a play
- go to a music festival
- take up a new sport
- start a local group to raise money for wildlife

b Listen again. Which activities has Paula already done? Which things does she decide to put on her list?

c You're going to discuss bucket list ideas. Think about the following:
- what you'd like to include on your bucket list and why
- what experiences you could recommend to your partner

SPEAK

8 a Work in pairs. Share ideas for your bucket lists. Use the Useful phrases to help you.

> **Useful phrases**
> Would you like to (take up a new sport)?
> Have you thought about (joining a drama club)?
> You should add that to your list.
> Yes, that has to go on my bucket list.
> That's *not* going on my bucket list.

b Compare your bucket list with other students. Which of your ideas are the same?

Develop your reading
page 92

3B Catching up

> **Goal:** talk about what you've been doing recently
>
> **Grammar:** present perfect continuous and present perfect simple
>
> **Vocabulary:** keeping in touch/catching up

Vocabulary

1 **Look at the photos and discuss the questions.**
  1 What situations do they show?
  2 What do you think the people are talking about?
  3 How do you think they feel?

2 **Read the comments. Are any similar to your experiences?**

  1 It's sad, but I've **lost touch with** a lot of friends from school now. We **get on really well**, but it's hard to find the time to **see each other**. We sometimes chat online but it's not as good as meeting.

  2 These days I **spend** more **time with** my colleagues than my friends. We **hang out** after work or go for lunch together. It's easy because we're all in the same place.

  3 I try to **keep in touch with** my old friends. We talk a lot on social media and I **catch up with** a lot of their news there. We don't **get together** very often, but when we do it's a lot of fun!

  4 I haven't got much time to **get to know** new people as I'm usually so busy with my job and my family, but I do **see a lot of** my good friends. They live nearby so it's easy to **meet up with** them.

3 a **Complete the sentences. Use the phrases in bold in Exercise 2 to help you.**
  1 How do you like to keep _____ with friends and family – by phone, instant messaging, email, writing letters, sending cards?
  2 Who do you _____ well with in your family?
  3 Do you keep _____ with people you _____ to know at school or university? Why/Why not?
  4 Are there any friends or former colleagues you've _____ with? Would you like to _____ up with them again?
  5 Do you _____ of your close friends? How often do you _____ together with them?
  6 Where do you usually _____ up with them? Do you like to just _____ time at each other's homes and chat or go out?
  7 Who do you most enjoy _____ out with? What do you like to do?
  8 How did you _____ your best friend? When and where did you meet?

  b **Work in pairs. Ask and answer the questions.**

  Go to your app for more practice.

Listening

4 🔊 **3.3** Listen to the conversation between Alan and Beth. Tick the topics they talk about.
- work
- travel
- family
- friends they have in common
- free-time activities
- films they've seen

5 a Listen again. Who asks these questions, Alan (A) or Beth (B)?
1. What have you been doing since I last saw you?
2. Have you been anywhere exciting?
3. So, what about you? How's your work going?
4. And what about your brother Dave, what's he been doing?
5. Have you seen Joanne recently?
6. Have you been doing anything else interesting lately?

b Match questions 1–6 in Exercise 5a with answers a–f. Then listen again and check your answers.
a I've been travelling quite a lot for work.
b He's been studying hard for his final exams for months. The bad news is, he and his girlfriend split up two months ago.
c I've been taking Spanish lessons! A friend has been helping me with my studies.
d She's been very busy getting ready for the wedding.
e I went to New York for work last month.
f My boss has been trying to persuade me to move to the Mexican office for ages. I've just accepted the job.

Grammar

6 Read the grammar box and choose the correct alternatives.

Present perfect continuous and present perfect simple

Form the present perfect continuous with the ¹*present simple/present perfect simple* of *be* + verb + *-ing*.
*What **have** you **been doing** since I last saw you?*
*I**'ve been travelling** quite a lot for work.*
***Have** you **been doing** anything interesting?*
Use the ²*present perfect continuous/present perfect simple*:
- to emphasise that an action or situation that started in the past is still in progress.
*I**'ve been taking** Spanish lessons.*
- to emphasise the length of time of an action.
*He**'s been studying** hard **for** months.*
- for repeated recent actions.
*He**'s been trying** to persuade me to move.*

Use the ³*present perfect continuous/present perfect simple* to focus on the finished result of an action.
*I**'ve** just **accepted** the job.*
Use the present perfect simple with verbs that don't usually take the continuous form e.g. *have, want, know* etc.
*I**'ve known** him for three months.*
*I**'ve had** a car for a few years now.*

7 a 🔊 **3.4** Listen and notice the pronunciation of *been*.
1. What have you been doing?
2. I've been travelling a lot.
3. He's been studying hard.

b Listen again and repeat.

8 Complete the email with the correct form of the words in brackets.

Hi Sam,
Lovely to hear from you! Thanks for getting in touch. We're both fine, thanks, though we ¹_____ (not be) anywhere interesting this year. We ²_____ (not have) time. Oh, I don't know if I told you, we ³_____ just _____ (buy) a new apartment in Florida! We ⁴_____ (put) in a new bathroom and kitchen and we're so happy with them. We ⁵_____ (look) for new furniture as well! Apart from that, I ⁶_____ (take up) golf! How about that? What about you? What ⁷_____ (happen)?
Love, Marion

9 a Put the words in the correct order to make questions.
1. a long time / for / Have / you / been / studying English / ?
   Have you been studying English for a long time?
2. been / this year / you / have / abroad / How many times / ?
3. recently / seen / any interesting films / you / Have / ?
4. How many of / your old friends / you / this month / have / got in touch with / ?
5. in your job / How long / working / been / have / you / ?
6. working on / any interesting projects / you / recently / Have / been / ?

b Work in pairs. Ask and answer the questions.

📱 Go to page 120 or your app for more information and practice.

Speaking

PREPARE

10 What have you, your friends and family been doing recently? Make notes about:
- travel – business or pleasure; trips or weekend breaks.
- social life.
- free-time activities.
- entertainment – books, films, TV programmes.

SPEAK

11 a Work in pairs. Talk about what has been happening in your lives recently. Use the Useful phrases to help you.

Useful phrases
What have you been doing recently?
I got together with (my friends last week).
I've been spending time with (my parents/best friend recently).

b Report back to the class. Who has been doing the most interesting things?

Develop your listening page 93

3c My kind of town

> **Goal:** talk about a favourite town, city or neighbourhood
> **Grammar:** articles
> **Vocabulary:** features of a town

Vocabulary

1 Read the comments. Which is closest to what you think about cities? Why?

1. Cities are noisy, crowded and dirty, but I feel at home there!
2. Everything you need is in a city – culture, shopping, restaurants and fun!
3. I only go to the city when I need to. They are very stressful places.
4. I like visiting big cities, but I'm happy I don't live in one!

2 Find the words and phrases in the box in photos A–I.

> art gallery   cycle lane   landmark   neighbourhood
> outdoor café   pedestrian street   skyline   square
> suburb   traffic jam

3 a Choose the correct alternatives.

1. I think we need more *cycle lanes/traffic jams*. People are nervous about using their bikes in the city centre because they feel it's dangerous.
2. I hate sitting in *traffic jams/art galleries* for hours when I'm trying to get to work in the morning.
3. I'd like to move from the *pedestrian street/suburbs* to the city centre, my *square/neighbourhood* is really boring!
4. When it's sunny, it's nice to sit in an *outdoor café/landmark* in one of the local *art galleries/squares*.
5. It's a small town, so there aren't many famous *landmarks/suburbs*.
6. The city doesn't have too many tall buildings, so the *skyline/cycle path* isn't that amazing.
7. We need more interesting places to visit in town, like museums and *pedestrian streets/art galleries*.
8. If we had more *pedestrian streets/suburbs*, it would be easier to walk around the city centre.

b Which of the sentences are true for you and your home town?

> *Number 1 is definitely true, we really need more cycle lanes in my town!*

Go to page 138 or your app for more vocabulary and practice.

Listening

4 a 🔊 3.9 Listen to a radio programme and put a–e in the order that you hear them.

a. Is there anything you don't like about it?
b. What do you like about your city?
c. Tell us what people usually notice about your city.
d. What does it mean to be a New Yorker?
e. Anything else?

b Listen again. Tick the things Tony mentions.

1. the high buildings on the New York skyline
2. having family connections in the city
3. what he did at school
4. the number of people from different parts of the world living in the city
5. eating at Chinese restaurants
6. a lot of cultural activities
7. slow-moving traffic
8. the friendliness of the people living there

Grammar

5 Read the grammar box. Match statements a–g with examples 1–7.

Articles

Use *the*:
a when both the speaker and listener know which thing they are talking about.
b with buildings or landmarks.
c with something when it is the only one.

1 when I come back to **the** city from the airport
2 all over **the** world
3 **the** Empire State Building and **the** Statue of Liberty

Use *a/an* with:
d something mentioned for the first time.
e one person or thing.

4 I'm **a** New Yorker actually.
5 We've got oranges, apples and bananas here. Would you like **an** orange?

Use no article with:
f people or things in general.
g uncountable nouns.

6 **Tourists** come to the city.
7 There's **art**, **music** and **theatre**.

6 a 🔊 3.10 Listen and notice the pronunciation of *a*, *an* and *the*.

1 It's at the end of the street.
2 It was difficult in the beginning.
3 People like to have a chat.
4 It's an amazing place!

b Listen again and repeat.

7 Complete the text with *a*, *an*, *the* or no article.

I live in ¹_____ neighbourhood near ²_____ city centre. I don't want to live in ³_____ suburb! ⁴_____ people usually notice two things about my neighbourhood. There is ⁵_____ café on every corner and it is very green. There are ⁶_____ parks and ⁷_____ squares everywhere. It's an old neighbourhood and I like that. I haven't lived in ⁸_____ neighbourhood very long, but I can see it's ⁹_____ real community – everyone knows each other. It's also got ¹⁰_____ great nightlife. There are all kinds of restaurants. People come here from all over the world. A lot of people from ¹¹_____ Spain and ¹²_____ Italy live here and there are ¹³_____ Italian and ¹⁴_____ Spanish restaurants. There are lots of small galleries and ¹⁵_____ theatres, too. What don't I like? I don't like the factories by the river very much. They're very ugly! Living in ¹⁶_____ neighbourhood is great, especially if you're ¹⁷_____ young person!

8 Complete the sentences with your own ideas. Use *a*, *an*, *the* or no article.

1 The best thing about my town/city is …
2 If you want to relax, we have …
3 Our town/city needs …
4 … often come to my town/city to see …
5 One famous landmark I'd love to visit is …
6 If you want to get from the airport to the city centre you can take …

📱 Go to page 120 or your app for more information and practice.

Speaking

PREPARE

9 You're going to talk about your favourite town, city or neighbourhood. First, think about the questions below and make notes.

- Where is your favourite town/city/neighbourhood?
- What type of people live there?
- What do you like about it? Think about landmarks, cafés/restaurants, places to visit, things to do, nightlife, transport etc.
- Is there anything you don't like about it? Why?
- What's the most important thing about it for you?
- Do many people visit? If so, what type of people, and why do they come?
- What do people who visit usually notice about it?

SPEAK

10 a Work in pairs. Tell your partner about your favourite town, city or neighbourhood. Use the Useful phrases to help you.

Useful phrases
My favourite (restaurant/park/landmark) is …
I like/don't like (the nightlife/traffic).
I don't really like (the town centre/traffic).
The (old buildings/parks/town square) are/is really important to me.

b What is important to your partner about a town, city or neighbourhood? Do you both agree?

Develop your writing page 94

3D English in action

> **Goal:** ask for, follow and give directions

1 Look at the pictures and discuss the questions.
  1 What problem do the people have?
  2 How are they trying to solve their problem?

2 🔊 3.11 Listen to a man asking for directions and answer the questions.
  1 Where does he want to go?
  2 How many people does he have to ask?
  3 Why is he in a hurry?
  4 How far is it to the station?

3 a Listen again and complete conversations 1–3.
  1 **A:** Excuse me, _____ you _____ me _____ _____ get to the train station, please?
      B: Sorry, I don't know. I'm not from round here.
  2 **A:** Excuse me, _____ the quickest way _____ the train station?
      B: Just go straight _____ and _____ the first road _____ the left.
  3 **A:** Excuse me, I'm _____ _____ the train station!
      B: Don't worry, it's only _____ _____ walk … The train station's _____ _____ the bus station. You can't miss it!

b Work in pairs and compare your answers. Then listen again to check.

c Work in pairs. Practise the conversations in Exercise 3a.

4 Look at the Useful phrases for asking for directions. What kind of information is missing?

Useful phrases
Asking for directions
What's the best/quickest way to … , please?
Where's the nearest … , please?
How do I get to the … ?
Can you tell me how to get to the … ?
Can you tell me the way to … , please?
Excuse me, I'm looking for the …

Giving directions
Go straight on.
Take the first/second road on the left/right.
Turn left/right when you get to the … /after you pass the …
Walk along the street until you get to/see …
Cross over the road at (the traffic lights).
It's the first/second building on the right/left.
It's next to/across from/opposite the …
It's not far. It's about five/ten minutes' walk.

5 Work in pairs. You're visiting Edinburgh on holiday. You need to ask for directions to the places you want to visit. Student A: Turn to page 151. Student B: Turn to page 153. Ask for and give directions.

6 Work in pairs. Choose a place near your school and ask a partner for directions to get there.

Go online for the Roadmap video.

Check and reflect

1 a Complete the conversations with the past simple or present perfect form of the words in brackets.

1. **A:** When _____ (be) your last holiday? Where _____ (you / go)?
   B: I _____ (go) to Turkey with my family. _____ (you / ever / be) there?
2. **A:** How long _____ (you / live) in your flat?
   B: We _____ (be) there about five years, I think.
3. **A:** _____ (you / see) any good films recently?
   B: I _____ (see) a great film last night, actually, on Netflix. However, I _____ (not / go) to the cinema for a while. In fact, I don't think I _____ (be) since I _____ (see) the new James Bond film.
   A: Ah, I _____ (not / see) it yet. Is it any good?

b Work in pairs. Ask and answer the questions in Exercise 1a. Find out more information.

2 a Match the sentence halves.
I'd like to ...
1. apply   a. the piano.
2. take up   b. in a TV reality programme.
3. perform   c. on stage at the theatre.
4. take part   d. living in another country.
5. experience   e. to be a police officer.

b Complete sentence beginnings 1–5 with your own ideas. Work in pairs and discuss your sentences.

3 Complete the sentences with the words in the box.

catch   got   hang   keep   lost   meet   spend

1. I first got to know Peter at primary school. We _____ on well from the first time we met.
2. I _____ in touch with my friends mainly on social media. It's a great way to _____ up.
3. The friends I _____ most time with are Dasha and Olga. We usually _____ up every couple of days and we _____ out at one of our houses.
4. Unfortunately, I've _____ touch with an old friend called Erica.

4 Complete the questions with the words in brackets. Use the present perfect simple or the present perfect continuous.

1. **A:** _____ (you / travel) abroad much?
   B: I guess I _____ (go) to about five or six countries.
2. **A:** What _____ (you / do) recently?
   B: I've got exams, so I _____ (work) hard for those.
3. **A:** _____ (you / go) to any concerts recently?
   B: Yeah, I _____ (go) to a few. And, hey, did you know I _____ (just / join) a band?
4. **A:** What _____ (the weather / be) like recently?
   B: Well, we _____ (have) a bit of rain, but on the whole it _____ (be) pretty good.
5. **A:** _____ (you / follow) the news for the past few days?
   B: No, I _____ (be) too busy. What _____ (happen)?

5 a Complete the text with the words and phrases in the box. One of the words or phrases isn't necessary.

cycle lanes   landmarks   neighbourhood
outdoor cafés   pedestrian streets   suburb
traffic jam   square

There's an old ¹_____ at the centre of my town, which has a few ²_____ where people can sit and drink a coffee. Around the square are some ³_____ , where cars aren't allowed. These streets do have ⁴_____ though, so there are often a lot of cyclists there. My town has a few interesting ⁵_____ , such as an old bridge and a small castle, which are popular with visitors. I live in a quiet ⁶_____ about 20 minutes' walk from the centre. I love living here - I never want to move to a _____ , I like being near the shops and restaurants.

b Write some sentences about your town with the words and phrases in Exercise 5a.

6 Complete the text with *a*, *the* or no article.

I live in ¹_____ Oxford in ²_____ UK and I'm ³_____ student. I'm studying education at Brookes University and I want to be ⁴_____ teacher when I finish ⁵_____ course. ⁶_____ university is very international and it has many students from overseas, particularly from ⁷_____ China and other countries in ⁸_____ Asia. ⁹_____ Chinese students are the biggest overseas nationality. The university is about a mile from ¹⁰_____ city centre and is next to ¹¹_____ park which has a great view of ¹²_____ Oxford skyline and some of its buildings and landmarks, such as ¹³_____ Bodleian Library and the colleges.
¹⁴_____ park is very popular with ¹⁵_____ students and ¹⁶_____ other people who live nearby for walking, relaxing and playing ¹⁷_____ games.

Reflect

How confident do you feel about the statements below? Write 1–5 (1 = not very confident, 5 = very confident).

- I can talk about experiences.
- I can talk about what I've been doing recently.
- I can talk about a favourite town, city or neighbourhood.
- I can ask for, follow and give directions.

Want more practice?
Go to your Workbook or app.

4A The internet generation

> **Goal:** discuss and compare lifestyles
> **Grammar:** comparatives
> **Vocabulary:** lifestyles

Vocabulary

1 a Look at the photos. What kind of lifestyles do they show? Use the adjectives in the box to help you.

active	busy	easy-going	energetic	fun
healthy	inactive	quiet	sensible	simple
sociable	stressful	unhealthy		

b Which of the adjectives describe your lifestyle? Why?

2 a Choose the correct alternatives.

1 Leading a *healthy/stressful* lifestyle can help you live longer.
2 Many office workers have an *inactive/active* lifestyle sitting at a desk all day.
3 It's important to eat *a quiet/an unhealthy* diet and get plenty of exercise.
4 When people retire, they often prefer *an energetic/a quiet* lifestyle.
5 Many people prefer life in the city because it's *fun/simple*.
6 Small towns often have a relaxed, *easy-going/stressful* atmosphere.
7 Life in the city can seem *busy/quiet* after living in the country.
8 After a long tiring day at work, I don't always want to go out and be *sensible/sociable*.

b Complete the sentences with your own ideas.

1 A stressful day is when …
2 I don't think it's sensible to …
3 The problem with a busy lifestyle is …
4 Sociable people …
5 If you want a healthy lifestyle, don't …
6 Many people prefer a simple lifestyle because …

c Work in pairs and compare your sentences.

📱 Go to your app for more practice.

Reading

3 a Read the title and introduction of the article. How old are millennials?

WHO ARE THE MILLENNIALS?

The term *millennials* describes people born between the 1980s and the mid-2000s. They're also known as the *internet generation*. What's special about them?

❤ HEALTH AND WELLBEING
Millennials are more interested in health and fitness than previous generations. They exercise more regularly than any other generation. They eat better than older generations, too. Instead of buying fast food, they cook their own food – it's healthier and less fattening.

♻ THE ENVIRONMENT
Millennials are more worried about the environment than older age groups. More millennials are happy to pay a higher price for products that are good for the environment.

🐦 SOCIAL MEDIA
Millennials are the first generation born after the internet revolution. They're more connected than any generation before them and they start to use new digital and mobile tools faster. They're also more likely to use social media.

£ LESS IS MORE
Millennials aren't buying as much as older generations. They're not as interested in owning things as their parents. They care about interesting experiences more than cars, phones and expensive clothes.

🏠 HOUSE AND HOME
Fewer adults in this age group own their own home. Many still live with their parents or share a rented flat. Millennials are just as hard-working as their parents, but they earn less money.

6 a 🔊 **4.1** Listen and notice the pronunciation of *than* and *as*. Are they stressed?
1. Millennials eat better than older generations.
2. They're not as interested in things as their parents are.
3. They're just as hard-working as their parents.

b Listen again and repeat.

7 Rewrite the sentences using the words in brackets so they mean the same.
1. Other generations aren't as interested in the environment as millennials. (more)
   Millennials are more interested in the environment than other generations.
2. Older generations aren't as healthy as millennials. (less)
3. They go to the gym less often than millennials. (as)
4. They don't buy as much fresh food as millennials. (less)
5. Millennials don't own as many things as their parents. (fewer)
6. They earn less money than their parents. (as)
7. Older generations don't work harder than millennials. (as)

8 a Write sentences to compare two things.
1. young people / older generations
   Young people work as hard as older generations.
2. home-cooked food / fast food
3. living with family / renting a flat
4. cycling / driving
5. the weather in my country / the weather in the UK
6. life in the country / life in the city
7. going out in the evening / staying at home

b Work in pairs and compare your sentences.

📱 Go to page 122 or your app for more information and practice.

b Read the article. Are the sentences true (T) or false (F)?
1. A healthy lifestyle is very important to millennials.
2. They don't want to pay more for healthy products.
3. They are good with technology.
4. Owning things is important to them.
5. Many millennials don't have enough money to buy their own home.

4 Work in pairs. Are the sentences in Exercise 3b true for millennials in your country?

Grammar

5 Read the grammar box and choose the correct alternatives.

Comparatives

Form the comparative of most short adjectives and adverbs like *tall*, *long* or *fast*, by adding **¹**-*er*/-*ier*.
*Millennials are happy to pay a **higher** price for products that are good for the environment.*
When an adjective ends in -*y*, change -*y* to **²**-*ier*/-*iest*.
*Millennials cook their own food - it's **healthier**.*
Form the comparative of adverbs ending in -*ly* and longer adjectives, by adding **³***more*/*much* or *less*. Use *than* to make a comparison with something else.
*Millennials exercise **more regularly than** any other generation.*
*Fresh food is **less fattening**.*
Some adjectives and adverbs are irregular, e.g.
- *good/well* → *better*
- *bad/badly* → **⁴** *worst*/*worse*

*Their diet is **worse than** younger generations'.*
Use (*not*) *as* + adjective/adverb + **⁵***as*/*than* to make comparisons.
*Millennials are **as hard-working as** their parents.*
We can also compare nouns.
***More millennials** are happy to pay a higher price …*
***Fewer adults** in this age group own their own home.*
*Millennials earn **less money**.*

Speaking

PREPARE

9 a 🔊 **4.2** You're going to discuss and compare lifestyles with a partner. First, listen to two people comparing their lifestyles. What topics in the article in Exercise 3a do they mention?

b Listen again. How are their lifestyles similar? How are they different?

10 Look at the words in the box and make notes about your lifestyle.

| exercise | food | free time | home | technology |
| work | | | | |

SPEAK

11 a Work in pairs. Tell your partner about your lifestyle.

b How are your lifestyles similar? How are they different? Tell the class.

Develop your listening page 95

4A | The internet generation

4B Popular brands

> **Goal:** express preferences about brands
> **Grammar:** superlatives
> **Vocabulary:** products and services

Reading and vocabulary

1 a Read the definition and discuss the questions.

> A **brand** is a type of product made by a particular company that has a particular name or design.

1 Are brands important to you? Why/Why not?
2 What are your favourite brands? Why do you like them?

b Look at the photos. What brands can you think of for these types of products?

2 a Read the article. What makes a strong brand?

What is brand loyalty?

Many of us have *brand loyalty* to certain products and services. Two pairs of sports shoes might be made of exactly the same material and be made in similar factories by people with similar skills, but because we like the brand we will always choose pair A over pair B. That's why it's so important to have a good brand and that's why companies spend millions of pounds on it.

Today, people have more choice than ever before. That's why it's important for companies to have a clear and easy-to-recognise brand to attract the most customers. So, what makes a strong brand? Here are some of the most important things that companies need to think about.

1 Brand identity – a logo or a phrase that everyone knows
2 Brand personality – what people think the product is like, e.g. fun, cool, healthy
3 Brand values – what the people making the product believe in, e.g. they take care of the environment, they give money to charity, etc.

b Do comments 1–3 refer to brand identity, personality or values?

1 'We want our toys to help children learn and to do the best they can.'
2 'We're the country's friendliest restaurant with the greatest customer service. Think of us and you think of fun and good times.'
3 'We make the strongest, loudest bikes for the strongest, loudest guys.'

3 Read the sentences. Are the words in bold positive or negative when used to describe brands?

1 Electric cars are more **environmentally friendly** than cars that use petrol.
2 This digital camera takes **high quality** photos and it's very **easy to use**. It's also **good value** at under £200.
3 The company's new family car model is **poorly designed** and **poor value** for money. It uses a lot of petrol and is **not environmentally friendly**.
4 This company offers **excellent service** to all its customers. That's why it's so **popular**.
5 Their products look beautiful, are **well designed** and very **reliable**. You can be sure they will last for years.
6 It's not a good idea to buy second-hand electrical goods like washing machines because they are **unreliable** and break down more often.

4 Choose the correct alternatives.

1 They are so *reliable/easy to use*, they never break down.
2 They're very *good value/high quality* for money; similar brands are twice the price.
3 They have excellent *quality/customer service* – they're really helpful when you have a problem.
4 The website is *easy to use/environmentally friendly* – you can find everything you need really quickly.
5 These products are *good value/unpopular* because they are so *hard to use/easy to use*.
6 The company has excellent brand values. Their products are *environmentally friendly/not environmentally friendly* and *poor/high* quality.

5 a 🔊 4.6 Listen and underline the stressed syllables.

1 reliable
2 well designed
3 environmentally friendly
4 high quality
5 good value

b Listen again and repeat.

📱 Go to page 139 or your app for more vocabulary and practice.

Grammar

6 Read the grammar box and choose the correct alternatives.

Superlatives

Use *the* + adjective +¹ *-er* or *-ier*/ *-est* or *-iest* to form the superlative of most short adjectives and adverbs.
They're **the strongest**, **loudest** bikes ...
We're **the** country's **friendliest** restaurant.
Use *the* + ² *most*/ *more* + adjective to form the superlative of longer adjectives and adverbs ending in *-ly*.
Here are some of **the most important** things.
Use *the least* to form the superlative of adjectives and adverbs. It is the opposite of *the most*.
What are **the least popular** brands?
Some adjectives and adverbs have irregular superlatives.
- good/well → ³ the best/ the better
- bad/badly → ⁴ the worse/ the worst

We want our children to do **the best** they can.
Use a superlative adjective with the present perfect tense.
It was **the worst** customer service we**'ve ever had**.

7 a 🔊 4.7 Listen and notice the pronunciation of *most*. How is the pronunciation of *most* different in sentences 1 and 2?

1 Here are some of the most important things to think about.
2 It's one of the world's most popular brands.

b Listen again and repeat.

8 a Complete the sentences with the superlative form of the words in brackets.

1 It's _____ (popular) brand in my country.
2 They're _____ (bad) value for money.
3 I think it's _____ (good) brand of sunglasses I have ever worn.
4 I think design is _____ (important) thing a company has to think about.
5 It's not the cheapest, but it is _____ (easy) to use.
6 Yes, they're the cheapest, but they're not _____. (environmentally friendly)

b Make questions using the prompts. Use the superlative.

1 What / popular / car / in your country?
What's the most popular car in your country?
2 What / good / item of clothing / ever / bought?
3 Which / phone company / reliable / customer service?
4 What / funny / advert / see / recently?
5 Who / do the food shopping / often / in your family?
6 What / bad / shopping experience / ever / have?

c Work in pairs. Ask and answer the questions.

📱 Go to page 122 or your app for more information and practice.

Speaking

PREPARE

9 a 🔊 4.8 You're going to compare some brands. First, listen to two people comparing brands and answer the questions.
1 What product do they talk about?
2 How many brands do they mention?

b Listen again. What does Charlie think about each brand? Which brand does he recommend? Why?

SPEAK

10 a Work in groups. Choose a product or service. Think of some popular brands for that product or service.

b Compare the brands you have chosen. Put them in order from best to worst (1 = the best). Use the Useful phrases to help you. Think about the following:
- brand identity/values
- quality
- cost
- customer service

Useful phrases
What do you think about (this brand)?
I think ... is good because (it's reliable/good value).
I'm not sure about that.

c Which product or service was top of your list?

Develop your writing page 96

4c Favourite films

> **Goal:** describe the plot of a film
> **Grammar:** defining relative clauses
> **Vocabulary:** types of film

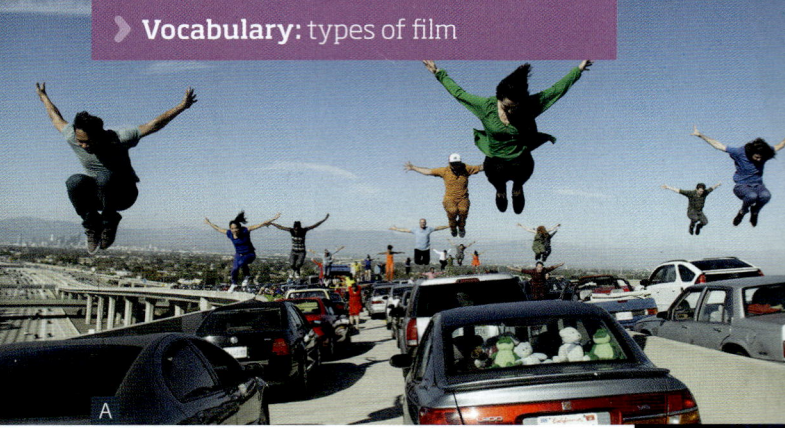

Vocabulary and listening

1 Read the comments. Which do you agree with? Which do you disagree with? Why?

1. I love watching old films. They're really interesting!
2. I like films that make me laugh. I don't like anything sad.
3. I guess I go to the cinema about once a week. I like to see all the latest films.

2 a Work in pairs. Match photos A–F with the types of film in the box.

> action   animation   biopic
> comedy   documentary   fantasy
> historical drama   horror   musical
> romantic comedy   science fiction
> thriller   war film

b Match the types of film in Exercise 2a with descriptions 1–6.
1. It's a film which has exciting car chases, good guys, bad guys and explosions.
2. It tells the story of someone's life.
3. It's a film about love, it's funny and it usually has a happy ending.
4. It's a type of film that often has robots, space ships and aliens.
5. It's a scary film, which you should never watch alone.
6. It's a film which is set in the past, often during an important event.

c Work in pairs. Which is your favourite type of film? Are there any types of films you don't like? Why?

3 a 🔊 4.9 Listen and underline the stressed syllables.
1. fantasy
2. science fiction
3. horror
4. documentary
5. animation

b Listen again and repeat.

4 a 🔊 4.10 Listen to Taylor talking about her favourite film. What does she like about it?

b Listen again and make notes about:
- the type of film.
- where the film is set.
- the actors.
- the story of the film.

c Work in pairs and compare your notes. Listen again to check your answers.

📱 Go to page 139 or your app for more vocabulary and practice.

Grammar

5 Read the grammar box and choose the correct alternatives.

Defining relative clauses

Use defining relative clauses to give information about a person, place, thing or moment in time.
- Use *who* or *that* for ¹*people/times*.
  *It shows people **who** feel really lost.*
- Use *that* or *which* for ²*things/reasons*.
  *I think it's a film **which** is funny and also says something about life.*
- Use *whose* to show possession.
  *She plays a woman **whose** husband is a photographer.*
- Use *when* for time and *where* for ³*places/amounts*.
  *My favourite scene is the one **when** they meet …*
  *It's a city **where** they both feel a bit lost.*

The relative pronouns *who*, *which* and *that* can be omitted when they come before a noun or a pronoun.
*It's one of the first films (**which/that**) Scarlett Johansson appeared in.*

6 a 🔊 4.11 Listen to the sentences. Are the words *who*, *which* and *that* stressed?

1 It's about a man who wins the lottery.
2 It's a film which I really enjoyed.
3 She plays the scientist that discovers the cure.

b Listen again and repeat.

7 a Join the sentences with a relative pronoun in the box. Sometimes more than one pronoun is possible.

| that | when | where | which | who | whose |

1 It's a film. I saw it when I was young.
   It's a film which I saw when I was young.
2 It's a film. It always makes me cry.
3 It's about a man. The man's brother has disappeared.
4 He lives in a town. Strange things happen in the town.
5 She's a student. She wants to escape from her small town.
6 They find a robot. The robot can tell them what will happen in the future.
7 The robot comes from a different time. Only robots live on Earth then.
8 It's a film. I'd recommend the film to anyone.

b In which two sentences can you leave out the relative pronoun? Why?

8 a Complete the sentences with your own ideas.
1 I like films that …
2 I don't enjoy films which …
3 Good actors are people who …
4 I saw a great film set in a place where …
5 It's a story about two people whose …
6 I saw the film on a day when …

b Work in pairs and compare your sentences.

📱 Go to page 122 or your app for more information and practice.

Speaking

PREPARE

9 You're going to describe one of your favourite films. First, read the questions and make notes.
- What kind of film is it?
- Who is the director?
- Who are the actors?
- Where is it set?
- What is it about?
- What happens?
- How does it end?
- Why do you like it?

SPEAK

10 a Work in groups. Tell your group about your film. Use the Useful phrases to help you.

Useful phrases
OK, so tell us about your film.
So, one of my favourite films is …
It's a very special film for me because …

b Which film would you most like to see? Why?

Develop your reading
page 97

4D English in action

Goal: ask for and give opinions

1 Look at the photos and discuss the questions.
1. What activities can you see?
2. Do you enjoy doing these activities in your free time? Why/Why not?

2 a 🔊 4.12 Listen to some people discussing things they have done recently. Which activities do they mention?

b Listen again. How did the speakers feel about the book, film or event they mentioned?

c Works in pairs and compare your answers.

3 a 🔊 4.13 Try to complete the sentences from the conversations. Then listen and check your answers.
1. Oh, I want to read that! How _____ it?
2. Um, it was OK, _____ guess.
3. I mean, it's good, just not his _____ .
4. No, was _____ good?
5. Amazing! I really _____ it. Best film I've seen in ages.
6. Did you _____ it?
7. Yeah, to be _____ , I found it a bit boring.

b Listen to the sentences again. In which sentences do the speakers show that they are excited or interested?

c Listen again and repeat.

4 Look at the Useful phrases. Can you think of any other expressions to add to each section?

Useful phrases

Asking for opinions
What did you think of it?
Did you like/enjoy it?
How was it?
Was it good?

Expressing opinions
Negative
I thought it was awful/terrible, to be honest.
It's not my kind of thing.
I found it a bit boring.
I was a bit disappointed.
Positive
I really enjoyed it.
It was amazing!
Best film/book I've seen/watched in ages.
I thought he was really good.
Neutral
It was OK, I guess.
It's good, but/just not her best.

5 a Choose two categories below and make lists.
- TV programmes I've watched recently
  Game of Thrones, Humans, The Vikings ...
- books I've read
- films I've watched
- cultural events I've been to

b Work in pairs. Tell each other about your lists.
A: *I saw Brubaker last week.*
B: *Oh, how was it?*

c Which of your partner's programmes/books/films/events would you like to see/read/go to? Why?

Go online for the Roadmap video.

Check and reflect

1 Complete the sentences with the words in the box.

| active | busy | fun | healthy | inactive | sociable |
| stressful | unhealthy | | | | |

1. She has a very _____ and _____ lifestyle. She always eats well and gets lots of physical exercise.
2. He sits at home all day, eats lots of fast food and never does any exercise. He has a really _____ and _____ lifestyle.
3. I have a very _____ and _____ lifestyle. I have a lot of pressure at work and I never have enough time to relax.
4. They have a _____ and _____ lifestyle, always meeting friends and going to parties.

2 a Complete the conversations with the correct form of the words in brackets and any other words needed.

1. **A:** Which is _____ (big), China or the US?
   B: I don't think China is _____ (big) the US.
2. **A:** Do you think people today are _____ (healthy) they used to be?
   B: Well, people certainly live _____ (long) they used to. So, I'd say yes, I guess people must be _____ (healthy) these days.
3. **A:** Which do you prefer, football or rugby?
   B: I think rugby is much _____ (interesting) football. It's much _____ (exciting) to watch.
4. **A:** Do you think people spend _____ or _____ (money) they used to on socialising?
   B: That's a good question. I think today, young people especially, spend _____ (time) at home using social media, so maybe they spend _____ (money) as they are not going out.

b Work in pairs. Do you agree with the ideas and opinions in Exericse 2a?

3 a Complete the sentences with the words in the box.

| brand | designed | popular | quality | reliable |
| use | | | | |

1. My mobile phone is well _____ .
2. My running shoes are high _____ .
3. Our television is a top _____ .
4. Coffee shops are very _____ .
5. My camera is easy to _____ .
6. The internet at home is really good. It's very _____ .

b Write sentences about things that you own or services or companies that you have used.

4 Complete the quiz questions with the superlative form of the adjectives in brackets. Then choose the correct answer.

1. _____ (expensive) car ever sold is (a) Italian (b) British (c) German.
2. _____ (big) selling English-language book of all time is by (a) JRR Tolkien (b) Charles Dickens (c) JK Rowling.
3. _____ (old) shopping mall in the world is (a) Galleria Vittorio in Milan (b) GUM in Moscow (c) Houston Galleria in Texas.
4. After water, _____ (popular) drink in the world is (a) fruit juice (b) coffee (c) tea.
5. _____ (happy) countries, according to the World Happiness Report, are (a) Finland and Norway. (b) Spain and Italy (b) Australia and New Zealand.
6. According to research, _____ (good) time of day to study is in the (a) morning (b) afternoon (c) evening.

5 Complete the sentences with the words in the box.

| biopic | fantasy | horror | musical | science fiction |
| thriller | | | | |

1. My favourite _____ is *The Theory of Everything* about the life of Stephen Hawking.
2. I really like the singing and dancing in *La La Land*. It's probably my favourite _____ .
3. I love _____ films, especially ones which are about space. I think *Interstellar* is probably my favourite.
4. My favourite _____ films are all the classic old 1970s ones about Dracula and Frankenstein.
5. My favourite _____ is *No way out*. It's about looking for a spy in the Pentagon in the US. It's very exciting.
6. The Lord of the Rings films are my favourite _____ films. I just love all the magic and the special effects.

6 Join the sentence halves with a relative pronoun.

1. I prefer books
2. I get on best with people
3. I really love days
4. I like visiting places

a. I have nothing to do.
b. like the same music as me.
c. are about real events and people.
d. there is a lot of history and culture.

Reflect

How confident do you feel about the statements below? Write 1–5 (1 = not very confident, 5 = very confident).
- I can discuss and compare lifestyles.
- I can express preferences about brands.
- I can describe the plot of a film.
- I can ask for and give opinions.

Want more practice?
Go to your Workbook or app.

5A How does it look?

- **Goal:** make guesses about people
- **Grammar:** modal verbs: possibility and deduction
- **Vocabulary:** describing clothes and appearance

Vocabulary

1 Discuss the questions.
1. Do you prefer smart or casual clothes?
2. What clothes do you wear at different times, for example, at work or at home?
3. Can you tell what people are like from their clothes?

2 a Read the comments. Which of the descriptions is closest to your own style?

1. I want to look good so I like **fashionable** clothes. I always want to look modern and **stylish**. It's important for me to have a **matching** bag and shoes, too, so these have to be the same colour as the other clothes I'm wearing.

2. I don't like to **dress up** in **smart** clothes, like a suit and tie. I prefer relaxing in some **casual** old jeans.

3. I like to wear vintage clothes ... you know, the kind of clothes people wore forty years ago. I don't think they're **old-fashioned** and I like to look a bit different.

4. I don't really care what I've **got on**, just as long as I'm comfortable. That's why I never wear **tight** clothes – they stop me moving easily. I prefer to wear big, **loose**, comfortable clothes.

b Work in pairs. Do you know anyone who matches descriptions 1–4 in Exercise 2a?

3 Choose the correct alternatives.

My mum thinks I need to ¹*dress up / wear* and look more ²*stylish / old-fashioned* for my new job. She thinks my clothes aren't modern enough, so she took me shopping yesterday to buy some ³*smart / casual* clothes for the office. She says I can't just wear old jeans to work! And she says I have to have ⁴*tight / matching* shoes and bags, too. You know – everything in the same colour. That's not really my style at all! Anyway, we went to about ten different shops. I didn't like anything and, in the end, we only bought one jacket. I really like it! It's orange. It's ⁵*loose / tight*, so I can wear a thick sweater under it when it's cold. It doesn't match anything though!

4 Work in pairs. Describe what you've got on today.

📱 Go to page 140 or your app for more vocabulary and practice.

Reading and listening

5 Read the first paragraph of the story. Who do you think the girl is? What do you think is wrong?

One cold day in the city, passers-by notice a young girl standing on the main street, outside one of the biggest buildings. She's wearing casual clothes. She's got an old denim jacket on and a grey sweater, tight jeans and flat black shoes. She is thin, with long blonde hair. She is pale and looks cold. She looks lost and confused.

She looks as if she is about 14 or 15 years old. The people who see her think she must be in trouble, or they think she may be ill or lost. They are worried about her. Someone calls the police. The police take her to hospital. She only starts to speak a few days later, but it is clear that she doesn't speak English, so she can't give the police any information about herself. She communicates through drawings. From the drawings, the police guess that she must be running away. The police think she must be from another country. She definitely can't be English-speaking because she doesn't understand them. However, she could be from somewhere else in Europe.

They start a search to find out who she is so they can return her to her family. Three weeks later they still don't know who she is, so they take an unusual step. They put her photo in the newspapers and on TV.

6 Read the next part of the story and answer the questions.
1. Where is the girl?
2. How does she look?
3. Do people think something is wrong? Are they sure about this?
4. How does she communicate with the police?
5. What guesses do the police make about her? Why?
6. What unusual step do the police take?

7 a 🔊 **5.1** Listen to the end of the story and choose the correct alternatives.
  1 The woman *called/ didn't call* the police.
  2 The girl *was/ wasn't* older than she looked.
  3 She *was/ wasn't* doing a test of how people behave to strangers.
  4 This *wasn't/ was* part of her university course.
  5 Her family *knew/ didn't know*.

b What do you think about the girl's experiment? Was it a good idea?

Grammar

8 Read the grammar box and choose the correct alternatives.

Modal verbs: possibility and deduction

Use *may, might, could* + infinitive ¹*with 'to'/ without 'to'* to make guesses about present and future situations.
*She **may be** ill.*
*She **might be** lost.*
*She **could be** from somewhere else.*
*She **might not be** here tomorrow.*
Use *seem to* to express strong possibility.
*She **seems to be** very cold.*
Use *must* + infinitive without *to* when you ²*are sure/ are not sure* that something is true.
*She **must be** from another country.*
Use *can't* + infinitive without *to* when you are sure that something isn't true.
*She definitely **can't be** English-speaking because she doesn't understand them.*

9 a 🔊 **5.2** Listen and notice the pronunciation of the letters in bold.
  1 She could**n't** be from anywhere else.
  2 She definitely ca**n't** be English-speaking.
  3 She mu**st** be from another country.

b Listen again and repeat.

10 Choose the correct alternatives.
  1 I'm not sure. I suppose they *can't/ might not* know the answer.
  2 *Could/ Must* he be lost? He's looking at his phone.
  3 She seems *be/ to be* happy — she's smiling.
  4 They're wearing coats so it *can't/ must* be cold there.
  5 It's not very clear and they may not *to be/ be* able to see the boat.
  6 I think they *look/ might* be scared.

11 Write responses to the situations. Use *may, might, could, must* and *can't*.
  1 Your friend is late for a dinner at your house. She's been to your house before.
     She can't be lost. She knows the way.
  2 You meet your friend outside on a freezing cold day and he's wearing only shorts and a T-shirt.
  3 A family you don't know are standing outside the house next door. They have suitcases with them.
  4 A woman dressed in very smart clothes comes to your work and goes to your manager's office.
  5 You see some people singing on your street.
  6 A man is standing outside a very expensive restaurant. He is wearing casual clothes and looks cold and hungry.

📱 Go to page 124 or your app for more information and practice.

Speaking

PREPARE

12 🔊 **5.3** You're going to make guesses about people from their photos. First, listen to two people doing the same. Tick the points they mention.
  - how old they are
  - who they are with
  - their clothes
  - their hairstyles
  - where they are
  - the time of day
  - their expressions
  - what they are doing

SPEAK

13 a Look at the photos on page 154 and make guesses about the people.

b Read the facts about the people on page 152. How close were your guesses?

Develop your writing
page 98

5A | How does it look?

5B Living space

- **Goal:** discuss advantages and disadvantages
- **Grammar:** zero and first conditional
- **Vocabulary:** places to live

Vocabulary and listening

1 Discuss the questions.
1. What type of accommodation do you live in?
2. What do you like and dislike about it?

2 a Find the things in the box in the photos A–J. What can't you see?

| air conditioning   balcony   block of flats   ceiling |
| central heating   cottage   detached house |
| entrance   floor   patio   roof   staircase   studio |
| terraced house |

b Complete the table with the words and phrases in the box in Exercise 2a.

Types of buildings	Things you find in/around buildings

c Work in pairs and discuss the questions.
1. Which of these words would you use when you are describing your own home?
2. Which of the homes in the photos would you like to live in?
3. What would your ideal home be like?

3 a Choose the correct alternatives.
1. Noisy neighbours make living in a *block of flats/ detached house* very difficult!
2. We don't have *air conditioning/central heating* so the house gets very cold in winter.
3. I just want one room so a *studio/terraced house* is fine for me.
4. I want to sit outside, but I don't want a garden. A *patio/ roof* is what I want.
5. A pretty country *cottage/entrance* with a garden is what I'm looking for.
6. I like space, so I don't like to leave too many things on the *floor/ceiling*.
7. My flat has got a big *staircase/balcony* full of plants.

b Work in pairs. Which of the sentences in Exercise 3a are true for you?

Go to your app for more practice.

4 a You're going to listen to a radio programme about small homes. First, think of possible advantages and disadvantages of living in a small home.

b 5.4 Listen to the programme. Were any of your ideas mentioned? What other ideas did they talk about?

5 Work in pairs. Which do you prefer, a small home in an area that you like, or a large home in an area you don't like? Why?

Grammar

6 Read the grammar box and choose the correct alternatives.

Zero and first conditional

Use *if/when* + present simple + **¹***present simple/will* to talk about something that is always true or that always happens.
When you **live** in a small space, you **don't need** so much furniture.
Do you **pay** a high rent **if** you **live** in a small house or flat?

Use *if* + **²***present simple/will* + *will/may/might/could* + verb to talk about the possible or likely future result of another action. *Will* is more certain than *may/might/could*.
You **won't** have so many rooms **if** you **go** small.
Use *unless* to mean **³** *if/if not*.
Unless you **are** a very tidy person, a tiny house **will become** messy very quickly.

7 a 🔊 **5.5** Listen and notice the pronunciation of *will*.
1 Your heating will cost less.
2 Having more space will make you much happier!
3 The bills will be much lower.

b Listen again and repeat.

8 a Match the sentence halves.
1 If you have a big house,
2 If we get a place in the centre of town,
3 If we get a place without air conditioning,
4 Terraced houses are nice if

a you have more rooms to clean!
b we'll be really uncomfortable in summer.
c we will be closer to everything we need.
d you don't mind noisy neighbours.

b Which of the sentences are about:
a a situation which is always true?
b a possible future situation?

9 Complete the sentences with your own ideas.
1 If you live in a block of flats, …
2 If you live in a small flat, …
3 Unless you buy a …
4 If your neighbours aren't friendly, …
5 If a flat has a big balcony, …
6 When people live in a detached house in a suburb, …

📱 Go to page 124 or your app for more information and practice.

Speaking

PREPARE

10 You're going to look for somewhere new to live. First, think about what things are important to you. Make notes about:
- where (town/country/city centre/suburbs)
- type of accommodation (flat/cottage/studio/detached house)
- size (small/tiny/large; number of rooms)
- characteristics (balcony/patio/garden/modern/old)
- cost (what is your budget?)

SPEAK

11 Work in pairs. Student A: Turn to page 151. Student B: Turn to page 152.

12 Report back to the class. Which of the places did you choose? Why did you choose it?

Develop your reading page 99

5c Eating well

> **Goal:** plan a special occasion
> **Grammar:** quantifiers
> **Vocabulary:** describing food

Vocabulary and reading

1 a Look at the photos. What food can you see?

b What other food can you name? Think about the categories below.

| dairy products | fish | fruit | meat | seafood |
| vegetables | | | | |

2 a Read comments 1–8. Which are true for you? Compare your ideas with a partner and check the meaning of the words in bold if necessary.
   1 'I mostly eat **vegetarian** food, but I do eat meat sometimes.'
   2 'I don't like **sweet** food much. I prefer **savoury** snacks, salty things like crisps and nuts.'
   3 'I love the taste of **fresh** bread when it's just come out of the oven.'
   4 'I like **spicy** food because it's really **tasty**, but I can't eat it if it's too **hot**!'
   5 'I avoid eating too much **fried** food as I don't think it's **healthy**. I prefer **grilled** fish to fried fish.'
   6 'I love my mum's **homemade** cakes. My friends do, too!'
   7 'I don't like anything with a **bitter** taste, like coffee.'
   8 'I prefer to eat something **light** at night. I don't sleep well on a full stomach.'

b Answer the questions about the words in bold in Exercise 2a.
   1 Which words describe how something tastes?
   2 Which words describe how food is cooked?
   3 Which words are often used in a positive way?

📱 Go to page 140 or your app for more vocabulary and practice.

3 a Read the extract from a food blog and the comments. Which comment best matches your lifestyle and diet?

b What does 'eating well' mean for you?

What does 'eating well' mean for you?

These days there's lots of advice about how to eat well. Every day it seems there's a new piece of advice. Eat a varied diet with plenty of fruit and vegetables. Eat regular meals, don't eat too much or too little per meal. Don't eat any snacks between meals. Don't eat too much sugar and dairy …

However, is there such a thing as the perfect diet? I believe there are many different ways to eat well – the right diet is the one that works best for you and your lifestyle. What makes you feel good?

> I agree a balanced diet is good. I know eating a lot of sweets and chocolate is bad for you, but you have to enjoy life as well, don't you? I often have a chocolate bar in the afternoon, but I go to the gym regularly so I don't worry about it! – *Anna*

> My lifestyle is really busy, so I have very little time to shop or cook. I know I eat too many takeaways! However, I always eat Sunday lunch with my family. It's usually roast chicken with several different vegetables. That keeps me healthy and happy! – *Jan*

> I'm a vegetarian most of the time, so I don't eat any meat, eggs or dairy products. I eat a lot of vegetables and I love making interesting meals with them – my spicy curry with peppers, onions and carrots is famous in my family! I eat some fish now and then – grilled, not fried! I think I eat really well. My diet works for me. – *Sam*

> I work from home and I eat several small meals a day. It helps me to concentrate on my work. Eating a big meal makes me feel sleepy. There are a few foods that I avoid, like cheese. I like it, but I can only eat a little. – *Peter*

👍❤ 34

Grammar

4 Read the grammar box. Find examples of quantifiers in the comments in Exercise 3.

Quantifiers

Use these words in positive sentences:
- *some, a lot of/lots of, enough* + plural countable noun/uncountable noun
  Try to take **some** exercise every day.
  I eat **a lot of/enough** vegetables.
- *many, a few* + plural countable noun
  There are **many** different kinds of diet.
- *(a) little, a bit of* + uncountable noun
  I like **a bit of** sugar in my coffee.

Use these words in negative sentences and questions:
- *any, a lot/lots of, enough* + plural countable/uncountable noun
  Vegans **don't** eat **any** food from animals.
  Do you eat **enough** fruit?
- *many* + plural countable noun
  I don't eat **many** sweets.
- *much* + uncountable noun
  I don't drink **much** coffee.

Use *too much/too many* to say 'more than we need'.
Don't eat **too much** chocolate or **too many** sweets.
Use *How much/How many?* in questions and *Not much/many, A lot, A few/little* in short answers.
How much meat do you eat? **Not much/A lot**.

5 a 🔊 **5.6** Listen and notice the pronunciation of *of*.
1 Eat plenty of fruit and vegetables.
2 Eating a lot of sweets is bad for you.
3 I eat lots of vegetables.

b Listen again and repeat.

6 Complete the questions with *much, many, a lot of, a few* or *a little*.
1 Do you ever miss breakfast if you haven't got _____ time in the morning? Do you eat snacks during the day?
2 Do you eat _____ meat? Why/Why not?
3 How _____ portions of fruit and vegetables do you eat daily? Do you think you eat enough?
4 How _____ exercise do you take during the week? Do you need to take more?
5 Do you make a lot of different meals, or do you only do _____?
6 Do you add _____ salt to your cooking or only _____, or none at all? Why?
7 If a friend asks you for _____ suggestions for a healthy diet, can you think of two or three?

7 a Write three more questions with *much, many, a lot of, a few* and *a little*.

b Work in pairs. Ask and answer the questions in Exercises 6 and 7a.

📱 Go to page 124 or your app for more information and practice.

Speaking

PREPARE

8 🔊 **5.7** You're going to plan the food for a special event or occasion. First, listen to three friends planning a barbecue and answer the questions.
1 How many people are coming?
2 Why do they need to buy fish?
3 Why doesn't Vicky want to buy too much sweet food?

SPEAK

9 a Work in groups. Choose one of the events or occasions below or your own idea.
- a dinner party for friends
- a child's birthday party
- a barbecue in the garden
- visitors for the weekend

b Talk about who will be there and what you will provide to eat and drink. Use the Useful phrases to help you. Make a shopping list.

Useful phrases
Let's get lots of (fruit/sweets/cake).
How about some (savoury snacks)?
We should get something (healthy/vegetarian).
I don't think we need any (fruit/coffee).
I can bring a few (snacks/drinks).

c Tell the class about your event or occasion. Can they guess what kind of event it is?

Develop your listening
page 100

5D English in action

> **Goal:** give instructions and ask for information

1 Look at the pictures and discuss the questions.
1 Which of the cooks are you more similar to? Why?
2 What dishes can you cook well?

2 a 🔊 5.11 Listen to Carl telling his friend Sophie how to make an omelette. Put the instructions in the order that you hear them.

Making an omelette

- Then fold the omelette in half.
- First of all, you put the eggs, salt and pepper and water into a bowl.
- Take a fork and mix them all together.
- Next, add the cheese or mushrooms.
- When the butter is hot, add the eggs.
- While the eggs are cooking, keep moving them.
- Then put some butter into a pan.
- Finally, take it out of the pan and put it on a plate.

b Listen again and tick the Useful phrases that you hear.

Useful phrases

Asking for information
Could you tell me/Do you know how to make (bread)?
Could you give me the recipe for (this cake)?
What ingredients do I need?
How do I make (lasagne)?
How long does that take?
Is there anything else?

Giving instructions
First (of all), you …
Then …
Next, …
While the … is cooking, wash/chop …
Finally, …
That's it.

Confirming understanding
OK, I've got that.
Right/OK, go on.
Right, that's clear.

c 🔊 5.12 Listen to the sentences. Are the words *first*, *next* and *then* stressed?
1 First, you put some oil in a pan.
2 Then, you leave it for five minutes.
3 Next, you add some onion and garlic.

3 a Choose the correct alternatives.
A: Could you ¹*tell/give me* the recipe for your mushroom risotto? What ²*ingredients/foods* do I need?
B: Well, you need risotto rice, onions, mushrooms and stock.
A: OK, is there ³*more/anything* else?
B: No, I think that's it.
A: And how do you ⁴*make/do* it?
B: Well, ⁵*one/first*, you fry an onion for five minutes and ⁶*than/then* add the rice. Then add the stock little by little. ⁷*If/While* you are doing this, fry some mushrooms. Keep adding more stock until the rice is cooked.
A: How long does that ⁸*take/wait*?
B: Maybe about 20 minutes. Then ⁹*finally/in the end*, add the mushrooms and cook for a few more minutes. And ¹⁰*that's/what's* it.

b Work in pairs. Practise the conversation in Exercise 3a.

4 a Work in pairs. Student A: Turn to page 155. Read the recipe notes and give your partner instructions. Student B ask your partner questions. Use the Useful phrases to help you.

b Swap roles. Student B: Turn to page 156. Read the notes and give your partner instructions. Student A ask your partner questions.

Go online for the Roadmap video.

Check and reflect

1 a Complete the sentences with the words in the box.

casual   dress up   fashionable   loose
old-fashioned   smart   tight

1. I generally like to wear _____ clothes, like a suit and tie. Or maybe just a jacket and tie. I rarely wear jeans.
2. I'm not interested in being _____ or stylish. I really don't care if people think I look _____ .
3. I generally prefer more _____ clothes like jeans and a T-shirt. However, I do like to _____ from time to time, maybe for a special occasion.
4. I don't really like _____ clothes because you can't move so easily and freely. I generally prefer _____ clothes. I find them more comfortable.

b Which of the sentences in Exercise 1a describe you and your attitude to clothes?

2 Complete the conversation with *must, might, could* or *can't*.

A: When did the World Wide Web start? Was it 1981, 1991 or 2001?
B: Well, it ¹_____ be 1981, there wasn't even the internet then. I suppose it ²_____ be 2001, but I'm pretty sure it was before then. So I guess it ³_____ be 1991.
A: That's correct! Next question. Which team has won the most World Cups?
B: Well, it ⁴_____ be my country – we've only won it once. It ⁵_____ be Germany or Italy … Oh, wait, it ⁶_____ be Brazil, they've won it so many times!

3 a Choose the correct alternatives.

I live on the fifth floor of a ¹*block of flats/studio*. I live in a small ²*patio/studio*, which is just one room with a living area and a small kitchen area. The sleeping area is above the living area and there is a ³*staircase/balcony* to get to it. There's also a bathroom, of course. It gets quite cold in the winter, so I have the ⁴*central heating/air conditioning* on to keep the place warm. And it gets hot in the summer, so I use the ⁵*central heating/air conditioning* to keep things cool.

b Work in pairs and talk about your home.

4 a Complete the sentences with the correct form of the words in brackets.

1. If I _____ (can / eat) healthily at home, then I _____ (not / have to / worry) about what I eat when I go to restaurants.
2. If there _____ (be) chocolate in the house, I _____ (eat) it. I just can't stop.
3. A house _____ (not / be) a home unless it _____ (feed) the mind as well as the body.
4. When someone _____ (come) to visit me, they _____ (have to / bring) some cake or biscuits. All my friends know that they _____ (can / not / stay) in my house if they _____ (not / bring) me some.

b Which of the ideas in Exercise 4a do you agree with or like the best? Why? Work in pairs and discuss your ideas.

5 a Complete the sentences with the words in the box.

bitter   savoury   spicy   sweet

1. Small quantities of _____ foods, such as biscuits and cake, is OK, but too much sugar is bad for you.
2. _____ foods such as lemon, some green vegetables and dark chocolate are actually good for you.
3. If you eat hot and _____ foods, such as curries in a hot climate, they can make you feel cooler.
4. _____ foods such as crisps and chips are the most popular snacks all over the world.

b Work in pairs and think of more foods that are savoury, sweet, spicy, bitter, etc.

6 a Choose the correct alternatives.

1. A healthy, balanced diet means eating *much/a lot of* different foods.
2. Make sure you don't eat *too much/too many* of one type of food.
3. Drink *many/lots of* water, this is really important!
4. There are *many/much* types of food which are healthy.
5. A *lot of/Any* people eat unhealthy food.
6. He doesn't eat *too much/enough* fruit and vegetables.
7. *A little/A few* sugar is OK, but you shouldn't have too much.
8. Be careful not to eat *too much/too many* things which are high in fat.
9. I have a *few/little* recipes which are healthy and delicious.
10. I don't eat *any/little* junk food. I like the taste, but it makes me feel terrible later.
11. I'd like to do *some/any* classes to help me cook better, when I have the time.

b Which of the advice in Exercise 6a do you follow?

Reflect

How confident do you feel about the statements below? Write 1–5 (1 = not very confident, 5 = very confident).
- I can make guesses about people.
- I can discuss advantages and disadvantages.
- I can plan a special occasion.
- I can give instructions and ask for information.

Want more practice?
Go to your Workbook or app.

6A Life without ...

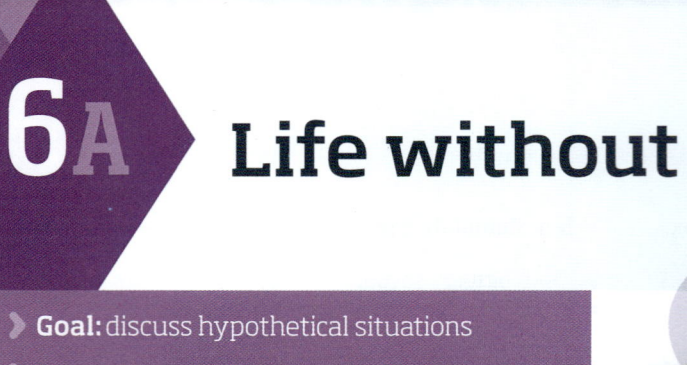

- **Goal:** discuss hypothetical situations
- **Grammar:** second conditional
- **Vocabulary:** everyday activities

Vocabulary

1 Look at the photos and discuss the questions.
1. What electrical equipment can you see?
2. Which of the things do you have?
3. Which do you sometimes use?
4. Which do you never use?
5. Which do you use every day?

2 Read comments 1–8. Which are true for you?
1. 'I bought a dishwasher to make life easier but loading and unloading it takes so much time.'
2. 'I don't mind housework, and I enjoy doing small jobs around the house, vacuuming, loading the washing machine and things like that.'
3. 'My mobile phone is useless. I have to charge it all the time.'
4. 'I don't want a car. You have to fill it with petrol, oil and water all the time.'
5. 'I don't like switching on the air conditioning because it's so expensive. I just use a fan – I think they are better.'
6. 'I don't like wasting energy. I never fill the kettle with more water than I need and I always switch everything off before I go to bed.'
7. 'I work from home. The first thing I do in the morning is have a cup of coffee and switch on my laptop.'
8. 'I always turn the radio up when I'm driving.'

3 Match the verbs in the box with appliances 1–5. Some verbs go with more than one appliance. Use the comments in Exercise 2 to help you.

| charge   empty   fill ... with   load/unload   switch on/off   turn down/up |

1. dishwasher/washing machine
2. mobile phone/tablet/laptop
3. car
4. radio/TV
5. kettle

4 Complete sentences A–D with the verbs in Exercise 3.

A ^{1}_____ the washing machine – do not mix coloured and white clothes. Choose the correct programme and ^{2}_____ the machine. When the programme has finished, ^{3}_____ the machine before you open the door.

B Only ^{4}_____ your electric kettle _____ water. Do not use it for other liquids. Make sure you ^{5}_____ the kettle and ^{6}_____ the water before you clean it.

C Always ^{7}_____ your mobile phone and laptop or tablet before travelling. It can be difficult to find somewhere to power them when you are away from home.

D You can ^{8}_____ the volume of your ringtone if you don't want to disturb other people, or ^{9}_____ it _____ if you want to make sure you can hear it!

Go to your app for more practice.

46

Reading

5 Read Melanie's post below and her friends' responses. What issues are they discussing?

ABOUT	DISCUSSION	EVENTS

Melanie
Hi, guys! I've had a terrible week - I lost my phone! I couldn't contact anyone. Modern life's so difficult when things go wrong!

Comments

1 Rachel
I agree, losing your phone is pretty bad, but power cuts are worse. We had one last week and I have so many electrical appliances in my flat – it was a nightmare! We couldn't cook. The washing machine stopped working and I had to unload all the wet clothes. I couldn't charge my tablet. We couldn't even use the kettle to make a cup of coffee. It's the worst thing that can happen.

2 Samir
Well, OK, that's bad, but what would you do if you couldn't drive anywhere? My car broke down last month and I didn't get it back for two weeks. It took me hours to get to work. If I lived near the station, I would be able to go to work by train. However, I live outside the city and the public transport isn't very good. If I got up very early, I could get a bus, but it's so slow I'd spend three hours travelling to work! If I didn't have a car, I would have to move.

3 Harry
Has anyone thought that if we didn't have cars, we wouldn't have so much pollution? And if we didn't use our mobile phones all the time, we might meet our friends instead? Maybe I'm just old-fashioned, but I think we have too many things in our lives. What if we tried living without mobile phones, the internet and all our appliances for a week? Wouldn't life be better if we did that?

6 Read the text again and answer the questions.
1. Why did Melanie have a bad week?
2. What happened to Rachel?
3. What problem did Samir have?
4. What does Harry think?

7 Work in pairs. Do you agree with the last response? Why/Why not?

Grammar

8 Read the grammar box and choose the correct alternatives.

Second conditional

Use *if* + ¹*past/present* + *would* to talk about ²*real/ imaginary* situations in the ³*present/past*.
If we **didn't have** cars, we **wouldn't have** so much pollution.
What would we **do if** we **had** no electricity?
Use *if* + ⁴*past/present* + *would* to talk about ⁵*real/ unlikely* situations in the ⁶*past/future*.
I'd meet you tonight **if I had** my car.
When we want the situation to seem less possible, we can use *could/might* instead of *would*.
If I **got up** very early, I **could get** a bus, but ...
If we **didn't use** our mobile phones all the time, we **might meet** our friends instead.
When we are talking about imaginary ability, we use *could*.
If I **had** a car, I **could get** around more easily.
When using the second conditional, say 'If I were', rather than 'If I was'.

9 a 6.1 Listen and notice the pronunciation of *'d*.
1. You'd feel better if you didn't have so many things.
2. If I had my mobile phone with me, I'd call them now.
3. If you went by car, you'd get there faster.

b Listen again and repeat.

10 Complete the sentences with the words in brackets. Use the second conditional.
1. If you _____ (have) a dishwasher, you _____ (do) the washing-up faster.
2. If there _____ (not be) so many cars, there _____ (be) less pollution.
3. If we _____ (not have) the internet, we _____ (not be able to) get so much information.
4. If there _____ (be) no electricity, _____ our lives _____ (change) completely?
5. If you _____ (buy) a tablet, you _____ (be able to) go online whenever you wanted.

11 Work in pairs and discuss the question. What would life be like if we had no electricity, running water or petrol?

If we didn't have running water, we would need to carry it from rivers.

Go to page 126 or your app for more information and practice.

Speaking

PREPARE

12 a 6.2 Imagine you're going to give up three of your favourite things for a month. First, listen to two people discussing giving up things. Which things do they mention?

b What does Steve decide to give up? Why?

13 Think about your own daily life. Which of the things in the box would you most/least like to give up? Why?

air conditioning   car   dishwasher   electric cooker
electric kettle   laptop/tablet   mobile phone
the internet   TV   washing machine

SPEAK

14 a Work in pairs. Agree on three things to give up for one month. Use the Useful phrases to help you.

Useful phrases
If I had to give up (my car), I'd ...
It's more important to have a (kettle) than a ...
I'd definitely choose (the internet) because ...
I couldn't live without (my TV) because ...

b Report back to the class. Explain your choices.

Develop your listening
page 101

6B A difficult choice

> **Goal:** ask for and give advice
> **Grammar:** structures for giving advice
> **Vocabulary:** describing bad behaviour and crime

Vocabulary

1 a Look at the pictures. What are the people doing?

b Put the actions in order from most to least serious. Then compare your ideas with the rest of class.

2 a Match comments 1–6 with pictures A–F.
   1 'He's **cheating** in an exam. That's not **fair** to other students.'
   2 'She's **jumping the queue**. That's really **rude** – I was here before her. I hate it when people aren't **polite**.'
   3 'She's **stealing** something from a shop. That's **illegal**.'
   4 'I think it's really **wrong** to **drop litter** in the street.'
   5 'He's **speeding** on the motorway. That's **against the law**.'
   6 'He **lied** to the ticket inspector. That's just **dishonest**.'

b Which of the words in bold:
   1 are examples of bad behaviour?
   2 tell us what people think of bad behaviour?

3 Write the sentences in a different way using the vocabulary in Exercise 2a.
   1 He's putting rubbish on the floor.
      He's dropping litter.
   2 She's going too fast in her car.
   3 He's not telling the truth about his age.
   4 He copied his friend's answers during the test.
   5 He took some food from the supermarket without paying.
   6 She ignored the line of people waiting at the post office, and went straight to the front.

4 a Complete the sentences with your own ideas.
   1 *Texting* when you are driving is dangerous.
   2 I really feel that it's not polite to _____ on public transport.
   3 In my country, it's illegal to _____ .
   4 I find it rude when people _____ in a restaurant.
   5 Some people _____ in the cinema. I don't think that's fair to other people

b Work in pairs and compare your ideas.

c Work in pairs. What would you do if you saw someone doing the things in pictures A–F? Why?

📱 Go to page 141 or your app for more vocabulary and practice.

Reading and listening

5 Read the problems below and answer the questions.
   1 What is the problem in each situation?
   2 Which situation is more serious?

A I've got this colleague, let's call him 'David', who lies about how much work he's done. He always tells our boss that he finishes work after six most days and that he's got too much to do. However, I know that he usually leaves at five, and he looks pretty relaxed when he's working. He's a nice guy, but I don't feel happy about the situation. I think it's dishonest and it's not fair to everyone else.

B I think my friend is stealing from shops. I always see her wearing new clothes, and I know that she doesn't earn enough to buy many new things. I saw her coming out of a clothes shop last weekend – when she saw me she looked really embarrassed, like something was wrong. I mean, it's against the law! The thing is, she's my friend and I don't want her to get into serious trouble.

6 a 🔊 **6.6** Listen to two friends talking and answer the questions.
  1 Which of the problems in Exercise 5 are they discussing?
  2 What two pieces of advice does the man give?
  3 What does the woman think of the advice?

b 🔊 **6.7** Listen to two friends talking about the other problem in Exercise 5 and answer the questions.
  1 What two pieces of advice does the woman give?
  2 What does the man think of the advice?

c Work in pairs. What do you think the people should do in each situation? Why?

Grammar

7 Read the grammar box. Can you think of any more examples of language to give advice?

Structures for giving advice

Use *should* to ask for and give advice.
*So, what **should** I do?*
*She **should** pay for her shopping.*
Use *should/shouldn't* and *If I were you, I would …* to give advice.
*Perhaps you **should** report him to the manager.*
If I were you, I'd tell the store manager.
Use *could* to give less strong advice.
*You **could** call the security guard.*
Sometimes we use *ought to* instead of *should*.
*You **ought to** tell the teacher about him.*

8 a 🔊 **6.8** Listen to the sentences. What happens to the /d/ sound in bold before a consonant sound? What happens before a vowel sound?
  1 You shoul**d** ask her where she gets the money.
  2 You shoul**d** go to the police.
  3 You shoul**d** allow him to explain.
  4 You shoul**d** try to be nice.

b Listen again and repeat.

9 Complete the conversations with the correct words. Use the structures for giving advice in the grammar box.
  1 **A:** My neighbours are always playing loud music.
     B: Maybe you _____ ask them to turn it down. Or you _____ call the police.
  2 **A:** I haven't finished my report. My boss will be angry.
     B: If I _____ you, I _____ tell your boss immediately!
  3 **A:** My friend is always queue jumping.
     B: Tell him he _____ do that. It isn't polite.
  4 **A:** Is it OK to lie if telling the truth will hurt someone?
     B: I'm not sure. You _____ try to tell the truth.
  5 **A:** I'm just going to phone my friend.
     B: You _____ to park the car before you do that.
  6 **A:** What can I do about my noisy neighbour?
     B: Well, you _____ talk to him, but he might get angry …
  7 **A:** He was late again. I'm so annoyed.
     B: I'd tell his boss, if I _____ _____ .

10 a Read the situations and write two or three sentences giving advice to each person.
  1 A student in my class cheated in the end-of-term exam.
  2 I've found a wallet on the street. It doesn't contain much money but there's a credit card in it.
  3 I saw my best friend's boyfriend with a woman in an expensive restaurant.

b Work in pairs and compare your ideas. Give reasons. What is the best advice in each situation?

📱 Go to page 126 or your app for more information and practice.

Speaking

PREPARE

11 Work in pairs. Student A: Turn to page 155. Student B: Turn to page 156.

SPEAK

12 Take turns to discuss your problems. Think about the questions below. Use the Useful phrases to help you.
  • What could you/your partner do?
  • What is good or bad about each possible choice?

Useful phrases
You could (phone the school).
The thing is, my friend will/might (be angry).
I think/don't think you should (go to the police).
(Shoplifting) is wrong/illegal/dangerous.
If I were you, I would …

13 Did you agree with your partner's advice? Why/Why not?

Develop your reading page 102

6c Take action!

> **Goal:** plan a campaign
> **Grammar:** question tags
> **Vocabulary:** environmental issues

Vocabulary

1 a Match the issues in the box with photos A–E.

> air pollution   endangered animals
> extreme weather   global warming   plastic waste

b Discuss the questions.
1 What issues are most important to you/your country?
2 What can people do about them?

2 Read the information about saving the environment. Which three issues in Exercise 1a are mentioned?

3 a Read the information again. Which verbs in bold are used in a positive way and which are used in a negative way?

b Choose the correct alternatives.
1 Riding a bike helps to *reduce/destroy* pollution.
2 Do some research before you travel and you will *waste/save* time and money.
3 It's better for the environment to *throw away/recycle* paper, plastic and glass.
4 *Reuse/Damage* bottles, plastic containers and plastic bags and *waste/protect* the environment.
5 Be careful! Don't fall over and *support/injure* yourself.
6 Raising money is a good way to *support/destroy* organisations that *attack/protect* wildlife.
7 Strong winds and waves *killed/destroyed* the buildings.
8 Smoking can *save/damage* your health.

📱 Go to page 141 or your app for more vocabulary and practice.

HOW CAN YOU HELP?

1 Every year we **waste** huge amounts of food. We **throw away** millions of plastic bottles and plastic pollution **kills** thousands of fish, sea animals and birds. We need to **reduce** waste to **protect** the environment.

- Don't **throw away** plastic bags. **Save** them and use them again!
- Don't buy plastic bottles. Buy glass bottles that you can **reuse**.
- **Recycle** things you no longer need.

TAKE ACTION NOW!

2 We are **destroying** the places where animals make their homes. Building on countryside reduces the land available for wildlife to live on. Animals move onto farmers' fields and **damage** their crops and sometimes **attack**, **injure** or even **kill** people while searching for food. However, most people don't understand the problems that wildlife faces.

- Encourage your friends and family to **protect** the environment.
- Ask the government to **reduce** building development in the countryside.
- Ask politicians to **support** laws that protect endangered animals.

TAKE ACTION NOW!

3 Every time we drive our car to the shops, turn on the lights or use the washing machine, we make choices that increase air pollution. Air pollution **damages** our health and **kills** millions of people every year.

- **Reduce** air pollution by taking public transport, walk or cycle instead of driving.
- Use less energy at home. **Save** electricity: turn off lights, computers and other electrical equipment.
- Buy locally grown food – transporting it produces less pollution.

TAKE ACTION NOW!

Listening

4 a 🔊 6.9 **Listen to an interview with Jenny Hunter and answer the questions**
1. What is Jenny interested in doing?
2. Which environmental problem in Exercise 1 are they talking about?
3. What does Jenny want to do?
4. What can people do to help, according to Jenny?

b Listen again and complete questions 1–5 with the question tags in the box.

| can't we? | do you? | don't they? |
| hasn't it? | is it? | |

1. It's not just a problem in Africa, _____ .
2. Half a million elephants now live in the wild, _____ .
3. That has made life very difficult for many animals, _____ .
4. You don't think governments are doing enough, _____ .
5. We can all help, _____ .

Grammar

5 Read the grammar box and choose the correct alternatives.

Question tags
Use question tags:
- when we are asking someone to agree with us.
  *We **can** all help, **can't we**?* (= I think you agree.)
- to check a piece of information.
  *There **are** only about half a million wild elephants left, **aren't there**?* (= I'm not sure if the number is right.)

Form tag questions using auxiliary verbs or modal verbs (*be, do, have, can*, etc.). If the statement is positive, the question tag is [1]*positive/negative*.
*That **has** made life very difficult, **hasn't it**?*
If the statement is negative, the question tag is [2]*positive/negative*.
*You **don't** think governments do enough, **do you**?*

6 a 🔊 6.10 **Listen and notice the intonation. Which speakers expect the listener to agree? Which aren't sure they are right?**
1. People waste lots of food, don't they?
2. The climate is getting warmer, isn't it?
3. There are only about half a million wild elephants left, aren't there?

b Listen again and repeat.

7 a Complete the sentences with the correct question tags.
1. Animals are not as intelligent as people, _____ ?
2. Zoos help to save animals in danger, _____ ?
3. It isn't right to keep animals in cages, _____ ?
4. We shouldn't protect dangerous animals, _____ ?
5. Farming wastes a lot of water, _____ ?
6. Rich countries should do more to save water, _____ ?
7. In some countries, some people don't have clean water, _____ ?
8. The sun can damage our skin, _____ ?

b Do you agree with the sentences in Exercise 8a?

8 Work in pairs and discuss these topics. Use question tags.
1. People are more important than animals.
2. We can all help to stop global warming.
3. We should only buy local products.
4. Everyone should stop eating meat.
5. It's wrong to keep money you find in the street.

📱 Go to page 126 or your app for more information and practice.

Speaking

PREPARE

9 a 🔊 6.11 **You're going to plan a campaign about an issue you feel strongly about. First, listen to some friends talking about their plans and answer the questions.**
1. What issue do they talk about?
2. What do they want to do?
3. What actions do they decide to take?

b Listen again and check your answers. What do you think about their ideas?

SPEAK

10 a Work in groups. Decide what issue you want to campaign about. What are you most concerned about?

b Think about your ideas. What do you want to achieve? What actions can you take? Make a list. Use the Useful phrases to help you.

Useful phrases
I think we should do something about (plastic waste).
OK, so any ideas (on how to educate people)?
How can we persuade people to take part?
I think it would be difficult to (avoid plastic waste completely).

11 Tell the class about your campaign.

Develop your writing page 103

6D English in action

> **Goal:** make and respond to requests

1 a Look at the cartoon and discuss the questions.
  1. What situation does it show? Where do you think the woman is going?
  2. Who do you think she is phoning?
  3. What do you think she wants that person to do for her?

b What do you ask other people to do for you when you are going away? Use the ideas in the box to help you.

> close the curtains at night   collect a parcel
> collect the post from the letterbox   feed the cat
> water the plants

2 a 🔊 **6.12** Listen to Chrissy talking to her neighbour and answer the questions.
  1. What does Chrissy ask Ed to do?
  2. What does Ed agree to do?
  3. What can't he do? Why not?

b Complete the sentences from the listening. Use the Useful phrases to help you.
  1. Do you _____ could do me a big favour?
  2. It _____ what it is.
  3. _____ you feed the cat for me, please?
  4. _____ you _____ watering my plants, too?
  5. Oh, just one more thing, if it _____ be too much trouble?
  6. _____ it be possible for you to be there to collect it?
  7. I'm _____ _____, but I've got to go town on Saturday morning.

> **Useful phrases**
>
> **Asking someone to do something**
> Could you (help me with this)?
> Would you mind (looking after my rabbit)?
> Do you think you could do me a big favour?
> Just one more thing, if it wouldn't be too much trouble?
> Would it be possible for you to (post this letter)?
>
> **Responding to requests to do something**
> Yes, sure, no problem.
> Yes, of course, happy to.
> It depends what it is.
> I'm really sorry, but (I'm too busy right now).
> I'm afraid I can't do that.

c Listen again and check your answers

3 🔊 **6.13** Listen to sentences 1, 3 and 4 in Exercise 2b. How does the speaker use his voice to make the requests sound polite?

4 a Work in pairs, A and B. Read the situations below and think about what you'd say.

Student A
You're really busy in the office. You have a deadline and can't leave your desk. Ask you colleague to help you by:
- getting you a sandwich for lunch.
- paying a bill at the bank.
- getting something from the chemist.
- collecting a book from the library.

Student B
You want to visit a friend in another town. Your car has broken down and the trains aren't very reliable. Ask you friend to help you by:
- driving you to the other town.
- picking you up later.
- taking you to the garage the next day to pick up your car when it's repaired.

b Take turns to ask for help. Use the Useful phrases to help you.

5 Have you experienced any similar situations? Tell your partner about a time when you asked someone for a favour. What was their response?

> Go online for the Roadmap video.

Check and reflect

1 a Complete the sentences with the correct form of the verbs in the box.

| charge | empty | load | switch off | switch on |

1 I have to _____ my phone at least once a day. Sometimes the battery only lasts a few hours.
2 I hardly ever _____ my phone. I usually leave it on all the time.
3 One of my jobs in the house is to _____ and _____ the dishwasher.
4 The first thing I do each morning is _____ the radio and listen to the news.

b Write down things you can switch on, switch off, empty, load, charge, etc.

2 Complete the sentences with the correct form of the verbs in brackets.

1 If I _____ (not / be) so busy all the time, I _____ (read) a lot more.
2 If I _____ (can / go) anywhere in the world, I _____ (go) to Australia.
3 If we _____ (not / have) computers, life _____ (be) very different.
4 If I _____ (speak) perfect English, I _____ (not / study) it.

3 a Complete the sentences with the words in the box.

| illegal | polite | fair | wrong |

1 She always says *thank you*. She's very _____ .
2 The law says you can't use a mobile phone while you are driving. It's _____ .
3 We do the same job, but I get paid less than the others. It's not _____ .
4 You shouldn't borrow something without asking. It's _____ .

b Think of activities that can be described by the words in the box in Exercise 3a.

4 a Complete the responses with the correct word in the box.

| could | ought | should | were |

1 **A:** I feel tired all the time these days.
   B: You _____ do more exercise.
2 **A:** I found a smartphone in the street.
   B: If I _____ you, I'd take it to the police.
3 **A:** I've got really bad toothache.
   B: You _____ to go to the dentist.
4 **A:** Can you recommend a good restaurant?
   B: Well, you _____ try that new Indian one, but do you like spicy food?

b Work in pairs. Take turns to read the problems in Exercise 4a and give your own advice.

5 a Complete the sentences with the verbs in the box.

| damage | protect | recycle | reduce | save |
| support | waste | | | |

1 _____ electricity by turning off lights when you are not in the room.
2 Don't _____ food. Only buy what you need.
3 _____ things made of paper, glass and plastic.
4 Help to _____ pollution by sometimes walking or cycling instead of driving.
5 _____ organisations that help to _____ the environment.
6 Don't use products that _____ the environment.

b Which of the things in Exercise 5a do you do? How else can we help the environment?

6 a Complete the responses with the phrases in the box and a question tag.

| at the weekend | eighteen | football | Scotland |
| sunny and warm | | | |

1 **A:** What's the weather going to be like at the weekend?
   B: It's going to be _____ ?
2 **A:** What's our country's national sport?
   B: It's _____ ?
3 **A:** How old do you have to be to drive in your country?
   B: You have to be _____ ? Like in most countries.
4 **A:** When did it last rain?
   B: It rained _____ ? We were out walking, remember?
5 **A:** Where's Julia, our teacher, from?
   B: She's from _____ ? She told us a few weeks ago.

b Work in pairs. Ask the questions in Exercise 6a and give true answers using a question tag.

Reflect

How confident do you feel about the statements below? Write 1–5 (1 = not very confident, 5 = very confident).
- I can discuss hypothetical situations.
- I can ask for and give advice.
- I can plan a campaign.
- I can make and respond to requests.

Want more practice?
Go to your Workbook or app.

7A New skills

> **Goal:** discuss study options
> **Grammar:** modal verbs: ability
> **Vocabulary:** skills and abilities

Vocabulary

1 Read the leaflet and discuss the questions.
1. Who is the leaflet for?
2. What can people learn at the adult education centre?
3. Have you learnt any of the skills in the leaflet?
4. Have you ever learnt skills outside of your work or studies? Where/How did you learn them?

2 a Cross out the incorrect alternative for each verb.

1. **work on**   your language skills/an office/your singing
2. **gain**   confidence/experience/a competition
3. **improve**   how to design a website/your speaking skills/your maths
4. **develop**   practical skills/your interview skills/English
5. **prepare**   delicious dishes/for an interview/the violin
6. **edit**   photos/your conversation skills/your work
7. **design**   a story/a website/your own clothes
8. **learn**   how to change a plug/the drums/your English
9. **take**   photos/skills/a course

b Can you think of any other words and phrases that can go with the verbs in Exercise 2a?

3 a Complete the sentences with your own ideas.
1. I need to work on my …
2. I've never designed …
3. I'd love to learn how to …
4. Lots of people do courses to help them prepare …
5. The last course I took was in …
6. I'm quite happy with my … skills. I don't think I need to improve them.

b Work in pairs and compare your answers.

Go to your app for more practice.

It's never too late to learn something new! At **Newington Adult Education Centre,** we offer a wide range of high-quality adult education courses for people of all ages. Sign up today!

Cookery
We offer a range of cookery classes, including Chinese, Indian and Thai cooking. Learn how to prepare delicious dishes from around the world. Gain confidence and experience during the course.

Do-it-yourself basics
Develop practical skills to look after your own home. Learn basic painting, how to change a plug and how to put up shelves.

Music
We offer courses in guitar, keyboards, drums and vocals. Develop the technical skills you need to play an instrument and learn a range of popular songs.

Modern foreign languages
Choose from courses in 20 languages including German, Italian, Spanish, Chinese and Russian. All levels from Beginners to Advanced. Work on your language skills and improve your speaking skills before you go on holiday!

Information technology
Courses include how to use popular software packages and how to design your own website.

Photography
Improve your skills to take better photographs and learn how to edit your photos. You will need to bring your own digital camera.

Listening

4 a 🔊 **7.1** Listen to two friends, Janet and Sam, discussing the courses in the leaflet. Which courses do they mention?

b Listen again. Are the sentences true (T) or false (F)? Correct the false sentences.
1. Janet can play the piano and the drums.
2. Sam would like to be able to play the guitar.
3. Janet likes Indian food but she isn't able to cook it.
4. Janet could speak another language well in the past but she can't now.
5. Sam was able to help his sister with her new flat.

c Work in pairs. Which courses would you recommend for Janet and Sam?

5 a 🔊 **7.2** Listen to the rest of the conversation and answer the questions.
1. What do Janet and Sam decide to do?
2. What reasons do they give for their decisions?

b Who says sentences 1–3 below, Janet (J) or Sam (S)?
a 'I'll be able to join my brother's band.'
b 'I'll be able to order in a restaurant, ask for directions …'
c 'I'll be able to do my own painting and decorating.'

Grammar

6 Read the grammar box and choose alternatives.

Modal verbs: ability

Use *can*, *could* and *be able to* to describe ability.
In the **¹**present/past, use *can*/*can't* to say that you know or don't know how to do something.
*I **can** speak French very well.*
*I **can't** play any instruments.*
Also use *be able to* to talk about present abilities. This is less common than *can*.
*I'**m able to** speak three languages fluently.*
Use *could* or *was*/*were able to* for general ability in the **²**past/future.
*I **could**/**was able to** play the piano when I was younger.*
*I **couldn't**/**wasn't able to** swim until I was ten.*
Use *was able to* to talk about ability to do a **³**single action/repeated actions in the past.
*The manager was there, so I **was able to** explain the problem to her.*
*I **wasn't able to** help my sister put up shelves.*
Use *will be able to* for a future ability.
*I**'ll be able to** order food in Spanish.*
Use a form of *be able to* with the present perfect and infinitive.
*I**'ve** never **been able to** cook well.*
*I hope **to be able** to order a meal in French!*

7 a 🔊 **7.3** Listen and notice the pronunciation of *to*.
1. Were you able to get the adult course programme?
2. I've always wanted to be able to speak Russian.
3. I wasn't even able to help her put up some shelves!

b Listen again and repeat.

8 Complete the sentences with the correct form of *can*, *could* and *be able to*.
1. My brother _____ play the piano when he was eight.
2. After this course, I _____ speak English much better.
3. Not many people _____ make their own clothes!
4. I'd like to _____ speak Chinese.
5. I _____ read until I was six years old.
6. After lots of practice and several attempts, I _____ pass my driving test.

9 a Complete the sentences with your own ideas.
1. I can't _____ but I'd like to learn.
2. I can _____ very well.
3. I couldn't _____ until I was _____ .
4. I've always wanted to be able to _____ .
5. If I _____ , I'll be able to _____ .
6. I hope to be able to _____ one day.
7. I wasn't able to _____ yesterday.
8. I'd love to be able to _____ .

b Work in pairs and compare your sentences.

📱 Go to page 128 or your app for more information and practice.

Speaking

PREPARE

10 You're going to choose and sign up for a course. First, look at the leaflet again. Think about the questions and make notes.
- Which activities can you do well? Do you want to develop your skills?
- What could you do well when you were younger but have forgotten how to do? Would you like to improve your skills/knowledge?
- What can't you do at all? Would you like to be able to do them? Why?

SPEAK

11 a Work in pairs and discuss the questions in Exercise 10. Talk about the courses you could do. Say how useful they would be for you and why. Choose a course to sign up for.

b Tell the class which course you chose. Which course is the most popular? Why?

Develop your writing
page 104

7A | New skills

55

7B Life events

> **Goal:** talk about life events
> **Grammar:** past perfect
> **Vocabulary:** milestones

Vocabulary

1 Discuss the questions.
1 What life events can you see in the photos?
2 Which of the following things have you done/experienced?
- get married/engaged/divorced
- have children
- move house
- graduate from university/college
- find/lose/get your first job
- pass a driving test/an exam
- win an award
- go travelling/abroad
- start a business
- leave school/home
- fall in love

2 Choose the correct alternatives.
1 Pete *won/lost* his job last month so he's really worried about money.
2 The only time I've ever *taken/won* an award was at school for writing the best story in the class.
3 After I finished studying, I decided to *pass/go* travelling.
4 Jen has always wanted to be her own boss; that's why she's *had/started* a business.
5 Carlo *finished/graduated* from university when he was 21; then he *won/got* his first job.
6 Beata and Tom met and *fell/took* in love on holiday and now they're *doing/getting* married.

Go to your app for more practice.

Listening

3 a 🔊 7.4 Listen to Rob, Sarah and Chris being interviewed about important things in their lives. Match them with topics a–d. There is one extra topic.
a a job
b going travelling
c having children
d starting a business

b Listen again. Are the statements true (T) or false (F)?

Rob
a He is successful.
b He worked in hotels.
c He passed his driving test.
d He had some special talents at school.
e He started selling street food.

Sarah
a She graduated from university.
b She decided she wanted to make a lot of money.
c She wanted to do something she loved.
d She gets paid a lot of money.
e She found her dream job.

Chris
a He went travelling.
b He travelled through Europe.
c He went to South Africa.
d He wouldn't do it again.
e He lived in Dalston.

Grammar

4 Read the grammar box and choose the correct alternatives.

Past perfect

Form the past perfect with *had* and the **¹***past/present* participle of the verb.

I'd had holiday jobs working in restaurants.

To make it clear that one event happened before another in the past, use the **²***past perfect/past simple* to show what happened first, and the **³***past simple/past perfect* to show what happened second.

Before I **decided** to go to South America, I **had travelled** through Europe.

I travelled through Europe
PAST ↓   PRESENT
                ↑
      I decided to go to South America

You can also use time expressions like *before*, *after*, *by the time*, *by this time* and *already* to show the order of the actions.
After I'**d left**, I didn't really know what to do.
By the time I was sixteen, I **had** already **left** school.

5 a 🔊 7.5 Listen and notice the pronunciation of *had*.
1 By the time I was eighteen, I'd left school.
2 I'd had holiday jobs working in restaurants.
3 By the time I finished, everybody had left.

b Listen again and repeat.

6 Complete the sentences with the past perfect form of the verbs in brackets.
1 By the time I arrived home, she ___had left___ (leave).
2 After I _____ (finish) school, I went to college.
3 Luckily, when I arrived at the station the train _____ (not go).
4 By the time he was 22, he _____ already _____ (win) lots of competitions.
5 They _____ (met) on a course earlier that year and got married early the next year.
6 Before I worked as a teacher, I _____ (be) an engineer.
7 By the time I was ready to get married, she _____ already _____ (meet) someone else.
8 Before we moved to Brazil, we _____ never _____ (study) Portuguese.

7 a Write three things that could happen before events 1–4. Use the past perfect.
1 She left the house.
She had eaten breakfast.
She had got dressed.
2 He lost his job.
3 They got married and had children.
4 He finally passed his driving test!

b Combine the past simple and past perfect sentences in Exercise 7a. Use phrases like *before*, *after* and *by the time*.
After she had eaten breakfast, she left the house.

📱 Go to page 128 or your app for more information and practice.

Speaking

PREPARE

8 a You're going to talk about your life events. First, make a list.
getting my first job, going travelling

b Choose one event. What was happening around that time? What had you done before? What were the reasons for the event? Make notes.

SPEAK

9 a Work in pairs. Tell your partner about your life events. Use the Useful phrases to help you.

Useful phrases
Before I …, I had already …
By the time I …, I knew I wanted …
I had always wanted to …
So, I started …

b Which of your life events are the same/different?

Develop your reading
page 105

7C Trip of a lifetime

> **Goal:** decide what to take on a trip
> **Grammar:** expressing purpose
> **Vocabulary:** outdoor equipment

Vocabulary and reading

1 Discuss the questions.
1. What can you see in the photos? Where is this place?
2. Would you like to visit a place like this? Why/Why not?

2 a Match the words in the box with photos A–K.

> backpack   camping stove   insect repellent
> portable charger   sleeping bag   sunglasses
> sunscreen   tent   torch   walking boots
> waterproof jacket

b Complete the definitions with the words in the box in Exercise 2a.
1. A _____ fills your mobile phone or tablet with electricity. It's _____, so you can carry it with you.
2. A _____ is a large bag you carry on your back. You can put your hiking clothes and equipment in it.
3. Insect _____ stops insects attacking you.
4. _____ protects your skin from the sun.
5. You can cook food on a _____ when you are camping.
6. A _____ jacket doesn't let the rain through.

c Work in pairs. Which items would be useful if you were visiting the place in the photos?

3 a Read Alison's question. Where is she going? What advice does she need?

b Read the replies to Alison's question. What things do people recommend she takes? Why?

c Can you think of any other things Alison should take?

Go to page 142 or your app for more vocabulary and practice.

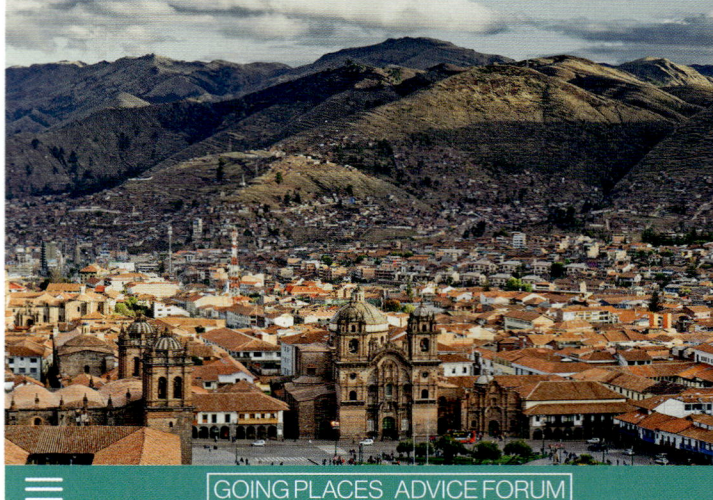

GOING PLACES ADVICE FORUM

Hey, has anyone been to Peru? I'm going there next month on a guided tour to see the Amazon jungle and to visit the Inca city of Machu Picchu. I need to travel as light as possible but take everything I'll really need. What I should take? – **Alison**

You'll need a good quality backpack and some comfortable walking boots ... and the right clothes for all the different places you're planning to visit. – **Max**

Yes, it's very hot and humid in the Amazon. Take fast-drying clothes so you can wash and dry them quickly overnight. – **Penny**

Remember that you'll need extra clothes to keep you warm in Machu Picchu as it gets cold at night. – **Sue**

You can buy sweaters and gloves quite cheaply in Peru so you don't need to pack those. Wait until you get there so you can save space in your luggage. – **Zak**

I recommend taking plastic bags for keeping your documents, cash and phone safe and so they don't get wet. Don't forget to take a portable charger so that you can recharge your phone. – **Maggie**

Insect repellent is very important to keep insects away from you but you can probably buy it there. – **Tom**

Make sure you take a hat and sunglasses to protect you from the sun. You should also take a waterproof jacket for when it rains in the jungle. – **Charlie**

You'll need a good digital camera in order to take really high-quality photos of the wildlife. – **Isa**

6 a Rewrite the sentences using the words in brackets so that they mean the same.
1 I'm learning English so that I can get a better job. (in order to)
I'm learning English in order to get a better job.
2 I'd like to stay in the UK for a while to improve my speaking skills. (so)
3 I'm saving up money to buy a new car. (so that)
4 I go to the gym regularly so I can keep fit. (to)
5 I need a visa in order to visit the US. (so that)

b Complete the sentences with your own ideas.
1 I'm learning English so I _____ .
I'm learning English so I can get a better job.
2 I got home early so that I _____ .
3 I'd like to visit _____ to _____ .
4 If you go walking in the mountains, you need something to _____ .
5 On holiday I always bring _____ with me in order to _____ .
6 For a long flight, it's a good idea to take something to _____ .

c Work in pairs and compare your ideas.

Go to page 128 or your app for more information and practice.

Speaking

PREPARE

7 a 7.7 You're going to plan what equipment to take on a trip. First, listen to two friends discussing what to take to a music festival. Write a list of the things they decide to take.
1 photo ID
2 cash
3 waterproof jackets

b 7.8 Listen to the last part of the conversation and answer the questions.
1 What's the problem?
2 What do they decide to do?
3 Which item do they decide not to take?

SPEAK

8 a Work in pairs. Choose one of the trips below or use your own idea.
- a hiking expedition in the mountains
- a cycling tour of a European country
- a camping trip by the sea

b Make a list of all the equipment you might need to take. Discuss why you need these things.

c You have to travel light. Decide what equipment on your list is essential and what isn't. Give reasons.

Grammar

4 Read the grammar box. Underline more examples of language for expressing purpose in the posts.

Expressing purpose

Use *(in order) to* + infinitive to state the purpose of an action. *In order to* is usually more formal.
*I'm going to Peru **to visit** Machu Picchu.*
*You'll need a good digital camera **in order to take** really high-quality photos.*

To express purpose, also use *so (that)* + modal verb. There is no difference in meaning between *so* and *so that*.
*Take fast-drying clothes **so that** you **can** wash and dry them quickly*
*Take a portable charger **so** you **can** recharge your phone.*

Use *to* + infinitive or *for* + verb + *ing* to talk about the purpose of something.
*You'll need extra clothes **to keep** you warm.*
*I recommend taking plastic bags **for keeping** your documents safe.*

5 a 7.6 Listen and notice the pronunciation of *to*, *for* and *that*.
1 Take plastic bags to store your documents.
2 You'll need a pair of good binoculars for watching wildlife.
3 Take a portable phone charger so that you can recharge your phone.

b Listen again and repeat.

Develop your listening
page 106

7D English in action

> **Goal:** ask for information

1 **Discuss the questions.**
  1 When did you last need to ask for information?
  2 What kind of information did you need to find out?

2 a 🔊 **7.11 Listen to the first part of a conversation. What does the speaker want information about?**

  b 🔊 **7.12 Listen to the rest of the conversation and complete the notes.**

NEWINGTON ADULT EDUCATION CENTRE

Course: _____
Level: Beginners stage _____
Start date: second week of _____
End date: first week of _____
Day(s): Tuesdays and _____
Times: from _____ p.m. to 9 p.m.
Venue: Adult Education Centre, Room _____
Fee: £ _____
Enrolment: Starts _____

  c Work in pairs and compare your answers.

3 a **Listen again and complete the sentences from the listening. Use one, two or three words in each gap.**
  1 I'm _____ in learning Spanish.
  2 I'm _____ to find out what courses you offer.
  3 I _____ if you _____ give me some advice?
  4 _____ you _____ me when the next course starts?
  5 OK, thanks, Tuesdays and Wednesdays. _____ that.
  6 _____ you tell me what time they start?
  7 Thank you very much _____ your help.
  8 Would you _____ sending me a brochure?

  b Work in pairs and compare your answers.

4 **Think of information you might ask for in these places and how you might ask for it. Use the Useful phrases to help you.**
  - a restaurant
  - a train station
  - a supermarket
  - a tourist information centre
  - a department store
  - a museum
  - a hotel

Useful phrases

Asking for information and advice
Hello, I'm calling to find out (about your courses).
Can you give me some information about (the fees)?
I wonder if you could give me some information about (the timetable).
Can/Could you tell me when/how much …?
I'd like to find out (about your language classes).
I'm interested in (studying poetry).
Do you offer (discounts for students)?
Would you mind telling me (when the course starts)?

Responding to a request for information
Hello, this is … How can I help?
Can I help you?
Let me see/check.
Is there anything else I can do for you?

Repeating back to confirm understanding
OK, thanks, [repeat]. Got that.
So, [repeat].

Thanking
Thanks very much for your help.

5 🔊 **7.13 Listen to the requests and repeat. Copy the intonation.**
  1 Would you mind sending me a brochure?
  2 I'm calling to find out what courses you offer.
  3 Do you offer night classes?
  4 I'm interested in studying part time.

6 **Work in pairs. Student A: Turn to page 153. Student B: Turn to page 154.**

▶ Go online for the Roadmap video.

Check and reflect

1 Complete the sentences with the words and phrases in the box.

| edit | improve | prepare | take (x2) | design |

1 I've always wanted to _____ an Asian cookery course so I can learn how to _____ dishes from different countries.
2 I'd really like to _____ my IT skills and _____ a website.
3 I'd like to learn how to _____ and _____ photos.

2 Complete the sentences with *can, can't, could, couldn't* or the correct form of *be able to*.

1 I _____ play a lot of different instruments, but I _____ play anything well.
2 I _____ cook at all. In fact, I'm probably the worst cook in the world. I _____ make toast, but that's all.
3 I've always _____ sing. Apparently, I _____ sing before I _____ talk.
4 I called the office but I _____ speak to the manager as he'd gone home.
5 Do you think you _____ to finish it by tomorrow?
6 I hated maths at school, I _____ understand it at all.
7 I'd like to _____ to play the violin really well.
8 I _____ run really fast when I was young.

3 Complete the words with the missing letters.

1 I f_ _ l in love, g_t married and h_d children all within a couple of years.
2 I st_ _ _ _d my own business after I l_ _t my job a few years ago.
3 As a child, we m_ _ _d house several times. We never stayed in the same place for more than two years.
4 I p_ _ _ _d my driving test the first time!

4 Complete the sentences with the correct form of the verbs in brackets. Use the past perfect to show which action happened first.

1 Kirkpatrick Macmillan _____ (invent) the modern bicycle in 1839 after he _____ (watch) some children playing on a bicycle.
2 The Titanic _____ (sink) at 2.20 a.m. on 14th April 1912 after it _____ (hit) an iceberg. Over 1,500 people _____ (lose) their lives.
3 At 20.18 on 20th July 1969, Neil Armstrong _____ (become) the first person to walk on the Moon. They _____ (land) six hours earlier. Armstrong and his partner Buzz Aldrin _____ (return) to Earth just over eight days after they _____ (leave).
4 Dr Seuss _____ (write) the book *Green Eggs and Ham* after a friend _____ (ask) him to write a book using no more than fifty different words.
5 In the story *The Wizard of Oz*, Dorothy's friend _____ (be) a dog called Toto. In the original version of the story, her friend _____ (be) a cow called Imogene.

6 Before Elizabeth II _____ (become) queen, her father, George VI _____ (be) king.
7 Until we _____ (have) running water, people _____ (collect) water from wells and rivers.
8 By the time he _____ (retire), Pele _____ (score) more than 1,200 goals.

5 a Complete the sentences with the words in the box.

| backpack | bag | binoculars | charger | torch |

1 You'll see the animals better on the safari if you take some _____ .
2 There's no lighting on the campsite, so make sure you take a _____ .
3 Try not to use your phone much, but just in case, take a portable _____ .
4 It's going to be cold in the tent, so make sure you have a warm sleeping _____ .
5 I've got quite a lot of clothing and equipment, but it should all fit in my _____ .

6 a Complete the responses with phrases a–d.

1 Why do people go on holiday?
   To _____
2 Why are you studying English?
   So _____
3 What do you mostly use your mobile phone for?
   For _____
4 Why do people have jobs?
   In order to _____
5 Why do people go to the countryside?
   To _____

a earn money.
b messaging and texting.
c relax and have a break from their routines.
d I can pass my English exam.
e get some peace and quiet away from the city.

b Work in pairs. Ask and answer the questions in Exercise 6a.

Reflect

How confident do you feel about the statements below? Write 1–5 (1 = not very confident, 5 = very confident).

- I can discuss study options.
- I can talk about life events.
- I can decide what to take on a trip.
- I can ask for information.

Want more practice?
Go to your Workbook or app.

8A Changing rules

> **Goal:** talk about rules
> **Grammar:** modals verbs: obligation and necessity
> **Vocabulary:** multi-word verbs

Vocabulary

1 Look at the photos and discuss the questions.
1. Where are the places in the photos?
2. What is happening?
3. How are the people behaving?

2 a Read the rules. Are they for the classroom, a home or an office?
1. When you have finished cooking, please **clear up** any mess.
2. Please **take out** the rubbish every evening.
3. When customers leave messages, **call** them **back**.
4. **Shut down** all computers before leaving.
5. **Join in** all class activities.
6. Don't leave personal possessions in the reception area. Please **put** them **away** in the cupboards.
7. Don't **throw away** used bottles. Recycle them.
8. Please **put** documents **back** in the right files.
9. **Give out** books and worksheets to your classmates when the teacher asks.
10. Be polite when **dealing with** customers.
11. **Hand in** homework at the correct time.

b Complete the sentences with the correct form of the phrases in bold in Exercise 2a.
1. I've decided to _____ some old clothes.
2. After you've washed and dried the plates, please _____ them _____ .
3. The teacher _____ the exam paper five minutes before the exam started.
4. Remember to _____ your computer at night so you don't waste electricity.
5. The phone company never _____ you _____ after you try phoning them.
6. James never _____ his homework _____ on time.

3 Work in pairs and answer the questions.
1. Look at the rules in Exercise 2a again. Have you ever had to follow any similar rules? When/Where?
2. Have you ever broken any rules? Which ones and why?

Go to page 143 or your app for more vocabulary and practice.

Listening

4 a 🔊 8.1 Listen to the first part of a radio discussion about rules. What places do Natalie and Tania talk about?

b Listen again. Tick the rules that Natalie and Tania mention.
Natalie
1. Take out the rubbish.
2. Only watch one hour of TV every day.
3. Eat at the table.
4. Be quiet at meal times.

Tania
5. Follow rules at home.
6. Arrive at school on time.
7. Stand up to speak to the teacher.
8. Wear a uniform.

5 🔊 8.2 Listen to the second part of the discussion. Are the sentences true (T) or false (F)?
1. Children still have to follow a lot of rules at home.
2. They don't go to school if they don't want to.
3. Students at school don't have to follow a lot of rules.
4. Natalie and Tania agree that rules are necessary.

Grammar

6 Read the grammar box and choose the correct alternatives.

Modal verbs: obligation and necessity

Use *must*, *need to* and *have to* to talk about something that is ¹*necessary/not necessary* in the present.
*I **must/need to/have to** go home soon.*

Use *don't need to* and *don't have to* to talk about something that is ²*necessary/not necessary* in the present.
*Children **don't need to/don't have to** wear school uniform on Fridays.*

Use *must not* (*mustn't*) to talk about something we should not do. Note that we usually use *must* and *mustn't* to talk about an obligation which is personal.
*I **mustn't** forget to shut down my computer.*

Use *had to* and *needed to* to talk about something that was ³*necessary/not necessary* in the past. Don't use *must* in the past.
*We all **had to/needed to** do jobs around the house.*

Use *didn't have to* and *didn't need to* when something was ⁴*necessary/not necessary* in the past.
*We **didn't have to/didn't need to** eat all our food.*

Use *be allowed to* or *could* to express permission.
*We were **allowed to/could** do what we liked.*

7 a 🔊 8.3 Listen and notice the pronunciation of *didn't, mustn't, wasn't* and *aren't*.
1 He didn't have to wear school uniform.
2 I mustn't forget to shut down my computer.
3 I wasn't allowed to watch TV.
4 They aren't allowed to have pets in the flat.

b Listen again and repeat.

8 Choose the correct alternatives.
1 Yesterday, I *have to/had to* finish work early.
2 You *don't have to/aren't allowed to* smoke here.
3 We *didn't have to/mustn't* stay, so we went home.
4 I *must/could* remember to lock the door when I leave. I forgot yesterday.
5 I remembered that I *needed to/must* do that yesterday!
6 You *don't need to/mustn't* come if you don't want.

9 a You used to rent a flat where there were a lot of rules. Look at the list below and write sentences about each rule using modals of obligation and necessity.
I wasn't allowed to have pets in the flat.

1 No pets in the flat.
2 Please take the rubbish out every evening.
3 Please wash and put away your dishes.
4 Don't worry about loud music.
5 There is a cleaner so it's not necessary to vacuum.
6 Please turn off the heating at night.

b Work in pairs. Imagine you now live on your own. How have the rules changed?

📱 Go to page 130 or your app for more information and practice.

Speaking

PREPARE

10 You're going to discuss how rules have changed. First, think about the situations below. What rules were there in the past? What rules are there now? Make notes.
• work • home • school/university

SPEAK

11 a Work in groups and discuss the questions. Use your notes and the Useful phrases to help you.
1 How have rules at work, home, school and university changed?
2 Do you think things are better now than in the past?
3 Do you think there should be any new rules? If so, why?

Useful phrases
In the past, people had to …
When I was younger, I was allowed to …
I think things are getting worse/better because …
These days, people don't have to …

b Share your ideas for new rules with the class. Which ideas do you think would work?

Develop your writing page 107

8B Who says I can't?

> **Goal:** talk about someone's life
> **Grammar:** passives: present and past
> **Vocabulary:** comment adverbs

Reading

1 Look at the photos and discuss the questions.
   1 What are the people doing?
   2 What connects all the people in the photos?
   3 Have you done any of these things? What happened?

2 a Read the article about someone who overcame a difficult challenge. Which of the people in photos A–F is it about?

Hugh Herr was born in Pennsylvania, USA. Since he was a child, he had loved rock climbing, and by age 17 he was considered one of the best climbers in the country. Then something terrible happened. In 1982, he and a friend were caught in a snowstorm during a climb. They got lost in the woods for three nights in below-zero temperatures. Thankfully, they were found by the rescue team just in time and taken to hospital by helicopter. Unfortunately, by the time they were rescued, they were badly injured. Herr lost both legs because of the extreme cold. Sadly, one member of the rescue team was killed by an avalanche.

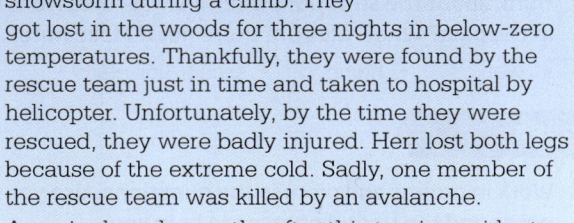

Amazingly, only months after this tragic accident, Herr was climbing again! He had designed special false new legs, which helped him to climb better than ever before!

After his climbing career ended, Herr decided to help other disabled people by developing better arms and legs for them. At that time, computer technology wasn't being used in this field. However, today, Herr runs a laboratory that designs and makes computer-controlled legs, arms and hands. He is recognised as a leader in the field. Because of him, many people are being given opportunities they never had before.

b Read the article again and answer the questions.
   1 What was Hugh Herr's favourite sport as a young man?
   2 Was he good at the sport?
   3 How did he lose his legs?
   4 How was he able to start climbing again?
   5 What did he do when his climbing career ended?
   6 Why is he famous today?

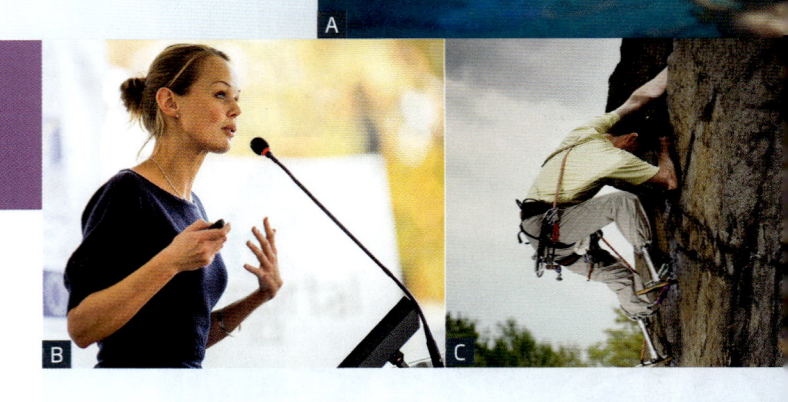

Grammar

3 Read the grammar box and choose the correct alternatives.

Passives: present and past

Use the passive voice:
- to focus on the [1]*person or thing that something happens to/the person or thing that does the action.*
   *... he and a friend **were caught** in a snowstorm.*
- when you [2]*know/don't know* who or what does/did the action.
   *... many people **are being given** opportunities they never had before.*
- when it is [3]*obvious/not obvious* or not important who or what does/did the action.
   *At that time, computer technology **wasn't being used** (by scientists/doctors).*

To mention who or what does the action, use *by*.
*They **were found by** the rescue team just in time.*

To form the passive, use the correct form of *be* + [4]*infinitive/past participle* of the verb.
Active: *They **recognise** him as a leader in his field.*
Passive: *He **is recognised** as a leader in his field.*

4 a 🔊 8.4 Listen and notice the pronunciation of *was* and *were*.
   1 Hugh Herr and a friend were caught in a snowstorm.
   2 They were found by the rescue team just in time.
   3 One member of the rescue team was killed.

b Listen again and repeat.

5 Complete the sentences with the passive form of the verbs in brackets.
1 Mont Aiguille in France _____ first _____ (climb) in 1492 by Antoine de Ville and a small team and the sport of mountaineering _____ (invent).
2 The swimmers _____ (follow) by a rescue boat as they were attempting to swim the Channel.
3 The climbing wall _____ (use) at the moment. They're taking a break.
4 Women _____ (allow) to compete in the Olympics until 1900, and then in only four events. In 1904, two events for women, golf and tennis, _____ (remove) from the programme.
5 In the 1970s, Billie Jean King was playing tennis to large crowds, but she _____ (not / pay) as much as the men. The Women's Tennis Association _____ (start) by King in 1973 to work for equal prize money in tennis.

6 a Change the sentences from active to passive.
1 He broke his arm in the crash.
His arm _was broken in the crash._
2 The police stopped their car.
Their car _____ .
3 A lot of his friends are helping him.
He _____ .
4 People are giving me some great advice.
I _____ .
5 They didn't speak English in that area.
English _____ .
6 Wild animals were following them.
They _____ .

b In which sentences in Exercise 6a is it important to include the word *by* + what/who did the action?

Go to page 130 or your app for more information and practice.

Vocabulary

7 a Look at the adverbs in bold. Does the speaker feel positive or negative?
1 **Thankfully**, they were found by the rescue team just in time ...
2 **Sadly**, one member of the team was killed ...

b Work in pairs. When would you use each of the adverbs in the box?

amazingly	fortunately/unfortunately
happily/sadly	hopefully	luckily/unluckily
obviously	strangely	(not) surprisingly
thankfully	tragically

8 Choose the correct alternatives.
1 She was in a bad car accident last year. *Thankfully/ Sadly*, she's now able to walk again.
2 Tom was in a car accident last year. *Luckily/Hopefully*, he wasn't badly injured.
3 *Hopefully/Surprisingly*, the Paralympics will encourage more disabled young people to start doing sport.
4 *Fortunately/Obviously*, providing sport for disabled people is very expensive.
5 *Strangely/Not surprisingly*, Vincent Van Gogh only sold one painting during his lifetime.
6 JK Rowling is a best-selling author with her Harry Potter novels. *Fortunately/Surprisingly*, several publishers refused to publish her first novel.

Go to your app for more practice.

Speaking

PREPARE

9 a 8.5 You're going to talk about the life of a famous person. First, listen to the story of Tanni Grey-Thompson and answer the questions.
1 Why is Tanni famous?
2 Why did she have to use a wheelchair?
3 What did she achieve in her career?
4 How have things changed for disabled athletes?
5 What does Tanni do now?

b Work in pairs and compare your answers. Then listen again and check. What adverbs in Exercise 7 does the speaker use?

10 Work in pairs. Student A: Turn to page 157. Student B: Turn to page 159. Read the information and make notes about the famous people. What adverbs in Exercise 7 could you use to describe events in the life of the person you read about?

SPEAK

11 Take turns to talk about the famous people. Use the Useful phrases and the adverbs in Exercise 7 to help you.

> **Useful phrases**
> I'm going to tell you about ...
> Who was he/she?
> Really?
> That's very sad.
> What an amazing person!

12 Work in groups. What are your reactions to the lives of these people? Do you know any other people who have overcome difficulties? Tell the group about them.

Develop your listening
page 108

8C Natural world

> **Goal:** describe and recommend places
> **Grammar:** non-defining relative clauses
> **Vocabulary:** geographical features

Reading and vocabulary

1 Look at the photos and discuss the questions.
  1 Where do you think these places are?
  2 Have you visited any places like these? Where?

2 a Read the extracts from travel guides and match them with photos A–C.

  b Work in pairs. Which of these places would you like to visit? Why?

3 a Which of the things in the box can you see in the photos?

bay	cave	cliff	coast	desert	forest	hill
island	lake	mountain	peak	rainforest	river
shore	valley	waterfall

  b Which of the words in the box can you match with the adjectives below?

  1 snow-covered _____   5 clear _____
  2 high _____   6 sandy _____
  3 deep _____   7 rocky _____
  4 steep _____   8 thick _____

4 Work in pairs and discuss the questions.
  1 Which of the geographical features in Exercise 3 do you have in your country?
  2 In which other countries can you see them?

📱 Go to your app for more practice.

COPPER CANYON — MEXICO

Discover what Mexico has to offer. You can find rainforests, deserts, high mountains and dark caves as well as all kinds of plants and animals. Explore some of Mexico's most fantastic natural scenery in the Copper Canyon, which is located in the state of Chihuahua. This is home to the Raramuri people, who live in the deep valleys, where they follow a traditional way of life.

One of the top sights is The Basaseachic Waterfall, which is the second highest waterfall in Mexico. It is surrounded by thick forest and hiking paths offer beautiful views of the falls.

To help you explore the Copper Canyon, you can hire a tour guide, whose knowledge of the area will make your experience even more interesting.

STEEPHILL COVE — UK

Visit Steephill Cove on the Isle of Wight, a small island off the south coast of England. The cove is hidden between high, rocky cliffs. To get there, you have to go on foot along a narrow path, which takes you down a steep hill to the village. When you get to the bottom, you will see a colourful bay with fishing boats floating near the sandy shore. Children love climbing over the rocks looking for rock pools, where they can find all kinds of small animals and swim in the clear waters.

GLACIER NATIONAL PARK — USA

For anyone who loves nature, Montana's Glacier National Park is an experience not to be missed. It has everything, including rocky mountains with snow-covered peaks, amazing waterfalls, clear rivers and deep lakes. The reserve, where you can see bears and other wildlife, is the perfect place for nature lovers to visit.

One of the best times to go is in September, when there are fewer tourists.

Grammar

5 Read the grammar box and choose the correct alternatives.

Non-defining relative clauses

Use non-defining relative clauses to add extra information about a person, thing or place.
Use **¹who/which** for people and **²who/which** for things. Don't use *that*.
*This ancient mountain, **which** is nearly 2,000 metres high, gives …*
*This is home to the Raramuri people, **who** live in the deep valleys …*
Use **³where/when** for places and **⁴where/when** for time.
*The reserve, **where** you can see bears, wolves and other wildlife, is …*
*One of the best times to go is in September, **when** there are fewer tourists.*
Use *whose* for possession.
*Here are some of the top spots, **whose** beauty you will never forget.*
Use commas to separate a non-defining relative clause from the rest of the sentence. They show that this is extra information and is not necessary for the sentence to make sense.

6 a 🔊 8.8 Listen and notice the pronunciation of the words *when*, *where* and *whose*. How do we pronounce the letters *wh*?

1. The reserve, **where** you can see bears and wolves …
2. One of the best times to go is in September, **when** there are fewer tourists.
3. Here are some of the top spots, **whose** beauty you will never forget.

b Listen again and repeat.

7 a Complete the sentences with the correct pronoun.

1. The Peak District National Park, _____ is 1,438 square miles in size, is in northern England.
2. This area, _____ you can enjoy beautiful scenery, was made a National Park in 1951.
3. Theodore Roosevelt, _____ was US President from 1901 to 1909, created five new national parks.
4. Our Egypt Tour includes a trip into the desert, _____ you will spend the night under the stars.
5. You will have your own guide, _____ speaks English well, and _____ knowledge of history is very good.

b Combine the sentences. Use non-defining relative clauses.

1. When I'm on holiday, I prefer to go somewhere quiet and peaceful. I can relax and enjoy nature there.
   When I'm on holiday, I prefer to go somewhere quiet and peaceful, where I can relax and enjoy nature.
2. One of my favourite places is the Greek island of Aegina. It's well known for its beautiful scenery.
3. There are lovely beaches. You can swim and relax.
4. I like the local people. They're very friendly and helpful.
5. To get there, you can fly to Athens. You can get a ferry to the island from there.
6. The best time to go is October. The weather is cooler.

8 Complete the sentences with your own ideas. Then join them using non-defining relative clauses.

1. There are some amazing _____ in the area. They're really popular with _____.
   There are some amazing mountains in the area, which are really popular with tourists.
2. There's a really nice area near my town called _____ .
   It has lots of _____ .
3. A beautiful part of my country is _____
   It's about _____ hours from my home.
4. _____ is famous for _____ .
   I was born there.
5. _____ is good to visit in summer.
   The weather is _____ at that time of year.

📱 Go to page 130 or your app for more information and practice.

Speaking

PREPARE

9 a 🔊 8.9 You're going to give a presentation about a place of natural beauty. First, listen to a presentation at a travel show and answer the questions.

1. What place does she recommend and why?
2. When is the best time to go?
3. How do you get there?

b Listen again and check your answers. How does the presentation end?

10 Think of a place of natural beauty that you know well. Prepare a short presentation. Make notes about the following:

- what you are going to say in your introduction
- where the place is and why it is special
- the best time of year to go
- how to get there
- what you're going to say at the end

SPEAK

11 Work in groups. Talk about your places. Use your notes and the Useful phrases to help you.

Useful phrases
So, I'm going to talk about …
I chose this place because …
I can highly recommend … because …
The best time to go there is …
You can take the bus from …

12 After listening to other groups, vote on the best place to visit.

Develop your reading page 109

8C | Natural world

8D English in action

Goal: make excuses and apologise

1 Look at the pictures and discuss the questions.
1. What's happening?
2. How do you think the people are feeling?
3. What do you think they are saying?
4. Have you ever done anything similar?

2 🔊 **8.10** Listen to two conversations. Answer the questions.

Conversation 1
1. What hasn't Alan done?
2. What excuses does he make?
3. What does his mother tell him to do?

Conversation 2
4. Why is Jackie annoyed?
5. What excuses does Scott make?
6. Why didn't he phone Jackie?

3 a Listen again and complete the conversations.

Conversation 1
1. What a terrible smell! _____ ?
2. I just _____ . I've been so busy at work!
3. Honestly, Alan! That's _____ .
4. Oh well, _____ .
5. I'm really sorry! It _____ again, I promise!
6. I _____ ! Just clear up now.

Conversation 2
1. _____ ? I've been waiting for ages.
2. I'm _____ I'm late.
3. _____ , it started to rain …
4. But _____ call me?
5. You'll _____ , I tried to phone you but …
6. Oh well, _____ .

b Work in pairs and compare your answers. Then listen again and check.

4 Look at the Useful phrases. Can you think of any other expressions to add to each section?

> **Useful phrases**
>
> **Making excuses**
> Well, you see …
> I meant to, but …
> I had to …
>
> **Apologising**
> I'm really sorry …
> It was very stupid of me.
> I won't forget/do it again, I promise!
>
> **Accepting and rejecting apologies and excuses**
> OK/Never mind. I understand.
> These things happen./It happens.
> That's no excuse.

5 a 🔊 **8.11** Listen to two people apologising. Which of the two speakers feels more sorry, A or B?

b 🔊 **8.12** Listen to the sentences and underline the stressed words.
1. I won't do it again, I promise.
2. I'm really sorry.
3. I'm so sorry I'm late.

c Listen again and repeat. Show that you feel really sorry.

6 a Look at these situations and think of excuses you can make for each situation.
1. You arranged to meet your friend in a restaurant at 8 o'clock. Your friend arrives late.
2. Your friend borrowed your mobile phone without asking and the bill is huge.
3. You let your friend borrow your car. When he/she brings it back, you can see it is damaged.
4. You asked a member of your team to prepare a report. It was due this morning, but he/she hasn't done it.
5. You lent a friend your camera and he/she has lost it.
6. It was your birthday yesterday. Your friend forgot about it and didn't get you a present.

b Work in pairs. For each situation in Exercise 6a, take turns to ask for an explanation and apologise/make excuses.

Go online for the Roadmap video.

Check and reflect

1 a Complete the sentences with the words in the box. You can use some words more than once.

| away | back | down | in | out | up |

1. Can you clear _____ the mess in the living room, please?
2. Can you hand _____ your essays on Friday, please?
3. Can you give _____ the books, please?
4. Shall I throw this old bread _____ ?
5. Don't forget to shut _____ the laptop before you go to bed.
6. Please put all the books _____ in the right places.

b Which of the sentences in Exercise 1a are you likely to hear (a) at home and (b) at school?

2 a Complete the sentences about UK law with the correct modal verb or a form of *be allowed to*.

1. You _____ go to school. You are _____ be educated at home. However, the parents _____ prove that the child is getting a good education.
2. You _____ wear a seatbelt in a car. It's the law nowadays, but you _____ wear one until the 1980s.
3. You _____ stand up when you hear the national anthem, but some people do.
4. You _____ carry ID with you. It's not necessary.
5. Everyone _____ have a birth certificate. However, you _____ have one until about 100 years ago.
6. You are _____ smoke in a public building or on public transport. It was banned in 2006.

b Work in pairs. Discuss whether the laws and rules in Exercise 2a are the same in your country.

3 a Choose the correct alternatives. Sometimes, two of the options are possible.

1. There will be snow and freezing temperatures. *Sadly/Hopefully/Amazingly*, this will last only until the weekend. *Unfortunately/Strangely/Amazingly*, the cold weather will return the following week
2. The damage to the building looked serious, but *obviously/unluckily/fortunately* it was not as bad as it looked.
3. The plane managed to land safely with only one wheel and *thankfully/luckily/sadly* no one was seriously injured.
4. Italy were losing 3-0 at half time but *amazingly/hopefully/happily* won the match after they scored four goals in just 15 minutes. Brazil were *sadly/obviously/unluckily* extremely disappointed to lose the game.
5. The election result was announced at midnight. *Unluckily/Not surprisingly/Hopefully*, the prime minister again won with a huge majority.

b Write three news extracts of your own that include adverbs like *Fortunately, Luckily, Amazingly*, etc.

4 a Complete the text with the correct form of the words in brackets.

Wimbledon ¹_____ (hold) every year in London and winning the tournament ²_____ (see) as the greatest prize in tennis. And one of the greatest victories ever was in 1985. Before that year's championships, 17-year-old German Boris Becker ³_____ (describe) by the media as a 'future Wimbledon champion'. And only three weeks later they ⁴_____ (prove) right. Becker was unknown and his early games ⁵_____ (hold) on the smaller courts with small crowds and little media interest. As the tournament went on, Becker ⁶_____ (talk) about more and more and went on to beat two previous champions before winning the final.

b Do you know any other great sporting achievements? Talk about them using the passive.

5 a Match the sentence halves.

1. We saw lots of snow-covered   a islands.
2. We sailed past some high   b hill.
3. It's a really deep   c mountains.
4. We climbed up a steep   d valley.
5. We swam in a lovely clear   e lake.
6. We sailed to several small   f cliffs.

b Work in pairs. Talk about places you know that you can describe using the sentences in Exercise 5a.

6 a Join the sentences where there is a (*) with non-defining relative clauses.

1. I live in Mariyno. *It is a district of Moscow. The district was originally a village. *It was named after Maria Yaroslavna, the mother of Ivan the Great.
2. My favourite place is Lindisfarne. *It is a small island off the north-east coast of England. It's got some lovely deserted beaches. *You can walk there for ages and see only one or two people.
3. My favourite book is *Wild Swans*. *It follows the lives of three generations of women in China. It was written by Jung Chang. *She was born in 1952.

b Write a short paragraph including non-defining relative clauses about your favourite place.

Reflect

How confident do you feel about the statements below? Write 1–5 (1 = not very confident, 5 = very confident).

- I can talk about rules.
- I can retell the main points of a story.
- I can describe and recommend places.
- I can make excuses and apologise.

Want more practice?
Go to your Workbook or app.

9A Shopping

› **Goal:** discuss and suggest improvements
› **Grammar:** the passive: all tenses
› **Vocabulary:** shopping

Vocabulary and reading

1 Look at the photos and discuss the questions.
1 What different ways of shopping do they show?
2 Do you usually shop on the high street, in a shopping centre or online? Why?
3 What kind of things do you usually buy in shops?
4 What kind of things do you buy online?

2 a Read the sentences. Check you understand the meaning of the phrases in bold. Are the sentences true (T) or false (F) for you?
1 I always **save up for** things I want to buy and wait until I have enough money.
2 I prefer to pay for my purchases **in cash** and not **by credit card**.
3 I always **keep the receipt** when I buy something in case I need to take it back and **exchange** it.
4 I always **look for bargains** and **special offers** when I shop. I love **a good deal**!
5 I usually wait for **the sales** before I buy anything because things are cheaper.
6 I like to replace my phone as soon as a new model **goes on sale**.
7 I usually buy heavy **goods** online – I don't have to carry them, they're **delivered** to my home.
8 I don't like buying clothes online – it often takes a long time to **get a refund** if you return them.
9 I once had to **cancel an order** because the goods didn't arrive on time.

b Work in pairs and compare your answers. Do you agree or disagree?

3 a Read the title of the article. What do you think the author of the article will say about shopping habits?

b Read the article and check your ideas.

Go to your app for more practice.

The future of shopping

Modern technology has changed the world around us in nearly every way and it has definitely changed the way we shop. In the past, most goods were bought on the high street, but what does the future of shopping look like?

Thanks to the internet, online shopping has grown fast. It's quick, easy and convenient, and it offers a huge range of choices and competitive prices. Mobile technology has also made it even easier to shop online and many experts predict that ninety-five percent of purchases will probably be made on the internet by 2040.

If today's trends continue, shops as we know them today will no longer be needed. Staff will be replaced by software and if that happens, thousands of high street jobs will be lost. In fact, many high street shops are already being used as places where customers can look at the products they are interested in, but the actual purchases are made online.

Many huge shopping centres have been built in the past thirty years. However, centres that were once busy and successful are now closing down. As a result, companies that run these centres are being forced to think differently about the way they plan and run their businesses. Shopping centres can no longer be just about shopping and the people who run them have realised that customers need to be given a more entertaining experience which offers both shopping and leisure.

Grammar

4 Read the grammar box and choose the correct alternatives. Then find examples in the article.

Passives: all tenses

Passives can be used with all tenses.
To form the passive, use the correct form of **¹**be/have + **²**past participle/infinitive.
Present simple: *The goods **are bought** online.*
Present continuous: *Many high street shops **are being used** as places where customers …*
Present perfect: *Many huge shopping centres **have been built** in the past thirty years.*
Past simple: *Most goods **were bought** on the high street.*
Future: *Ninety-five percent of purchases **will be made** on the internet.*
To form the passive with modal verbs, use the correct form of the modal + *be* + past participle.
*Thousands of high street jobs **could be lost**.*

5 a 🔊 9.1 Listen and notice the pronunciation of the words in bold. Which word is stressed?
  1 Most purchases **will be made** online.
  2 The goods **have to be paid** for online.
  3 Many huge shopping centres **have been built**.
  4 What **can be done**?
  5 Customers **must be given** a more entertaining experience.

b Listen again and repeat.

6 Rewrite the sentences using the passive and *by* when necessary.
  1 Technology has changed the way we shop today.
    The way we shop today has been changed by technology.
  2 Soon we will do most of our shopping online.
  3 Many people have already lost their jobs in shops.
  4 Online businesses must still solve some problems.
  5 Online customers often return clothes because they don't fit.
  6 They are now developing new software so it is easier to get the right size.
  7 Remote-controlled drones may soon deliver small parcels.
  8 They have already tested this technology in the US.

7 a Work in pairs and read the questions. Answer using the prompts and the correct form of the passive.
  1 What sort of things have always been done in high street shops?
    a goods / buy / sell
      Goods have always been bought and sold.
    b cash / accept
    c shops / close early / Sundays
  2 How will most shopping be done in the future?
    a products / buy / pay for / online
    b purchases / deliver / to your home
  3 What other services could be offered in shopping centres now or in the future?
    a play areas / provide / for young children
    b wider range of activities / offer

b Think of more ideas to answer the questions.

📱 Go to page 132 or your app for more information and practice.

Speaking

PREPARE

8 a 🔊 9.2 You're going to present your plans to improve your local bookshop. First, listen to a woman presenting her plans for changes to a clothes shop and answer the questions.
  1 What are the problems?
  2 What are her solutions?

b Your local bookshop is losing money. Look at some of its problems below and make notes about how you could improve it.
  • It only accepts cash.
  • It has no online services.
  • It's not comfortable to be in and it's old-fashioned.
  • It doesn't do any special promotions.

SPEAK

9 a Present your ideas to improve the bookshop to the class. Use your notes and the Useful phrases to help you.

Useful phrases
In the past, customers haven't been offered …
… could be given to regular customers.
Everyone should be given a free …
Books can be bought …

b Vote for the best idea.

Develop your reading page 110

9B What if ...?

> **Goal:** tell a story
> **Grammar:** third conditional
> **Vocabulary:** strong and weak adjectives

Reading

1 Look at the photos and discuss the questions.
  1. What kind of lives do you think the people in the photos have?
  2. Would you like to have the same kind of life as any of these people? Why/Why not?

2 a Read the story. What decision did Paolo make?

Do you ever wonder how your life could have been different? If you had chosen University A instead of University B, or gone out one night instead of staying home, would your life have changed in some way?

My friend Paolo often tells a story about a big decision. He was working for a big company and one day his boss asked him if he'd consider moving to their new office – in Singapore! Paolo thought about it for a long time. On the one hand, he thought it would be an excellent opportunity, but on the other hand, he liked his home town and he was very happy there. He had lots of friends and his family didn't want him to leave, either. So, what did he do? He tossed a coin. If it was heads, he'd go and if it was tails, he'd stay in his town. He threw it up in the air, caught it, closed his eyes for a second and when he opened them he saw it was heads. He was moving to Asia!

In Singapore, he met some people who had a great idea for a dating app (you probably know the one!) and within six months he had started a new business with them. Now he and his partners are very successful and Paolo travels all over the world for his business, including trips to his home town sometimes. He also met his future wife on the app!

I asked him one day if he ever regretted his decision and he said 'I think if I'd stayed in my home town, I might have been happy. It's a nice place and it's full of people I love. I'm glad that I made the decision to go, though. If I hadn't moved to Singapore, so many brilliant things wouldn't have happened in my life and I thank my lucky coin every day. I still keep it with me!'

b Read the story again and answer the questions.
  1. Why was it a difficult decision to make?
  2. How did Paolo decide whether to stay in his home town?
  3. Was Paolo's move to Singapore a success? Why/Why not?
  4. Does he feel he made the right decision? Why/Why not?

3 a Work in pairs and discuss the questions.
  1. How many of the decisions below have you made?
  2. What happened?
  3. How did you make your decision?

  - choose which subjects to study at school/university
  - buy a house/flat
  - choose what pet to get
  - change job
  - save or spend your money
  - move abroad for work/study
  - buy a new computer or go on holiday

b Discuss the questions. How do you make important decisions? Would you toss a coin to make a decision? Why/Why not?

Grammar

4 Read the grammar box and choose the correct alternatives.

Third conditional

To form the third conditional, use *if* + past perfect + *would/wouldn't have* + past participle.
*If I **hadn't moved** to Singapore, so many incredible things **wouldn't have happened** in my life.*
Use the third conditional to talk about actions or events in the ¹*present/past* that did or did not happen and the ²*imaginary/real* results of this action or event.
*If you **had chosen** University A instead of University B, **would** your life **have changed** in some way?*
*If Paolo **hadn't moved** to Singapore, he **wouldn't have started** his own company*
To make the result ³*more/less* likely, use *could* or *might* instead of *would*.
*If I'd stayed in my home town, I **might**'ve been happy.*

5 a 🔊 9.3 Listen and notice the pronunciation of *would have, might have* and *wouldn't have*.
  1. What would have happened?
  2. Things might have changed.
  3. We wouldn't have known.

b Listen again and repeat.

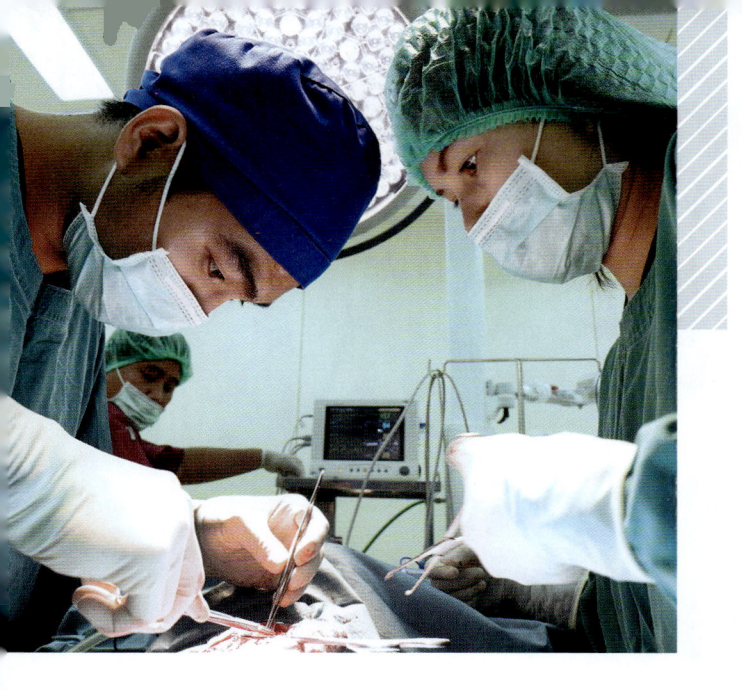

6 Complete the sentences with the correct form of the verbs in brackets.
1 If she _____ (take) the job, she would have moved to London.
2 If they _____ (not / read) the advertisement, they wouldn't have known about the opportunities abroad.
3 If I hadn't gone to Turkey, I _____ (not / meet) Andy.
4 I _____ (might / become) a scientist if I'd been better at science at school.
5 I'd have told you what happened if you _____ (ask) me.

7 Complete the sentences with your own ideas.
1 If I hadn't come here today, I …
2 If I'd studied harder at school, I …
3 My life would have been very different if I hadn't …
4 If I'd listened to my parents, I would have …
5 If I'd been born in another country, I would never have …

Go to page 132 or your app for more information and practice.

Vocabulary

8 Read the sentences. Match the strong adjectives in bold with the weak adjectives in the box.

| angry   bad (x2)   beautiful   big   frightened |
| good (x2)   happy   small   tired |

1 Going to Hawaii was a great idea. Everything was **wonderful**.
2 The restaurant was **terrible**. The portions were **tiny** and the food was **disgusting**!
3 The hotel was **excellent**. We had a **huge** room with a brilliant view of the sea.
4 We were **furious** about our flights being delayed.
5 He was **thrilled** when they offered him the job.
6 Jake was **terrified** about the idea of moving to a new country, but he soon relaxed when he arrived there.
7 Travelling around the world was a great experience, and we saw some **gorgeous** places, but we were **exhausted** by the time we had finished!

9 Complete the sentences with the adjectives in bold in Exercise 8.
1 It's been really cold for weeks. The weather is _____ .
2 They've been working day and night for a week. They're _____ .
3 Jamie has lost the camera I lent him. I'm _____ .
4 What a _____ dress! Where did you buy it?
5 I can't eat this. It's _____ .
6 He spent his life helping people. He was a _____ man!
7 Only one person can get into this lift. It's _____ !

10 Write six sentences about a time in your life when …
- you thought someone or something was gorgeous/ wonderful/terrible.
- you were furious/thrilled/terrified/exhausted.
- you ate something disgusting.
- you saw something huge/excellent/tiny.

Go to page 144 or your app for more vocabulary and practice.

Speaking

PREPARE

11 9.4 You're going to talk about a personal experience and how things might have been different. First, listen to two friends talking and answer the questions.
1 What had James never expected to do?
2 Who did James speak to? What was the result?
3 What did James find? What was the result?
4 What would have happened if he hadn't been walking through the park?
5 What would have happened if he hadn't been brave?

12 Think about something that happened to you. What might have happened if things had been different? Make notes about the following:
- what happened
- who was involved
- what could have been different
- how it made you feel – are there any strong adjectives you could use to describe the experience?

SPEAK

13 a Work in pairs. Tell your partner about your experience. Use your notes to help you. Discuss what could have been different and why.

I was offered a job in Belgium. I decided not to take it, and two months later I met my future wife, Jo Jo. If I'd taken the job, I would never have met the love of my life!

b Swap roles and repeat.

c Take turns to tell other pairs your stories.

Develop your writing page 111

9c Is it art?

› **Goal:** express agreement and disagreement
› **Grammar:** short responses with *so, neither/nor, too/either*
› **Vocabulary:** describing art

Vocabulary

1 a Discuss the questions.
1 What kind of art do you like/prefer?
2 Do you have favourite artists or works of art?

b Look at the photos. Which ones do you like best? Which don't you like? Why?

c Match definitions 1–4 with pieces of art A–D. Some definitions can match with more than one piece of art.
1 Sculpture is a piece of art that is made from stone, metal, wood, etc.
2 Realistic art shows people, places or things as they really are.
3 Public art is in a place where everyone can see it and enjoy it, usually outside.
4 Abstract art doesn't show real things or people but uses shapes and colours.

2 a Check you understand the meaning of the adjectives in the box. Are they positive, negative or neither?

abstract awful cheerful colourful creative fascinating old-fashioned original powerful realistic silly spectacular traditional ugly unoriginal weird

b Choose the correct alternatives.
1 Picasso painted in many different styles. He was a very *creative/unoriginal* artist.
2 Many people think his paintings of people are amazing, but I just find them *creative/ugly*.
3 Some people find modern art hard to understand because it's *realistic/abstract*.
4 That artwork is just really *weird/traditional*. I've no idea what it's supposed to mean.
5 It's important for modern art to be *original/awful*.
6 It's not exactly a new idea, is it? I mean it's completely *realistic/unoriginal*.
7 Her work is very *cheerful/powerful* – lots of people cry when they see it for the first time.
8 The recent exhibition at the Modern Art Museum was a *spectacular/silly* success.

c Work in pairs. Which adjectives in the box in Exercise 2A describe photos A–D?

Go to your app for more practice.

Listening

3 a 9.5 Listen to members of the public giving their opinions about a new sculpture in the city centre. How many people like it?

b Listen again and complete the extracts.

Conversation 1
1 **A:** The new sculpture? I think it's really weird.
   B: So _____ I!
2 **A:** I don't understand the point of it.
   B: Neither _____ I.
3 **A:** I think it's a waste of public money.
   B: Me _____!

Conversation 2
4 **A:** I went to see it when they first put it up.
   B: So _____ I. I think it's brilliant.
5 **A:** I've never been to Barcelona.
   B: Neither _____ I, actually.

Conversation 3
6 **A:** I think it's amazing, I really like it.
   B: I _____ too.
7 **A:** No, I didn't, to be honest.
   B: I _____ either.
8 **A:** I'm not really keen on that kind of traditional statue.
   B: _____ neither.

6 Complete the short responses.

1. **A:** I was good at art when I was at school.
   B: So _____ I.
2. **A:** I wanted to study art at college.
   B: I _____ . I hated art at school.
3. **A:** I don't like abstract art.
   B: Neither _____ I. I think it's all really strange.
4. **A:** I'd love to visit the Louvre in Paris.
   B: So _____ I. It'd be amazing.
5. **A:** I'm a big fan of the Spanish artist Dali.
   B: Really? I _____ . I don't understand why people like his work.
6. **A:** I like art which sends a positive message.
   B: So _____ I.
7. **A:** I don't go to see art exhibitions very often.
   B: I _____ . I go every week.
8. **A:** Sometimes I can't understand what an artist is trying to say.
   B: Neither _____ I sometimes!

7 a Complete the sentences with your own ideas.

1. I love …
2. I'd love to …
3. I've always wanted to …
4. I've never …
5. I'm (not) interested in …

b Work in pairs. Take turns to share your sentences. Respond and say if you agree or disagree using short responses.

Go to page 132 or your app for more information and practice.

Speaking

PREPARE

8 a 9.7 You're going to talk about proposals for a new piece of public art. First, listen to a discussion about a new piece of art and answer the questions.
1. What questions do they have to think about?
2. Which piece of art do they finally choose?

b Listen again and answer the questions.
1. How many speakers like each piece of art?
2. Why don't the other speakers like each piece?
3. What's the reason for their final choice?

SPEAK

9 Work in groups. Turn to page 158 and follow the instructions.

10 Tell the group which piece of art you chose. Which proposal is most popular with the class?

Grammar

4 Read the grammar box and choose the correct alternatives.

Short responses: so, neither/nor; too/either

To **¹**agree/disagree with someone, use:
- so + auxiliary verb + subject after positive statements.
  A: I love it. **B:** So do I.
- neither/nor + auxiliary verb + subject after negative statements.
  A: I didn't enjoy the exhibition. **B:** Neither/Nor did I.
- subject + auxiliary verb + too after positive statements.
  A: I love modern art. **B:** I do too.
- subject + negative auxiliary verb + either after negative statements.
  A: We didn't enjoy the film. **B:** I didn't either.

To **²**agree/disagree, use the positive form of the auxiliary verb if the statement is negative, and the negative form of the auxiliary verb if the statement is positive.
A: I didn't enjoy the exhibition. **B:** Oh, I did.
A: I love it. **B:** Really? I don't.

5 a 9.6 Listen and notice the extra sound between the first word and the verb.
1. So are we.
2. We are too.
3. I am too.

b Listen again and repeat.

Develop your listening page 112

9D English in action

> **Goal:** make complaints

1 Look at the picture and discuss the questions.
1. What is happening? Has something like this ever happened to you?
2. What other things can go wrong when you shop or use services?
3. What other situations can you think of when you might need to make a complaint?

2 🔊 **9.10** Listen to three conversations. Answer the questions about each conversation.
1. What is the customer's problem?
2. What does the assistant do/say?
3. What action does the customer ask for? Why?

3 a Listen again and complete the extracts from the three conversations.

Conversation 1
1. Hello. I'm _____ I've got a problem.
2. _____ but your order hasn't come in yet. We'll _____ as soon as it arrives.
3. I'd like to _____ immediately and get _____ please.

Conversation 2
4. I'd _____ replace them, please.
5. I _____ we don't have any more of these plates at the moment.
6. _____ order another box for me, please?

Conversation 3
7. Sorry, I'm afraid _____ .
8. I'm very sorry _____ . I'll _____ to the kitchen and order your fish.
9. Please _____ bring me my bill for the first course.

b Listen again and check your answers.

c Look at the extracts in Exercise 3a again. Who says each line, the customer (C) or the member of staff (S)?

4 Look at the Useful phrases. Where there is a gap, complete them with your own ideas.

Useful phrases

Complaining
I'm sorry, but there's been a mistake with …
I'm afraid that there's a problem with …
There seems to be a problem with …
Can I see your …, please?
I'd like to make a complaint.

Giving reasons for complaints
The problem is …
The … doesn't work.
The … is broken.
I've been waiting for …

Responding and offering solutions
I'm very sorry about that.
Unfortunately, we can't …
We'll give you …

Asking for action
I'd like to cancel the order/get a refund/speak to the manager, please.
I'd like you to (change it for a new one).
Please could you (bring the bill)?

5 a Work in pairs. Look at the situations below and think about what you'd say.

Student A
You're in a restaurant. There are some problems.
- You've been waiting half an hour for your food.
- Your steak is overcooked.
- Your soup is cold.
- You were given the wrong meal, but were asked to pay for it.

Student B
You're staying in a hotel. There are some problems.
- The shower is broken.
- The bed is uncomfortable.
- There is a lot of noise from other guests.
- You had asked for a room with a sea view, but you can only see the garden.

b Take turns to complain and ask for action. Use the Useful phrases to help you.

Go online for the Roadmap video.

Check and reflect

1 a Choose the correct alternatives.

I try to buy clothes in the ¹*sales/deals*, when they're much cheaper. I'm always looking for a ²*bargain/save* or for special ³*orders/offers*. I love a good ⁴*save/deal*! However, if there's something I really want, then I'll save ⁵*out/up* for it. I also buy clothes online, as they're ⁶*ordered/delivered* to my home. If you don't like it, you can send it back and get a ⁷*refund/return* or ⁸*exchange/refund* it for something else.

b Are your shopping habits similar to those in Exercise 1a? Work in pairs and compare your ideas.

I spend quite a lot on clothes, actually ...

2 a Complete the sentences with the correct form of the verbs in brackets.

1 If shoppers like the music that _____ (play) in a shop, they are more likely to stay longer and spend more.
2 Many shopping centres _____ (design) to make people lose their sense of time and location. Clocks _____ (remove) and windows _____ (cover) so you can't see out.
3 In recent years, seating areas _____ (remove) from many shopping centres, as people don't spend money when they're sitting down.
4 It _____ (predict) that in the future almost everything _____ (will / purchase) online.

b Do you agree with the ideas in Exercise 2a? What other ways do shops and online shopping sites try to make us spend more?

3 a Join the events using the third conditional.

1 Robert went to bed late last night → he overslept → he was late for work → he lost his job.
If Robert hadn't gone to bed late last night, he wouldn't have overslept. If he hadn't overslept, he ...
2 Alexa went to a piano concert → she decided to learn the piano → she became a professional pianist → she became rich and famous.
3 Bonny didn't revise for her exams → she failed them all → she didn't get into university → she started her own company → she became a millionaire.

b Write a sequence of events in your life that depended on each other using the third conditional.

4 Complete the responses with the adjectives in the box.

| exhausted | gorgeous | huge | terrible | terrified |

1 **A:** Were you tired? **B:** I was ____ !
2 **A:** Was it big? **B:** It was ____ !
3 **A:** Were you frightened? **B:** Frightened? I was ____ .
4 **A:** It's beautiful, isn't it? **B:** It is. It's ____ .
5 **A:** It was bad, wasn't it? **B:** Bad? It was ____ !

5 a Complete the sentences with the adjectives in the box.

| abstract | cheerful | colourful | powerful |
| realistic | unoriginal | weird | |

1 I've seen so many paintings like this. It's so ____ .
2 Her paintings of people are extremely ____ . They look like photographs.
3 It says it's a self-portrait, but it's just squares and triangles. I can't see a face. It's too ____ .
4 It's so ____ . Blues, reds, yellows, purples, oranges, ...
5 Why is there a horse coming out of someone's mouth? That's a bit ____ if you ask me.
6 That's a really ____ image of a battlefield. It really makes you think.
7 I love this picture. It's full of light and life – it's so ____ . It always puts a smile on my face.

b Work in pairs. Discuss works of art that you know that can be described by the adjectives in Exercise 5a.

6 a Complete the responses.

1 **A:** I'm not a fan of modern art.
   B: Neither ____ . I just don't understand it.
2 **A:** I can speak some Russian.
   B: So ____ , but I only speak a little.
3 **A:** I don't like going to museums.
   B: Oh, I ____ . I love them. Why don't you like them?
4 **A:** I can't stand most reality TV.
   B: Me ____ . It's just boring.
5 **A:** I went to a party last night.
   B: I ____ . Maybe we were at the same one.
6 **A:** I'd love to live abroad for a year.
   B: So ____ . Maybe for even longer.

b Work in pairs and take turns to read the sentences and give short responses that are true for you.

Reflect

How confident do you feel about the statements below? Write 1–5 (1 = not very confident, 5 = very confident).
- I can discuss and suggest improvements.
- I can tell a story.
- I can express agreement and disagreement.
- I can make complaints.

Want more practice? Go to your Workbook or app.

10A Education

> **Goal:** report opinions
> **Grammar:** reported statements
> **Vocabulary:** education

Vocabulary and reading

1 Discuss the questions. Do you think schooldays are the best days of your life? Why/Why not?

2 Match questions 1–4 with answers a–d.
1 What kind of school did you go to?
2 Did you enjoy your time at school?
3 Did your time at school help you in later life?
4 What advice would you give to students at school now?

a You shouldn't spend all your time **revising for tests** or worrying about if you're **doing well**. You should enjoy your life, too!
b Yes. It taught me that it's OK to **fail** as long as you don't give up. I didn't **pass** all my **exams** first time, but I **took** them again and got good results.
c Not really. I didn't like **secondary school** at all as it was all about **passing exams**. I **got low grades** because I found most subjects really boring.
d After **primary school**, I went away to a **boarding school**, a kind of private school that you live in. You **pay** high **fees** to go there so not many people can afford it. Some people think it sounds amazing, but I'd have preferred to **attend** a **state school** like my friends.

3 a What verbs can you use with the words in the box? Use Exercise 2 to help you.

| an exam | a subject | high grades |
| qualifications | school | |

attend/enjoy school, find school boring

b Read opinions 1–8 and choose the correct alternatives.
1 Going away to *boarding/secondary* school would be fun.
2 *Private/Primary* schools are better than state schools.
3 The most important thing about school is *passing/making* tests and *winning/getting* qualifications.
4 Doing *well/good* at school means you'll have a happy life.
5 Students spend too much of their time *revising for/having* and *getting/taking* tests.
6 If a student doesn't like a *subject/topic* at school, they should be able to choose to stop studying it.
7 It's wrong for rich families to be able to *pay/spend* fees to get a better education for their children.
8 Getting low *tests/grades* means you're not intelligent.

4 Work in pairs. Do you agree with any of the opinions in Exercise 3b? Which one(s)? Why?

📱 Go to page 145 or your app for more vocabulary and practice.

Looking back at your schooldays

Last month we asked people in our group about their experiences of school. Here are some of the results.

1 What kind of school did you go to?
Over half of the people said they had gone to state schools and about 30 percent told us they had gone to private schools. Some people said they had attended a private primary school followed by a state secondary school. Not many people in the group said they had gone to boarding school.

2 Did you enjoy your time at school?
Everybody said there were always good and bad things about school and that some subjects had been interesting and some hadn't been interesting at all! They had all sat exams and passed some and failed some. Generally, though, people say they enjoyed school. Most told us that the two things they really remembered were the teachers and then the fun they had had with their friends.

3 Do you feel your time at school has helped you in later life?
The majority of readers said they thought their schools had helped them to get to where they were. Most people told us that they now had interesting careers or were studying courses that they enjoyed and that school had helped them achieve this.

4 What advice would you give to students at school now?
Most people said that the best idea was to make the most of the opportunities school offers and try to do well. However, they also said those years had been the best time to make good friends and have fun!

5 Read the report about school experiences. What are your answers to questions 1–4 in the report?

6 Read the report again and answer the questions.
1 How many people attended state schools?
2 How many people went to boarding schools?
3 What did most people remember about school?
4 Did people think school had helped them?
5 What two pieces of advice did people give?

Grammar

7 Read the grammar box and choose the correct alternative.

Reported statements

To repeat what someone says to us, make the following changes:
1 Use *say* and *tell* to report what someone says.
2 Move all tenses one step back into the **¹***past/present*.
Present simple → Past simple
*'The best idea **is** to make the most of the opportunities school offers,' the majority said.*
*The majority said the best idea **was** to make the most of the opportunities school offered.*
Present continuous → Past continuous
*'We **are studying** courses we enjoy,' they said.*
*They said they **were studying** courses they enjoyed.*
Past simple → Past perfect
*'We **attended** a private primary school,' some people said.*
*Some people told us they **had attended** a private primary school.*
Present perfect → Past perfect
*'Our schools **have helped** us,' they said.*
*They said their schools **had helped** them.*
Will (future) → *Would*
*'We **will** get qualifications which will help us get good jobs,' these people said.*
*These people said they **would** get qualifications which would help them get good jobs.*
Sometimes it isn't necessary to change the tense, when what we are saying is still true now.
*Tom said that he **likes** school.* (Tom still likes school now.)
It also isn't necessary to change the tense if *say/tell* is used in the present tense.
*Some people **say** schooldays **are** the best days of your life.*

8 a 🔊 **10.1** Listen and notice the pronunciation of *'d*.
  1 Some people told us they'd gone to private schools.
  2 One person told me he'd failed some exams.
  3 Some people said they'd attended a private school.
  4 They said they'd enjoyed school.

  b Listen again and repeat.

9 Complete the texts with the correct form of the verbs in the box.

| be (x3) | do | like | say | study | tell |

1 A lot of people told us they ¹_____ not _____ very well at school because they ²_____ not _____ some of the subjects very much. Scientists have said that this ³_____ normal and that students ⁴_____ hard if they enjoy what they are learning.

2 Most people told us that their time at school ⁵_____ very happy. They ⁶_____ they had enjoyed most of the lessons. When we asked what they thought could be better, they ⁷_____ us that sometimes the classes ⁸_____ too large in schools in the city.

10 Write sentences reporting what each person said.
  1 'I don't want to go to university,' John told me.
     John told me he didn't want to go to university.
  2 'My mother didn't go to a boarding school,' Nina said.
  3 'Education will be free in the future,' Mark told us.
  4 'I'm still studying at university,' Jamie said. 'But my sister is working for a big IT company.'
  5 'Schooldays were the best days,' my grandmother says.

📱 Go to page 134 or your app for more information and practice.

Speaking

PREPARE

11 a 🔊 **10.2** You're going to discuss education. Listen to three people discussing whether a good education is important. What examples do they give to support their opinions? Make notes.

  b Listen again and check your ideas.

12 Read the questions below and make notes. Think of examples from your own experience to support your ideas.
  • What would you like to change about the education system in your country?
  • Do you think we need to go to school? Why/Why not?

SPEAK

13 a Work in groups. Discuss the questions in Exercise 12. Use the Useful phrases to help you.

Useful phrases
In an ideal world, I would change …
It would be a good idea to change …
School can help a child to …
I think school is … because …

  b What did you agree/disagree on? Tell the class.

10A | Education

Develop your writing
page 113

10B Green cities

> **Goal:** talk about improving your town or city
> **Grammar:** verb patterns
> **Vocabulary:** suggestions and improvements

Vocabulary and reading

1 Look at the photos and discuss the questions.
   1 What kinds of transport can you see? How often do you use them?
   2 What's public transport like where you live?

2 a Read the introduction to the article below. Which problems are mentioned? What suggestions and recommendations do you think people will make?

What can we do to make our cities greener?

As more and more people move to the city, the problems of air pollution, traffic jams and lack of green spaces are increasing. These problems will continue to get worse unless we find solutions. What can we do to make our cities greener?

Comments

We should **encourage people to join** car-sharing schemes. He should **refuse to allow** companies to build houses on parkland.

My parents have **warned me not to ride** my bike on busy main roads, it's too dangerous. The mayor must **promise to provide** more cycle lanes.

How about **persuading more employers to offer** loans to their employees to buy bicycles?

I **recommend providing** free parking facilities near metro and train stations.

I'd **advise the mayor to install** more charging points for electric cars.

I **suggest reducing** fares for public transport. People are always complaining that it's too expensive.

We should **consider raising** the price of parking in the city centre.

People need to **start thinking** about the environment more and **avoid using** their cars unless they really need to.

b Read the comments. Are any of your ideas mentioned? How would the suggestions help to solve the problems?
Encouraging people to join car-sharing schemes would help to reduce traffic jams.

c Have any of the solutions been successfully tried in your town or city?

3 Choose the correct alternatives. Use the phrases in bold in the article to help you.
   1 She *persuaded/warned* me to use my bicycle by telling me how much weight I'd lose.
   2 People *start/suggest* complaining when you tell them to stop using their cars.
   3 You should *promise/refuse* to go if they don't pay for your travel expenses.
   4 I *promise/refuse* to leave the car at home next week. I'll cycle to work instead.
   5 We should *encourage/warn* people to walk to work.
   6 Several people have *warned/promised* us not to cycle on the busy main road.
   7 I'm *considering/recommending* selling my car and buying a motorbike.
   8 You should *avoid/start* travelling at that time, unless you really need to.
   9 If you want to be greener, I'd *recommend/avoid* using public transport.
   10 I'd *advise/warn* you to think about how often you really need to use your car.

Go to your app for more practice.

Grammar

4 Read the grammar box and complete the information with the reporting verbs in bold in Exercise 2.

Verb patterns

When we use two verbs together, the second verb is usually either the *-ing* form or the infinitive form with *to*.

Verbs + *-ing* form
consider, recommend, start, avoid, [1]_____
I **recommend providing** free parking ...

Verbs + infinitive with *to*
promise, [2]_____
The mayor must **promise to provide** more cycle lanes.
Some verbs always need an object before the infinitive with *to*.
encourage, persuade, warn, [3]_____
We need to **persuade them to offer** loans.

To make an *-ing* form or infinitive negative, put *not* in front of it.
My parents have **warned me not to** ride my bike on busy main roads.

A few verbs take both the infinitive and the gerund.
They **started arguing** when they heard our suggestions.
They **started to argue** when they heard our suggestions.
When you learn new verbs, try to memorise whether they take a gerund or an infinitive, or both.

5 a 🔊 **10.3** Listen and notice the pronunciation of *to*.
1 They promised to provide more cycle lanes.
2 I suggest cycling to work.
3 They warned me not to ride my bike.
4 We tried to persuade her to take action.

b Listen again and repeat.

6 Complete the sentences with the correct form of the verbs in brackets.
1 He suggested _____ (travel) to work on foot.
2 We should encourage people _____ (walk or cycle) instead of using their cars.
3 A lot of people refuse _____ (give up) their cars and use public transport.
4 I recommend _____ (replace) buses with trams.
5 The government must promise _____ (not increase) train fares.
6 I think we should consider _____ (stop) cars from entering the centre.

7 a Think about how your town or city could be improved. Complete the sentences with your ideas.
1 We should encourage people to ...
2 I'd recommend ...
3 We need to start ...
4 We should persuade people not ...
5 We should consider ...
6 People should avoid ...

b Work in pairs and compare your answers. Give reasons for your ideas.

📱 Go to page 134 or your app for more information and practice.

Speaking

PREPARE

8 🔊 **10.4** You're going to suggest ways to make your town/city greener, cleaner and safer. First, listen to a group of residents having a meeting about their neighbourhood and answer the questions.
1 What problems do the speakers mention?
2 What solutions do they suggest?
3 What do they want their local council to do?

9 Think about ways to improve your city. Make notes about the following:
- pollution
- green spaces
- transport
- facilities for children

SPEAK

10 a Work in groups. Discuss your ideas for improvements and make a list of suggestions. Use the Useful phrases to help you.

Useful phrases
So, we're here to discuss ...
I worry about ...
We should ask/request the mayor/council to ...

b Report back to the class. Vote for the best ideas.

Develop your reading page 114

10B | Green cities

81

10C What's in a job?

> **Goal:** report the results of a survey
> **Grammar:** reported questions
> **Vocabulary:** work activities

Vocabulary

1 a Discuss the questions.
  1 How do people waste time at work?
  2 Which activities do you think waste the most time?

b Look at the survey and check your answers. Does any information surprise you?

We asked 2,000 employees how they spend their time at work.

Here are the top work time wasters.

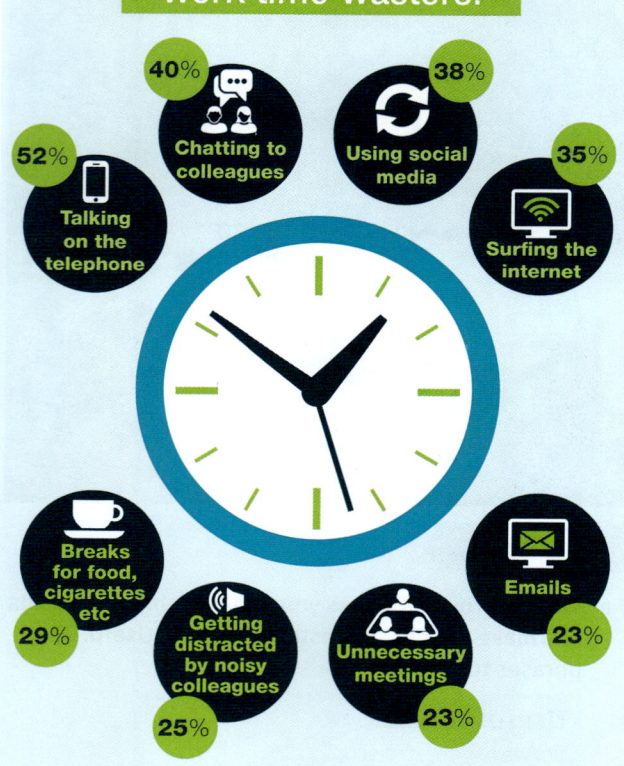

- Talking on the telephone — 52%
- Chatting to colleagues — 40%
- Using social media — 38%
- Surfing the internet — 35%
- Breaks for food, cigarettes etc — 29%
- Getting distracted by noisy colleagues — 25%
- Unnecessary meetings — 23%
- Emails — 23%

2 Look at the photos. Which of the activities in the box can you see?

> arrange (interviews/meetings)   do research
> employ people   give presentations
> interview people   manage (projects/people/a shop)
> offer someone a job   serve customers
> set up meetings   write reports   work in a team

3 Choose the correct alternatives.

A Market researcher
In my job, I *do research/set up meetings* for my company. I use different methods to get information. I often *offer someone a job/interview people* on the phone. I also use the internet to collect data. Then I have to *write a report/serve customers*. The documents contain all the details of my research. Sometimes I *do research/give presentations* to tell people about my results.

B HR officer
A big part of my job is finding suitable staff for the company. I *arrange interviews/work in a team* for jobs. If they're good, I *offer them the job/give presentations*. If they accept the job, the company then *employs/serves* them.

C Office manager
I'm very busy at work. I have to organise everything that happens in the office. I do things like *set up meetings/write reports* – I organise them and make sure everyone knows about them. When we need new staff, I also *arrange/offer* interviews for my boss.

D Project manager
In my job, I need to be very organised and have good communication skills. As my title says, I'm responsible for *managing projects/employing people*. I work with the *team/presentations* to get the project done and make sure everything runs smoothly.

E Shop assistant
I work in a busy bookshop so I *serve customers/work in a team* all day. My goal for the future is to *manage/employ* the bookshop myself.

4 Work in pairs. Have you done any of the activities in Exercise 2? Would you like to? Choose three activities and say when you do/did them or when/why you would like to do them.

📱 Go to your app for more practice.

Listening

5 a You're going to listen to Sharon describing her job in digital advertising. What activities do you think she does every day?

b 🔊 10.5 Listen and check your ideas.

6 a Match sentences 1–6 with answers a–f.
1 Tim asked Sharon to tell him what she did exactly.
2 Then he asked her what the second part of her job was.
3 He wanted to know how she did that.
4 Then he asked her to give him an example.
5 He wanted to know if Sharon enjoyed her job.
6 Finally, he asked her if she recommended the job to other people.

a She said there were two parts to her job. First, she wrote advertising texts for websites.
b Sharon said she loved it.
c She told him that she used key words in her texts.
d She said she would recommend it to anyone looking for a job in marketing.
e She explained that her job was to bring her customer's website to the top of online search results.
f She told him that a title like '10 ways to …' was good because people often searched for ways to do things.

b Work in pairs. Would you enjoy a job like Sharon's? Why/Why not?

Grammar

7 Read the grammar box and think of one more example of a reported question for rules 1–3.

> ### Reported questions
> **1** When a question that uses the auxiliary *do* becomes a reported question, the tenses are changed in the same way as when reporting a statement.
> The auxiliaries *do* (and also *did*) are removed to form a reported question.
> '*How **do** you **make** that?*' he asked her.
> *He asked her how she **made** that.*
>
> **2** Some questions don't use *do/did*. Change the order of the auxiliary verb and the subject (*are* and *you*), so that it looks more like a statement than a question.
> '*Where **are** you **going**?*' she asked him.
> *She asked him where she **was going**.*
>
> **3** Use *ask somebody to/for* to report requests.
> '*Could you give me an example?*'
> *I **asked her to** give me an example.*

8 a 🔊 10.6 Listen and notice the intonation in the direct and reported questions.
1 'Do you ever recommend it to other people?'
  I asked her if she ever recommended it to other people.
2 'How do you do that?'
  He asked her how she did that.
3 'Could you give me an example?'
  I asked her to give me an example.

b Choose the correct alternative.
In *direct/reported* questions the speaker's voice goes up then down at the end.

c Listen again and repeat.

9 Report the questions from a survey.
1 What time do you start work/studying?
  The interviewer asked me/wanted to know what time I started work/studying.
2 What time do you finish?
3 Where do you work/study?
4 Do you work with other people or alone?
5 What percentage of your time do you spend answering emails?
6 What do you spend most of your time doing?
7 Do you enjoy your work/study?

📱 Go to page 134 or your app for more information and practice.

Speaking

PREPARE

10 You're going to carry out a survey about people's work or study habits. Write six or seven questions to ask people. Use Exercise 9 to help you.

SPEAK

11 a Ask your questions from Exercise 10 to three or four students in your class. Make notes.

b Work in groups. Report the questions you asked and answers you received. Use the Useful phrases to help you. How many answers were the same/different?

> **Useful phrases**
> I asked him to tell me …
> I wanted to know if …
> I asked them if they enjoyed/wanted/liked …
> He said he spent … hours …

c Did any of the answers you heard surprise you? Why/Why not?

Develop your listening
page 115

10D English in action

Goal: ask and answer interview questions

1 Look at the photos. What skills and personal qualities do you think each person needs for their job?

2 🔊 10.10 Listen to the first part of a conversation. What is the situation?

3 a 🔊 10.11 Listen to the whole conversation. Tick the questions that the interviewer asks.
  1. What made you decide to become a civil engineer?
  2. Why do you want this job?
  3. Why do you want to work with this company?
  4. Which job are you interested in?
  5. So, could you tell me a bit more about your qualifications for this job?
  6. So how much experience have you had?
  7. What would you say you are best at?
  8. Can you speak any other languages?
  9. So, could you describe yourself in just three words?
  10. And what are your goals for the future?
  11. When would you be able to start?

b Complete the answers from the listening. Use the Useful phrases to help you.
  a Well, I've always wanted to do something practical. _____ , civil engineers build roads and bridges.
  b Your company is very well-known and _____ I'll have excellent opportunities to develop my skills.
  c _____ from my CV, I have a degree in civil engineering _____ get my Master's degree this year.
  d But _____ my greatest skill is organising projects.
  e Umm, I _____ that I'm well-organised and responsible. And I'm also creative.
  f I _____ manage my own projects and work with customers.

Useful phrases

Asking for information
What made you decide to …?
Can/Could you tell me why/about …?
What would you say …?
I'd be interested to know (if/what/how much) …

Giving information and explanations
I mean, …
As you can see, …
I can say …
I think I'd say …

Confirming what has been said
I see. So, …

Asking about future plans
Where do you see yourself in five years?
What are your goals for the future?

Expressing hopes for the future
I'm hoping to …
I want/hope/would like to …
Hopefully, …

4 a Match the answers in Exercise 3b with questions from Exercise 3a. Sometimes more than one question is possible.

b Listen again. What words and phrases does the candidate use to give her time to think before she answers the questions?

5 Work in pairs. Student A: Turn to page 157 and follow the instructions. Student B: Turn to page 159 and follow the instructions.

Go online for the Roadmap video.

Check and reflect

1 a Complete the sentences with the words in the box.

| fees | grades | pass | primary | private |
| secondary | state | subjects | take | university |

1. In the UK, you go to _____ school from 5 to 11, then you go to _____ school and then about a third of 18-year-olds go to _____ to study for a degree.
2. Over 90 percent of children in the UK go to a _____ school. A small number go to a _____ school, where you pay _____ .
3. Students _____ important exams called GCSEs when they are 16. If they get good _____ , they take their A levels. If they _____ their A level exams with good grades, they can go to university. Students usually study up to ten different _____ for GCSE and three or four for A levels.

b Work in pairs. How is education in the UK the same or different from your country?

2 Complete the reported statements.
1. 'I'm looking for a new job.'
   She told us _____ .
2. 'I've got a degree in biology.'
   She said _____ .
3. 'I've been to a few conferences.'
   Camilla told me _____ .
4. 'I'll be in touch sometime next week.'
   She said _____ .
5. 'I started teaching about 15 years ago.'
   Mr Williams told me _____ .

3 Choose the correct alternatives.
1. The government has *promised/demanded* to increase spending on education.
2. Because of the snow, police have *encouraged/advised* people not to drive.
3. The police have *warned/persuaded* people not to approach the escaped lion.
4. Smith said that he had *considered/recommended* resigning, but later changed his mind.
5. People should *avoid/refuse* travelling at night.

4 Complete the reporting sentences.
1. 'You should walk and cycle more.'
   He suggested _____
2. 'I might walk to work this week.'
   He's considering _____
3. 'OK, I'll give you a lift to the airport.'
   She's agreed _____
4. 'I think we'll arrive around 6.30.'
   She expects _____
5. 'If I were you, I'd wait a little longer.'
   He advised _____
6. 'Don't forget to book the taxi.'
   She reminded _____

5 Choose the correct alternatives.
1. He suggested *to walk/walking* to the beach.
2. I try to avoid *to eat/eating* too much at night.
3. She refused *to come/coming* with me to the party.
4. We recommend *to leave/leaving* quite early.
5. You should consider *to change/changing* those curtains.
6. She persuaded me *to go/going*.
7. You never encourage me to *try/trying* anything new.
8. You're not going to persuade *me to/to* change my mind.

6 Complete the sentences with the words in the box.

| customers | offered | presentations | report |
| set | team | | |

1. Giving _____ always makes me nervous.
2. Do you have to _____ many meetings in your job?
3. How often do you need to _____ reports?
4. I work in a shop and serve _____ all day.
5. I'm so happy - they _____ me the job!
6. I prefer working in a _____ to working alone.

7 Complete the reported questions.
1. 'Where do you live?'
   She wanted to know …
2. 'Have you got any hobbies?'
   He asked me …
3. 'Do you speak any foreign languages?'
   She asked me …
4. 'When did you leave school?'
   He wanted to know …
5. 'Have you ever lived abroad?'
   She asked me …
6. 'What do you think of your new boss?'
   Graham wanted to know …
7. `What are you doing?'
   He asked me …
8. `What did you eat?'
   She wanted to know …

Reflect
How confident do you feel about the statements below? Write 1–5 (1 = not very confident, 5 = very confident).
- I can report opinions.
- I can talk about improving my town or city.
- I can report the results of a survey.
- I can ask and answer interview questions.

Want more practice?
Go to your Workbook or app.

1A Develop your reading

> **Goal:** understand an article
> **Focus:** reading for general understanding

1 Which of the following are the most important qualities of a good friend?
   a They always tell you the truth.
   b They are good listeners.
   c They make time for you.
   d They are loyal and trustworthy.
   e They make you feel good about yourself.

2 You're going to read about the qualities of a real friend. First, read the Focus box. What kind of words help you get a general understanding of a writer's message?

Reading for general understanding

Before you read a text in detail, it is a good idea to look through it quickly first to get a general idea of the content and identify the writer's message.
To do this, focus on content words – adjectives, nouns and verbs – not grammar words.

*For many of us, **real friends** are like **family**. They are very **important** for our **health** and **happiness**. They **listen** to us when we **have problems** and they **help** us when we **need** it. They **celebrate** our **happy moments**, too.*

Don't stop if you don't understand a word. Keep reading. You don't have to understand every word to get the main ideas.

3 a Read the article and match sentences a–e in Exercise 1 with paragraphs 1–5.
   b Underline the words that help you identify the main idea in each paragraph.

4 Read the article again and answer the questions.
   According to the text, ...
   1 how are real friends like family?
   2 why are good friends important to us?
   3 why is it sometimes difficult to meet up with friends?
   4 in what way are friends good listeners?
   5 how do they make you feel good about yourself?
   6 why do they tell you when you do something wrong?
   7 why is it OK to tell your real friends secrets?

5 Work in pairs and discuss the questions.
   1 Which of the ideas in the article do you agree/disagree with?
   2 Do you have a best friend?
   3 Are your friends similar to you or very different?
   4 Do you think you are a good friend? Why/Why not?

The qualities of a real friend

Real friends are like family. You can always depend on them to be there for you. They are very important for our health and happiness. Here are five key qualities of real friendships.

1 We all lead busy lives, trying to deal with work and family, so it can be difficult to find the time to keep a friendship going. However, real friends always make time for you. They call you to chat about your latest news and take advantage of your shared interests and activities, like going to the cinema or the gym together.

2 Real friends are interested in what you say. They don't just talk about themselves. They listen to you as well and pay attention to what you say. They don't keep looking at their phones when you're talking.

3 Real friends encourage you and make you feel happy and self-confident. A real friend never makes you feel bad or stupid. When you're feeling sad and depressed, real friends try to make you feel cheerful again.

4 Good friends are honest with you. They tell you when you do something wrong, but they do it in a nice way. They don't do it to be cruel or unkind but because they want to help you be a better person. This kind of honesty is the sign of real friendship.

5 You can share your personal secrets with a real friend and trust them not to tell other people. You know your secrets are safe with them. And real friends don't say nasty things about you when you're not around.

1B Develop your writing

> **Goal:** write a job application
> **Focus:** using paragraphs in a job application

1 Discuss the questions.
1 Have you ever written a job application, either in your language or English?
2 What kind of information should you put in a job application?

2 Read the job application and answer the questions.
1 What type of job is the candidate looking for?
2 What kind of information does the candidate give?

Dear Mr Garsforth,
¹I'm writing to apply for the **position** which was advertised on your website on 5th July. Please find my CV attached.
²I am a graduate in Graphic Design from the University of Birmingham. **Currently**, I am working for BetaCore as a Junior Graphic Designer in their London office. I have been in this position for **approximately** two years.
³I feel I would be an excellent candidate for the position of designer **as** I have all the skills that you **require**. I'm also hardworking, creative and always happy to learn new things.
⁴Thank you for taking the time to **consider** my application and **I look forward to hearing from you** in the near future.
Yours sincerely,
Hannah Worth

3 Match words and phrases 1–7 with the words and phrases in bold in the job application.
1 think about
2 job
3 at the moment
4 need
5 because
6 I'm excited about getting an answer from you
7 more or less

4 Read the Focus box. What do paragraphs do?

Using paragraphs in a job application

Pieces of writing are usually organised into paragraphs. Paragraphs make it easier for a reader to find the information they need. Each paragraph usually deals with a different part of the topic, so it's easy for a reader to know where they can find the information they need. Many job applications are organised in the following way:
First paragraph: This tells the reader why you are writing.
Middle paragraph(s): This is where you communicate the main information, what makes you a good candidate for the job, including details of education and work experience.
Final paragraph: This tells the reader what you hope/want to happen next.

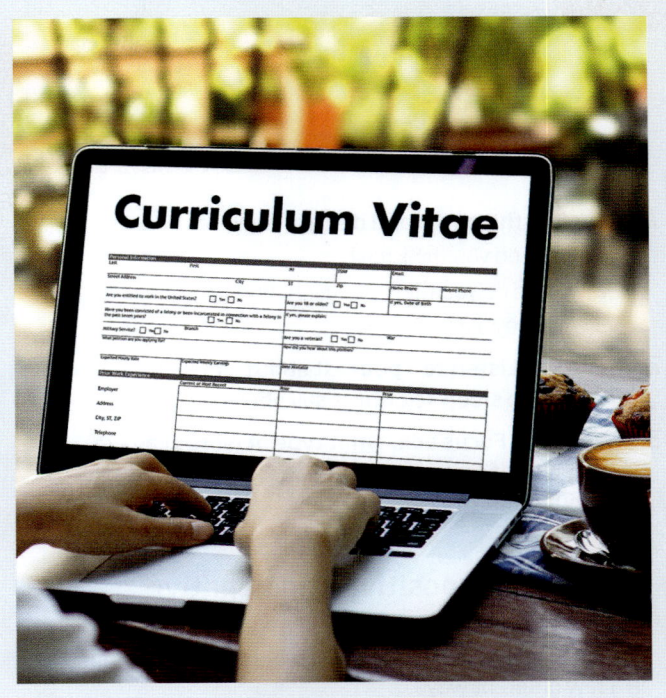

5 Look at the job application again. In which paragraph do you find the following information?
1 what you want to happen next
2 your reason for writing
3 a description of qualifications
4 a description of personality
5 a description of work experience
6 where you heard about the job

6 Look at the sentences and decide which paragraph of an application they might appear in.
1 I have very strong communication skills.
2 I'm writing to apply for the position of IT Instructor.
3 I am a qualified accountant.
4 I would be happy to attend an interview.
5 I saw the position advertised on Maspa.com.
6 I work well in a team.
7 Many thanks for your consideration.
8 Yours sincerely

Prepare

7 a You're going to write a job application for your dream job, or one of the jobs below. What qualifications, experience and personal qualities would you need for the job? Make a list.
- a nurse in a busy hospital
- a ski instructor
- a graphic designer
- a project manager

b What words and phrases from the application in Exercise 2 would be helpful for writing your own application? Make a list.

Write

8 Write your letter of application. Remember to organise your information into paragraphs.

1c Develop your listening

> **Goal:** understand a podcast
>
> **Focus:** recognising positive and negative attitudes

1 Look at the photo and discuss the questions.
1 What do you think it is?
2 Where do you think you might find them?
3 Are they a good idea?

2 🔊 1.7 Listen to a podcast about sleep. What two things do sleep scientists say about sleep?

3 Read the Focus box. What type of words can we listen for if we want to know how someone feels about what they are saying?

Recognising positive and negative attitudes

People show how they feel about what they are saying in a few different ways.

The way they introduce what they are saying

It's not good news for people who have a full-time job.
Unfortunately, these problems are getting worse.
The bad news is that people are not as healthy as they should be.

The adverbs and adjectives they use

People don't take enough breaks, which is **not great for them**.
I think that's going to be a very **positive** change.
They want us all to sleep at work. That's **an amazing idea**.
A lot of companies do this really **well**.
The situation is getting **better**.

The tone of voice they use

As well as listening to the words someone says, we can also listen to how they say them. Someone's face can also tell us a lot about how they're feeling.

---

4 Listen to the podcast again and complete the sentences. Tick the sentences where the speaker is talking about something positive. Put a cross where the speaker is talking about something negative.
1 … but the _____ is not many adults get eight hours a night.
2 This is not _____ for the evening people, but we all have to get up early to go to work.
3 And it's ____ that many of us go to bed late because we finish work late.
4 So, it seems like the situation is _____ for anyone: no one gets enough sleep!
5 However, the situation is getting _____ .
6 Isn't that a _____ ?
7 And another _____ change is that more people work online.
8 And the second thing sleep scientists tell us is that sleep is an _____ medicine.

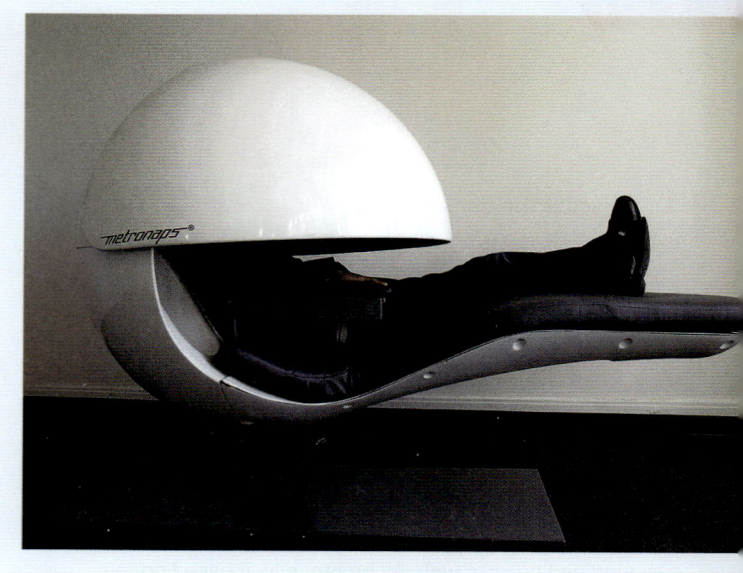

5 Listen again and answer the questions.
1 What is an evening type?
2 What is a morning type?
3 What often stops us getting enough sleep?
4 What are companies recognising about tired employees?
5 What will companies do?
   a let people sleep at work
   b check how long people sleep
   c give people more holidays
6 Why is working online a good thing for some people?

6 a 🔊 1.8 Listen to the comments of some listeners about the podcast. Choose the correct alternatives.
1 Speaker 1 is talking about sleeping at *work/home*. He feels *positive/negative* about this.
2 Speaker 2 is talking about being able to go to work *early/late*. She feels *positive/negative* about this.
3 Speaker 3 is talking about his *company/friends* knowing how much sleep he gets. He feels *positive/negative* about this.
4 Speaker 4 is speaking about what sleep scientists call *medicine/work*. She feels *positive/negative* about this.
5 Speaker 5 is talking about *sleeping/working* in the office. He feels *positive/negative* about this.
6 Speaker 6 is talking about *working/sleeping*. She feels *positive/negative* about this.

b Listen again and check your answers. Write down the words/phrases that helped you decide if the speaker felt positive or negative.

7 Work in pairs and discuss the questions.
1 Which of the comments about the podcast are closest to the way you feel?
2 How many hours of sleep do you need?
3 Are you a morning or an evening person?
4 What do you do when you can't sleep?

2A Develop your reading

> **Goal:** understand a news story
> **Focus:** reading for specific information

1 Discuss the questions.
  1 Have you read any interesting news stories recently? If so, who were they about and what happened?
  2 What kind of news stories are you interested in? For example, sport, politics, crime, funny stories etc.

2 Look at the photos and read the headline of the news story. What do you think it's going to be about?

3 Read the Focus box. What can help us find the key details in a news story?

Reading for specific information
When we read a news story, we look through it quickly to get the key information. To do this successfully, it helps to look for the answers to these *Wh-* questions:
Who is it about?
What happened?
Where did it happen?
Why/How did it happen?
When did it happen?
What happened in the end?

4 Read the news story and answer the questions. Underline the parts of the article with the specific information.
  1 Who is the article about?
  2 When did the event take place?
  3 Where did it take place?
  4 What happened to the Browns?
  5 Why did it happen?
  6 What happened in the end?

5 Read the story again and answer the questions. Underline the parts of the article with the specific information.
  1 Why did the Browns need to go back to their boat?
  2 Why didn't their boat come back?
  3 Why did they swim away from the shore?
  4 How did they feel while they were out at sea?
  5 How did they feel after their rescue?

6 Work in pairs and discuss the questions.
  1 Who was responsible for the situation in the story?
  2 How could you stop this situation happening again?
  3 Have you ever had a lucky escape? If so, what happened?

BRITISH DIVERS IN LUCKY ESCAPE

A British couple had a lucky escape last week after they were lost at sea for five terrifying hours. The couple, both in their thirties, were starting a ten-day diving holiday off the coast of Indonesia. With its warm waters and variety of fish and other sea life, this is an excellent place to go diving.

Jim and Sally Brown were looking forward to their holiday but on their first morning, they had a frightening experience. That morning, the Browns went out with a dive boat and entered the water to explore. However, after only a short time under water, they had to go back up to their boat because the sea was getting rough and they couldn't see well. However, when they got to the surface, their boat wasn't there any more. Unknown to them, it was taking other divers to different places along the coast.

The Browns were only a short distance from land but they had to swim away from the shore to avoid some nearby rocks. Then the waves pulled them further out to sea, the sky went very dark and it started to rain. Their five-hour nightmare began.

When people realised that the Browns were missing, two helicopters and more than 20 boats started searching for them. After five hours, the crew of one of the boats finally saw them. They pulled them out of the water and took them back to land. They were thirsty and tired – but they were alive!

According to Sally Brown, they were afraid they were going to die. They were looking out for sharks the whole time. 'We'd like to thank everyone who looked for us. We're very grateful,' she said.

2B Develop your writing

> **Goal:** write an essay
> **Focus:** writing paragraphs

1
a Discuss the questions.
1. What differences are there between the way we live now and the way we lived in the past?
2. Is life easier or more difficult now? Think about things like travel, free time interests, housework and cooking.

b Read the essay. Does it mention any of your ideas?

Was life really better?

[1] People often talk about how life was better in the past, but how true is that? Let's compare my grandparents' lives with my life today.

[2] Life was certainly different in my grandparents' day. There were no modern appliances such as washing machines and vacuum cleaners to make housework easy, so they had to work hard to keep their house clean and prepare their food. They also didn't have the same opportunities to enjoy themselves that we have. They couldn't travel to all the interesting places we go to on holiday and their summer holidays were usually spent at the same local beach every year. Life was harder and less interesting.

[3] Modern life is easier in many ways. Our kitchens are full of electrical appliances to make our lives easier, from fridges to dishwashers. We have more time to do the things we want and more things to do. We now have the opportunity to travel the world easily and experience new cultures. As a result, people are living less stressful and more interesting lives.

[4] I am not saying everything is perfect today, but for all the reasons above, I think I am very lucky compared to my grandparents!

2
Read the Focus box. How is a paragraph organised?

Writing paragraphs

A well-organised paragraph focuses on one subject (the topic).

Topic sentence
The first sentence of the paragraph usually gives the writer's main idea about the topic.
Life was certainly different in my grandparents' day.

Example sentences
The rest of the paragraph usually supports the main idea by giving reasons, examples and supporting details.
There were no modern appliances such as washing machines and vacuum cleaners to make housework easy, so they had to work hard to keep their house clean.

Conclusion sentence
A paragraph often finishes with a sentence that gives a result or conclusion.
Life was harder and less interesting.

3
Look at the third paragraph of the essay in Exercise 1b. Underline the topic sentence and example sentences. Is there a conclusion sentence?

4
Put the sentences in the correct order to make a paragraph.
a For example, there was no social media,
b In many ways life was easier in the past.
c People didn't have so many things going on in their lives like we do these days.
d so people didn't spend so much time checking what their friends were doing
e They also didn't spend so much time watching the millions of TV programmes that we have now.
f As a result, they spent more time talking to each other, and maybe that's a good thing.
g and worrying if they were 'doing enough'.

Prepare

5
a You're going to write an essay answering the question below. What's your opinion?

> People often talk about how life was better in the 'good old days', but how true is that?

b Look at the topics below. Write topic sentences about the difference between life in the past and life now.
- education
- technology
- communication
- entertainment/leisure

c For each of the topics, think of examples that will support your topic sentences.

Write

6
Write your essay. Use your topic sentences and examples to help you.

2c Develop your listening

> **Goal:** understand an interview
> **Focus:** understanding linkers

1 **Discuss the questions.**
  1 Do you think it's a good idea to take time off between finishing university and starting work? Why/Why not?
  2 What is the difference between a 'gap year' and a 'career break'?
  3 Is it usual for people to take gap years or career breaks in your country?
  4 When do you think is a good time in life to take a gap year or career break?
  5 What type of things might you do on a gap year or career break?

2 🔊 **2.7 Listen to two people being interviewed and answer the questions.**
  1 What are they describing?
  2 What did they do?

3 **Read the Focus box. How can linkers help when listening?**

Understanding linkers

Linkers can help us predict what's coming next when we're listening. Look at the beginning of the sentence below:

I liked my gap year, **but**/**although**/**however** ...

We can guess from the linkers that the speaker will now talk about something negative, perhaps the problems they had during their gap year.

Look at how the sentence changes if we change the linker:

I liked my gap year **and** ...

Now we might guess that the speaker will talk about the good times they had during their gap year or how it helped them.

Sometimes we will hear a linker that tells us about the result of an action:

I was very tired when I got off the plane, **so** ...

In this case, we can guess that the speaker will tell us about the result, perhaps that they went straight to bed when they got home.

Because tells us that we're going to hear the reason for something:

I didn't stay for a full year **because** ...

We might guess that this person became ill or got homesick.

4 **Look at the sentences. How do you think they might finish?**
  1 I didn't take a career break, because ...
  2 I was pretty tired, so ...
  3 We enjoyed the food and ...
  4 The first day we had lovely weather. However, ...
  5 The service in the restaurant was generally good, but ...
  6 We thought the film was good, although ...
  7 We didn't visit them again because ...
  8 The price of flights was really high, so ...
  9 They gave flowers to Julia, but ...
  10 They took his wallet and ...

5 a 🔊 **2.8 Listen and choose the linker that you hear.**
  1 and/but/so
  2 and/however/because
  3 however/so/because
  4 and/because/so

  b **Listen again. Work in pairs and predict how the speaker might finish the sentence.**

  c 🔊 **2.9 Listen and check. Were any of your ideas correct?**

6 🔊 **2.7 Listen to the interview again and answer the questions. Use the linkers you hear to help you.**
  1 Why did Rob decide to have a gap year?
  2 Rob found Mexico City quite busy. What did he decide to do?
  3 Why did Rob leave the job that he got?
  4 What else did Rob like about Brazil apart from the beaches?
  5 Was Sally's gap year similar to Rob's?
  6 Why did she decide to work during her gap year?
  7 What didn't she like about her job?
  8 Did they both enjoy their gap years?

7 **Work in pairs and discuss which kind of gap year you would choose. Say why.**

3A Develop your reading

> **Goal:** understand adverts
> **Focus:** recognising similar ideas

1 Read adverts 1–4 and answer the questions
  1 Have you done any of these activities?
  2 Which would you be interested in doing? Why?

1 Free sports coaching

Get involved in sport in your local area! We offer free coaching for team sports like basketball and football for beginners. Not a team player? You can also attend martial arts classes and marathon training, too.
Classes run from 6 p.m. on Mondays, Wednesdays and Fridays.
Visit our website to get details about days and times.

2 Volunteers needed for reading programme

We are looking for volunteers to travel abroad, have fantastic experiences and help out! Would you like to take part in a programme to help children with their reading skills? Accommodation and food will be provided and we promise you an amazing experience which you will remember forever.
The programme runs for a three-month period from the beginning of June.
Click here to get more information.

3 Summer work programmes

Would you like to spend the summer picking strawberries in Scotland or grapes in France? We organise summer work programmes for university students in several countries in Europe. In addition to your pay, you'll get free accommodation and a chance to meet people from lots of different countries! Programmes run from June to September.
Check out our website for more information.

4 Language and cultural exchange

We offer a cultural exchange programme for people from all over the world who want to learn a new language in exchange for teaching their own language. Right now, you can choose from languages such as English, Portuguese, Spanish, Japanese and Polish. As well as learning a new language, there will be an opportunity to find out more about the countries where it is spoken. You don't have to be a professional teacher, just excited about helping other people make their first steps in learning your language!
The group meets on Wednesdays and Thursdays from 6 p.m.–8 p.m. Contact us on our website and let us know what you can offer!

2 Read the Focus box. How do we know if two texts have the same ideas?

Recognising similar ideas

Sometimes we may want to compare different texts to see if they contain the same ideas. When we do this, it's useful to remember that there are different ways to express similar ideas in English.
*I'm really **busy** these days.*
*I **don't have much time** these days.*
In the example above, we use an adjective, *busy*, and a phrase, *don't have time*, to express the same idea.
Sometimes ideas will be expressed using different forms of the same word:
*I don't think it's **interesting**.*
*It doesn't **interest** me.*
Sometimes we can express the same idea using both positive and negative forms.
*I thought the service **was** pretty **bad** there.*
*That place **doesn't have** very **good** service.*

3 Compare the two comments below. Do they express the same opinions or different ones? How do you know?
  1 'The course doesn't look very useful. I think the level is too low and the price is very high for a ten-week course.'
  2 'The course looks pretty expensive and I don't think it's going to help me very much. I think it will be too easy.'

4 a Match comments a–d with the most suitable adverts 1–4.
  a 'I'd like to do something nice in the holidays before I go back to my studies, but the main problem is that I can't afford to just have a holiday and go and sit on a beach somewhere. I don't want to stay in my town and work, and I'd like to see a new place and new people.'
  b 'I need to do something new in the evenings instead of just relaxing on the sofa. I need to be active and healthy. The main problem is I don't have much money, so I don't want to spend thousands on a gym. I also get bored doing things on my own, so it'd be nice to find something I can do with other people.'
  c 'My perfect situation would be to go abroad for a few months. I'd love to go and live in a completely new town or city and learn about its history, as well as learning how to talk to local people! The problem is, my job makes that impossible. The next best option would be to do something similar here, I guess, maybe in the evenings or at the weekend.'
  d 'I think it'd be nice to go somewhere completely different before I get a full-time job, even to another country for a while. I'd like to do something helpful, not just work to earn money. I have a little money saved. It'd be nice to get involved in a project, maybe like coaching kids to play football.'

b Work in pairs. Discuss why you chose your answers and what connections you found between the language in the adverts and comments.

3B Develop your listening

> **Goal:** understand a conversation
> **Focus:** understanding discourse markers

1. What do friends usually talk about when they catch up?

2. a) 3.5 Listen to the conversation. Which topic do the men discuss?
   1. a holiday one person took
   2. a change to office rules
   3. a hotel they both like

   b) Listen again. Did the trip go well? Why/Why not?

3. Read the Focus box. What kind of things do discourse markers do?

> ### Understanding discourse markers
> People use words and phrases called 'discourse markers' when they speak, for example *well, it, actually* etc. Understanding these words can often help you know what's coming next in a conversation. There are several types of discourse marker:
>
> Words/sounds like *well, so, um* and *erm* give people time to think:
> A: How was the trip?
> B: **Well,** it was interesting ...
>
> A: Where's Basha?
> B: **Um**, I think she went home.
>
> *I mean* can be used to add extra details or make changes to what we've just said:
> I think it was a good show. **I mean**, it's not the best I've ever seen, but I liked it.
>
> The words *actually* and *in fact* tell you that you're going to hear information that contrasts with what you heard before, or what you expect to hear:
> A: So, was the team meeting boring, as usual?
> B: **Actually**, it was quite interesting.
>
> *Anyway* and *by the way* can be used to change the topic of a conversation:
> I don't think we'll go there again, it was terrible. **Anyway**, how was your weekend?
>
> Words like *Wow!* and *Really?* can also be used to react to what someone is saying:
> A: I think Penny is going to get fired.
> B: **Wow!** She's quite new, isn't she?

4. a) Look at the conversations below. What do you think B will say?
   1. A: Did you enjoy the film?
      B: Um, ...
   2. A: I guess Sandra was really annoying, as usual?
      B: Actually, ...
   3. A: The gym is nice, isn't it?
      B: Um, it's not amazing, I mean ...
   4. A: I'm pretty hungry, are you ready for lunch?
      B: No, not yet. By the way, ...

   b) 3.6 Listen and check.

5. a) 3.7 Listen to the next part of the friends' conversation. What's the best summary?
   1. They compare holidays they have had.
   2. They discuss a holiday plan.

   b) Listen again and tick the words and phrases that you hear.
   1. actually
   2. I mean
   3. in fact
   4. well
   5. so
   6. by the way
   7. anyway

6. a) 3.8 Listen to the last part of the conversation. Are the statements true (T) or false (F)?
   1. They both want to go straight home.
   2. They decide to invite someone else.
   3. Gigi is still working.
   4. The conversation topic changes.

   b) Complete the sentences from the conversation.
   1. _____ , I was thinking of getting something to eat. Do you want to come?
   2. Cool. Oh, invite her, too! _____ , if you want to.
   3. Ah, _____ she's just finished. I'll see if she wants to come.
   4. _____ , are you guys still planning to move in together?
   5. _____ , that's a long story. I'll tell you another time.

   c) Listen again and check.

7. Work in pairs and discuss the questions.
   1. Do you enjoy catching up with people when you meet in the street? Why/Why not?
   2. What do you do when you can't think of anything to say to someone that you've met by accident?
   3. What topics of conversation are typical for people from your country that may not be typical in other countries?

3c Develop your writing

> **Goal:** write a guide
> **Focus:** planning a piece of writing

1 Discuss the questions.
1 What sort of things do you like doing when you visit a new place?
2 What sort of information do you need/want when you are visiting a new place?

2 Read the brochure. Who is it for and what information does it provide?

3 Read the Focus box. What are the three stages of planning?

Planning a piece of writing

When we plan a piece of writing, we start by thinking about the reader. What topic areas would they be interested in?
After that, we decide what order to put the topics in. Each topic should have a separate paragraph, so we can call this our 'paragraph plan.' Then we can make notes about each topic area to help us think about what to write.
Look at the examples below for the guide to Bath.
Paragraph plan:
Paragraph 1: Introduction to Bath
Paragraph 2: Must-see sights
Paragraph 3: Getting around
Paragraph 4: Shopping
Notes about the topic 'Getting around':
Getting around
Explore on foot/cycle
Boat trip - on river Avon
Hot-air balloon!
When we have made these notes, we decide what order we'd like to present the information and then start to put our ideas into sentences.

4 Match notes 1–11 with the paragraph headings in the box.

accommodation   eating and drinking   events   introduction

1 nightclubs – The Roxy, The Zone
2 hotels – quite expensive in centre
3 music festival – May – rock
4 small guest houses – good value
5 lots of people visit – from all over the world
6 Christmas market – really pretty!
7 local restaurants – cheap, good food
8 capital city
9 1,000 years of history
10 international food – Central Food Market
11 book early – hotels get full quickly
12 summer fun fair – July

A WARM WELCOME TO BATH
UNESCO World Heritage Site

What is there to do on a visit to Bath? More than you can imagine! The city is famous for its beautiful buildings and interesting history. There are also plenty of other things to do in Bath, with fun for all the family. Why not start planning your visit today?

You'll find a museum, gallery or attraction on every corner. When the Romans founded the city over 2,000 years ago, they built a wonderful temple and baths on top of natural hot springs. Today the Roman Baths are one of the city's most popular places to visit.

Getting around Bath is easy. It's a perfect size to explore on foot or to cycle around. If you're feeling adventurous, you can take a boat trip on the nearby River Avon, or even go on a hot-air balloon ride over the city!

Bath is famous for its variety of shops. You can choose from well-known high street department stores or small independent shops. You won't have a problem finding the perfect gift for friends and family.

Prepare

5 a You're going to write a guide to your town/city or a town/city you know well. First, decide who you're writing for. Is it for someone visiting, or someone planning to live there?
b Make a list of topic areas you want to write about and make short notes for each one.
c Work in pairs and compare your notes. Have you chosen similar things to write about?

Write

6 Write your guide. Use your notes to help you.

4A Develop your listening

> **Goal:** understand a radio programme
>
> **Focus:** predicting information

1 Look at the photos. What do you know or what can you guess about the hippies of the 1960s? Think about the following:
- lifestyle
- beliefs
- music
- clothes
- diet
- the environment
- money
- work

2 Read the Focus box. How can you predict what information you are going to hear on a radio programme?

Predicting information

Before you listen, it can be useful to try and predict what you are going to hear. Think about what you know about a topic and what you can guess about it. Doing this gives you something to focus on, which is often better than just listening 'generally'.

For example, imagine you're going to listen to a radio programme about Italian food. What do you already know about the topic?

I know that pizza and pasta are popular dishes.

What can you guess the programme might tell you about?

Maybe the show will mention less popular dishes that are also good.

Maybe the show will discuss how they prepare their food.

3 a 🔊 4.3 Listen to the introduction to a programme about hippies' beliefs and lifestyle. Which topics do you think the speaker might mention?

b Predict the correct alternatives to complete the sentences.
1 The hippies *believed/didn't believe* in war.
2 They *wanted/didn't want* the same lifestyle as their parents.
3 They were *interested/not interested* in owning things.
4 They often lived together in *large groups/in their own homes*.
5 They *cared/didn't care* about the environment.
6 Music *was/wasn't* important to them.

c 🔊 4.4 Listen to the next part of the programme and check your answers.

4 a In the final part of the programme, the speakers compare hippies in the 1960s with modern-day hippies. Make a list of topics/opinions/facts you might hear them talk about.

b 🔊 4.5 Listen and check your ideas. Which things did you predict correctly?

5 a Match ideas 1–7 with the speakers, Maddy (M) or Lucas (L).
1 For today's hippies, it's just about fashion.
2 Today's hippies really believe in hippy ideals.
3 It's not enough to follow a healthy lifestyle.
4 Today's hippies care just as much about the environment as old hippies.
5 They do things that are bad for the environment.
6 They are more interested in owning things than older hippies.
7 Following a hippy lifestyle is good for young people today.

b Listen again and check your answers. Do you agree with Maddy or Lucas?

6 Work in pairs and discuss the questions.
1 Does the hippy lifestyle appeal to you? Why/Why not?
2 Are there any modern-day hippies in your country? How do you know they are hippies? How 'real' do you think they are?

4B Develop your writing

> **Goal:** write a biography
> **Focus:** using linkers

1 a What do you know about Steve Jobs' life and career?
b Read the biography and check your ideas.

Steve Jobs was, and still is, one of the most famous people in the modern world. He was a creative genius who changed the face of the computer industry.

He was born in 1955 and grew up in California. Although he was a very bright student, he was often bored with ordinary lessons. As a result, school was not a positive experience for him. After high school, he went to college, but because he didn't really know what he wanted to do with his life, he soon decided to leave. Later he spent some time travelling in India.

In 1976, he started Apple Computers with his friend, Steve Wozniak. They didn't have much money when they started, so they used the family garage as their office. It was difficult at first, but that didn't stop Apple becoming one of the most successful companies in the world. Their success didn't stop there. In addition to Apple, Steve Jobs started the famous Pixar animation studio that produced animated films like *Toy Story*.

Steve Jobs died in 2011. However, he will always be an inspiration to everyone who is looking for a direction in life.

2 Read the Focus box. Why do we use linkers?

Using linkers
Linkers are words like *and*, *but* and *because*. We use them to connect ideas in a text. Look at the examples below of how linkers can connect ideas.

Use *although, but* and *however* to show how one event is different from another.

Although he was a very bright student, he was often bored with ordinary lessons.
It was difficult at first, **but** that didn't stop Apple becoming one of the most successful companies in the world.
Steve Jobs died in 2011. **However**, he will always be an inspiration to everyone ...

Use *in addition (to)* to add information.
In addition to Apple, Steve Jobs started the famous Pixar animation studio.

Use *because* to show the reason for something.
He went to college, but **because** he didn't really know what he wanted to do with his life, he soon decided to leave.

Use *as a result* and *so* to show the result of an action.
He was often bored with ordinary lessons. **As a result**, school was not a positive experience for him.
They didn't have much money when they started, **so** they used the family garage as their office.

3 a Read the biography again and underline the linkers.
b Choose the correct alternatives.
1 He was tired of his town, *so/although* he moved away.
2 Their first company was a success, *but/as a result* their second company was less successful.
3 *However/Although* her first love was music, she actually decided to study dance.
4 She did very well at school, *so/although* she was offered the chance to go to a top university.
5 They toured all over the world. *However/In addition*, they recorded five hit records.
6 He was interested in acting. *However/But*, his family didn't have the money to send him to theatre school.
7 She was successful *because/in addition* she tried hard.

Prepare

4 You're going to write a biography of someone you admire. First, read the questions and make notes.
- Who is the person you admire?
- Why do you admire him/her?
- Where is the person from?
- What basic details do you know about him/her?
- What happened in his/her early life?
- What happened when they grew up?
- Why is he/she important to you?

Write

5 Write your biography. Use your notes to help you. Use linkers to connect your ideas.

4c Develop your reading

> **Goal:** understand a magazine article
> **Focus:** understanding paragraph structure

THE STARS BEHIND THE SCENES

1 a Discuss the questions.
  1 What are the Oscars?
  2 Who receives Oscar awards?

b Read the first paragraph of the article. What makes the Oscars awards special?

2 Read the Focus box. What does each kind of sentence in a paragraph do?

Understanding paragraph structure

Understanding the structure of a paragraph can help you to read a text more easily. Texts often contain topic sentences, example sentences and conclusion sentences.

Topic sentence
The topic sentence gives the writer's main idea.
When a film is successful it's usually the actors who get all the attention in the media, but at the Oscars this is different.

Example sentence(s)
An example sentence supports the main idea by giving more information, such as examples or reasons.
The actors are just one part of what makes a film successful. Behind the scenes there is a hard-working team that makes it all happen.

Conclusion sentence
A paragraph can also contain a sentence where the writer makes a conclusion which often relates to the example sentences.
They are just as important as the big stars and the Oscars recognise many of these people who we never usually consider.

3 a Read the first sentence of each paragraph in the article and match topics a–e with paragraphs 1–5.
  a making the film look perfect
  b making everything happen
  c the person who tells people what to do
  d it's not only about the actors
  e designing the actors' clothes

b Read the whole article and check your answers.

4 Read the article again. Are sentences 1–5 true (T) or false (F)? Underline the sentences in the article that help you decide.
  1 The actors are more important than the rest of the team.
  2 Directors only work with the film crew.
  3 The photography in a film is not connected to the story.
  4 Costume designers need a wide range of skills.
  5 The producer's role is only to find the money to pay for the actors.

5 Which of the jobs mentioned in the article do you find the most/least interesting? Why?

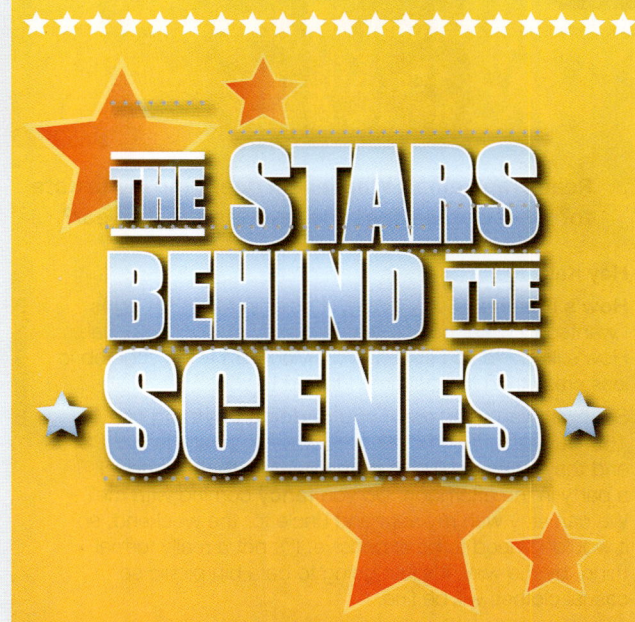

---

[1] When a film is successful, it's usually the actors who get all the attention in the media, but at the Oscars this is different. The actors are just one part of what makes a film successful. Behind the scenes there is a hard-working team that makes it all happen. They are just as important as the big stars and the Oscars recognise many of these people who we never usually consider.

[2] One of the most important people behind the scenes is the director. The director's job is to give directions to the actors and the film crew. However, a director doesn't work alone. He or she needs to work closely with lots of other people behind the scenes.

[3] All films need good photography to help develop the story. The cinematographer is the person who is in charge of shooting the film. He or she makes sure that the photography supports the story. The cinematographer has a lot of responsibility and leads the teams in charge of lighting and cameras.

[4] Another essential person that we often forget about is the costume designer – the person who designs what the actors wear. The costume designer needs to understand exactly what the director wants and design the most suitable costumes. The costumes have to be comfortable so the actors can move easily, but at the same time they need to match the characters the actors are playing. It's a job that requires imagination, research and you have to know how to make things!

[5] It could be said that the most important person in the creation of a film is the producer. Without a producer there would be no film at all! The producer steers the film through all its stages. He or she finds the money to finance the whole film and also works closely with many other people behind the scenes. During the whole filming process, it is the producer's job to make sure that everything goes well.

5A Develop your writing

> **Goal:** write a personal email
> **Focus:** using informal words and expressions

1 Read Fran's email. What event does Fran invite Kate to? What clothes does she say Kate should wear?

Hey Kate,

How's it going? Sorry I haven't been in touch **for ages**. I wanted to write, but it's been so busy at work as usual. How's life? Are you still enjoying Madrid? I hope your job is less crazy than the last time I talked to you!

So, I just wanted to ask if **you're doing anything** on 16th July. I have some relatives who live near Madrid and they've asked me to **come over to their place** for a party in the afternoon. Do you **fancy** coming with me? We can stay with my aunt and uncle for the weekend, so it wouldn't need to be expensive. It's not a really formal thing, by the way, it's just going to be a big picnic so casual clothes will be fine.

Anyway, let me know what you think and we can make some plans. It would be **awesome** to get together again!

Speak soon!
Lots of love,
Fran

2 Read the Focus box. What is the style of an informal email similar to?

Using informal words and expressions

When you write a personal email to someone you know well, you write as if you are speaking to the person directly. You can use many of the same words and expressions that you use when you are having a conversation. For example:

Start a new statement using so
So, I just wanted to ask if you're doing anything …

Show a change or contrast of topic using anyway, by the way
Anyway, let me know what you think.
It's not a really formal thing, by the way …

Ask direct questions
Are you still enjoying San Francisco?

Use short forms
How's life?
… they've asked me to come.

Use informal words and phrases
Hi Kate, how's it going?
I haven't been in touch for ages.
Do you fancy …?
It would be awesome.

3 Match the phrases in bold in the email in Exercise 1 with the less informal phrases below.

a long time   great   Hello   how are you?
Let's talk soon.   visit their house   want
you're free

4 Complete Gianni's email with the words and phrases in the box.

awesome   By the way   come over to my place
doing anything   for ages   how's it going
Hi   speak soon

¹_____ Tom,
²_____ ? I feel like we haven't spoken ³_____ !
I just wanted to ask if you're ⁴_____ next Saturday. I'm inviting a few people to ⁵_____ to watch the football and it'd be really ⁶_____ if you could come.
⁷_____ , Jenny will be there, so you guys can catch up. I don't think you've seen each other since our Paris trip, right?
Anyway, ⁸_____ and let me know if you fancy coming.
Gianni

5 Read a reply to an invitation. Replace the underlined words with the informal words and phrases in the box.

awesome   being in touch   Bye for now
get together   How's it going   I'm   It'll   I've
I'm sorry   you're

Dear Lucia,
¹I apologise for not ²writing before this. ³I have had a lot of work to do. ⁴How are you?
⁵I am very happy to hear that you are visiting soon. Let me know when ⁶you are arriving and I can come to London any time.
⁷It will be ⁸very good to ⁹meet again!
¹⁰Yours sincerely,
Sergey

Prepare

6 You're going to invite a friend to stay with you. Think about the questions below and make notes.
1 Who are you going to invite?
2 How long is it since you last saw him/her? Why?
3 When do you want them to visit?
4 What plans do you have for their visit?
5 What information do you want to give him/her?
6 Is there anything you want him/her to do for you?

Write

7 Write an email invitation to your friend. Use your notes to help you.

5B Develop your reading

> **Goal:** understand a factual article
> **Focus:** guessing unknown words

1 a How many kinds of home can you think of? Make a list.
  b Look at the photos. Where do you think these homes can be found?
  c Read the article quickly and check your ideas.
2 Read the part of the article about *tipis*. Can you guess what the words in bold mean?
3 Read the Focus box. How can you guess the meaning of a new word?

Guessing unknown words

If there's a word that you don't understand, there are different ways to check the meaning.

Explanations
Does the text explain the word?
Native Americans used to live in **tipis**, *which are a kind of tent.*
The text explains that tipis are tents.

Reason/cause and effect
Linkers like *so, because, as a result, that meant …* introduce a cause, reason or result that can help you work out the meaning.
They were **nomadic, so** *they needed homes that were easy to move from place to place.*
You can guess that *nomadic* means 'moving from place to place'.

Context
Can you guess the meaning from the words around it?
They used to **hunt** *and* **kill wild animals** *for food.*
Hunt is used together with *kill* and *wild animals*. From this we might guess that it means 'try to catch'.

Repetition
Is the same word repeated in the text, so you have another context to help you guess the meaning?

4 a Look at the words in bold in the first part of the article about tipis. Choose the correct definitions.
  1 roam: *move around/ stay in one place*
  2 poles: *long piece of wood/ young people*
  3 protect: *keep someone or something safe/ cool*
  4 reservation: *a kind of house/ a place for Native Americans to live*
  b Underline the other words in the article that helped you to guess the meaning of the words in Exercise 4a.
5 Use the methods in the Focus box to guess the meaning of the words in bold in the part of the article about tulou earth buildings.
6 What are traditional homes like in your country? Why are they like that?

Traditional homes are built in different ways around the world. Let's look at some examples of traditional homes from North America and China.

Tipis

Native Americans used to live in **tipis,** which are a kind of tent. They were **nomadic** so they needed homes that were easy to move from place to place. They used to **hunt** and kill wild animals for food and they **roamed** across the land following the animals.

They used the skins of the animals to build their tipis. They attached the skins to tall wooden **poles**. That meant they could put the tipis up and take them down again quickly.

Tipis were cool in summer and warm in winter. The shape of the tipis **protected** them from the cold winter winds.

Today, most Native Americans live in cities and towns of the US. Others live in houses on **reservations**, areas of land specially reserved for them.

Tulou earth buildings

The tulou homes of Fujian in Southern China **date back to** the twelfth century. At that time, thieves used to attack homes and steal food. So the people who lived there needed to **defend** themselves. The tulou were built in a circle. They were up to four stories high, with very thick earth walls. Tulou means 'earth building'. There was usually only one entrance gate into the building. This design helped to protect the **residents**.

The tulou design had another purpose as well: **communal living**. Many families lived together in the same tulou building. Although each family had their own rooms, the residents of the tulou met outside every day. They also used to get together for weddings and ceremonies.

Today there are still about 3,000 tulou homes in Fujian, but many of them are empty. The residents are moving to the cities to find jobs and they are **abandoning** their homes. As a result, the buildings are falling down. One man, Lin Lusheng, is trying to save them. He believes it's important for any country to **preserve** its traditional buildings and culture.

5c Develop your listening

> **Goal:** understand announcements
>
> **Focus:** listening for specific information

1 a Discuss the questions.
  1 Have you ever been to a food festival?
  2 What kind of events and activities would you expect to find there?
  3 Are food festivals popular in your country?

b Read the advertisement for a food festival and answer the questions.
  1 Where is it?
  2 When is it on?
  3 What kind of things can you do there?
  4 Which activities and events look interesting to you?

THE BIG Food LOVERS' FESTIVAL
THE BEST FOOD FESTIVAL IN THE SOUTH OF ENGLAND!

Watch live cooking demos
Watch famous TV master chefs cooking their favourite recipes in the Chef's Tent. Get signed copies of your favourite cookbooks!

Try exotic food
Explore dozens of food stalls in the Street Food Avenue and try food you've never tasted before.

Visit the cheese tent
Come and visit the cheese tent and watch a demonstration on how to make cheese, then try it yourself!

Walk on the wild side
Learn how to find safe and healthy wild food like mushrooms and herbs on the Wild Food Walk.

Plus:
- live music
- talks and presentations
- kids' play area

OPENING TIMES
Saturday 1st September
11 a.m.–11 p.m.
Sunday 2nd September
11 a.m.–7 p.m.

2 a Read the Focus box. When you listen for specific information, do you have to listen in detail to everything you hear? Why/Why not?

Listening for specific information
When you listen for specific information, you're often listening for facts, e.g. names, times, places, etc. For example:
- You listen to the weather report to get details about the weather in your area.
- You listen to an announcement to get details about time and place.

Before you listen, think about the kind of information that will answer your question(s). While you listen, focus only on the information which is important for you, and ignore anything that isn't important.

b You have decided to go to the Food Lovers' Festival this weekend. You're going to listen to the weather forecast. What information do you need to listen for? Think about the following:
- the area of the country you are interested in
- which days of the week you want to know about

c 🔊 **5.8** Listen to the weather forecast and decide which day(s) you want to go. What information helped you decide? What information was not relevant?

3 a You're at the festival and are listening for an announcement about the cookery event. Think about the information you'd like to know.

b 🔊 **5.9** Listen to three announcements. Which one is useful for you?

c Listen again and answer the questions.
  1 Where is the cookery event happening?
  2 What time does it start?
  3 How long is the event?
  4 What can you do afterwards?

4 a You are interested in going on the Wild Food Walk and the book signing with a famous chef. What information do you need to know about each event? Make notes.

b 🔊 **5.10** Listen to three more announcements. Which two are important for you?

c Listen again and note down the information you need.

5 Work in pairs and discuss the questions.
  1 Which events at the festival do you think will be the most popular?
  2 Which ones would you like to go to?
  3 What other events would you include if you were planning a food festival?

6A Develop your listening

> **Goal:** understand a short talk
> **Focus:** identifying the stages of a talk

1 a You're going to hear a short talk about the use of appliances in 'smart' houses. Look at the picture and discuss the questions.
  1 What do you think a 'smart' house is? What do you think it can do?
  2 How many household appliances can you name? Make a list.

b 6.3 Listen to the first part of the talk. What appliances are mentioned?

2 Read the Focus box. How do people make their talks easier to follow?

Identifying the stages of a talk

The purpose of a talk is usually to give the listener information and talks are usually organised into clear stages. There are some common phrases we use to help the listener follow a talk.

Beginning the talk
I'm going to be talking about technology in our homes.
I'm going to start by looking at technology in our homes.
Let's begin by looking at technology in our homes.

Changing between topics
And *that's the next thing* I want to talk about.
This brings me to my next point.
Another question is, how do we use technology?

Ending the talk
I'll end by answering my own question.
To sum up, technology is only as good as its user.

---

3 Complete the sentences with the correct words. Use the information in the Focus box to help you.
  1 _____ end by asking you a question. Could you live without your phone?
  2 Hi. So today I'm going _____ talking about how technology has changed the way we live.
  3 Let's begin _____ talking about the mobile phone.
  4 To _____, I think we have allowed technology to control us.
  5 This _____ to my next point. Has technology really made things better?
  6 _____ question is, is technology stealing our time?
  7 And that's the next _____ I want to discuss. Is it too late to change things?
  8 I'm _____ start by asking you to listen to the results of a recent survey.

4 a 6.4 Listen to the whole talk and tick the phrases in the Focus box that you hear.

b Listen again. Number the topics in the order you hear them.
  a the reason these things are important
  b what 'smart appliances' means
  c the results of a survey

5 6.5 Listen to four extracts from different talks. Choose the stage of the talk for each extract.
  1 a starting a talk   b ending a talk
    c in the middle of a talk.
  2 a starting a talk   b ending a talk
    c in the middle of a talk.
  3 a starting a talk   b ending a talk
    c in the middle of a talk.
  4 a starting a talk   b ending a talk
    c in the middle of a talk.

6 6.4 Listen to the whole talk again. Are the sentences true (T) or false (F)?
  1 Not many people have household appliances.
  2 People think kitchen appliances are more important than other kinds of appliance.
  3 People don't have a lot of time to spend on cooking and cleaning.
  4 Some smart fridges can tell you how to cook food.
  5 There is a touchscreen inside some smart fridges.
  6 Most people want their fridges to do a lot of different things for them.

7 Work in pairs and discuss the questions.
  1 Would you like to live in a 'smart' house?
  2 Would it change your life? Why/Why not?
  3 Do you think technology can be dangerous? Why/Why not?
  4 What appliance for your home would you really love to have?

6B Develop your reading

> **Goal:** understand a magazine article
> **Focus:** understanding linkers

1 a Discuss the questions. When you were at school, were you well-behaved? What things did you sometimes do wrong?

b Read the article. What was the problem with the girl?

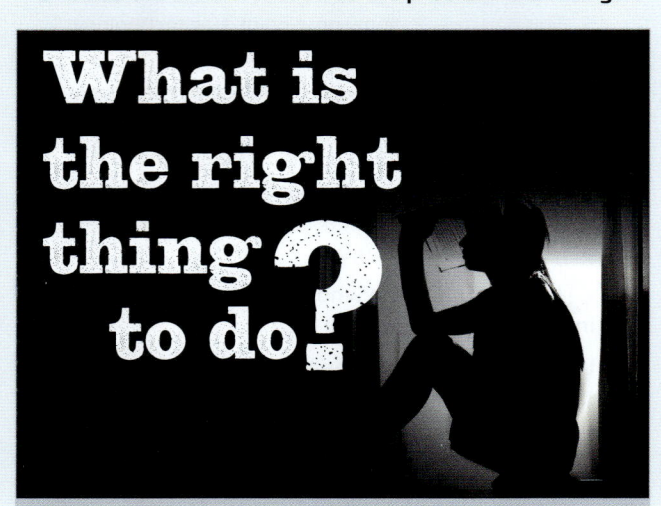

What is the right thing to do?

Making a choice about what is right and what is wrong is something we all have to do at some time or another. However, sometimes the results of the right choice and the wrong choice both seem bad. For example, if we see a friend, let's call him Brian, stealing, we know we should report him. That's the right thing to do. On the other hand, we like Brian. He's a nice person. If we report him, he may get into trouble and we don't want that to happen. What's more, Brian might never talk to us again! Choices like these are called 'moral dilemmas'. In a situation like this, most people will do nothing. However, sometimes people have to make a choice and it's not always easy.

Let's think about the case of one student. Lisa is a young girl I know. When she was at school, she had a very strong sense of right and wrong, so if she saw one of the other students doing something bad, she would report them to the teachers. For example, if she saw someone looking at the answers in a maths test, she would tell the teacher. Or, if a classmate told a lie or took another student's books without asking, she would report them. Because of this, the other students didn't like her and no one wanted to be her friend. She was very unhappy, but she wouldn't change her behaviour because she was sure that she was right.

Let's consider the teachers' choices. Should they thank Lisa for reporting bad behaviour? If they did that, Lisa would continue to be unpopular and unhappy. Or should they try to convince Lisa to stop reporting the other children? If they did this, Lisa would be happier, but they wouldn't know when the children were breaking the rules. In other words, both solutions have bad results for someone!

In the end, what do you think the staff at the school did?

2 Read the Focus box. Why are linkers important?

Understanding linkers

Writers use linkers (e.g. *because, but, so* etc.) to connect ideas in a text. They make it easier to understand what the writer wants to say. Linkers can be used to:

Show the order that things happen
First, he stole the painting.
After that, he sold it for a lot of money.
In the end, he built a school.

Give reasons for something
Because of her strange behaviour, she didn't have too many friends.
I didn't vote for him *because* I don't trust him.

Add more information
It was wrong, and *what's more* it was illegal.

Introduce different information
Telling lies is wrong, *but* sometimes it is the kind thing to do.
Telling lies is wrong. *However/On the other hand*, sometimes it is the kind thing to do.

Show the results of something
He woke up late *so* he had to run for the bus.

Explain in a different way
It is the right thing to do. *In other words*, it would be wrong not to do it.

3 Read the article again. Underline the linkers.

4 Put the sentences in the correct order to complete the story. Use the linkers in bold to help you.

a Lisa stayed the same and continued to be unhappy. **Then** one day a new student started who also reported the other students to the teachers!
b she refused, because she felt she had to do what was right. **Then**
c the staff spoke to her parents and explained what was happening,
d the other students were getting angry with her. **However**,
e **but** they couldn't change her mind either. **So,**
f **First** they spoke to her, and asked her not to report everything she saw **because**
g **Finally**, Lisa understood how her classmates felt and stopped reporting them. **In the end**
h she became more popular with other students and was happier, too.
i The staff of the school tried lots of things to help Lisa. 1

5 Work in pairs and discuss the questions.
1 What do you think of Lisa's behaviour? Was it 'wrong'?
2 Do you think the staff did the right thing trying to stop her?

6c Develop your writing

> **Goal:** write a for and against essay
> **Focus:** organising ideas

1 a Discuss the questions.
   1 Do you think zoos are a good thing? Why/Why not?
   2 What reasons can you think of for and against zoos?

b Read the essay. Does the writer mention any of your ideas?

Should we keep animals in zoos?

[1] Today we can watch animals on TV or the internet any time we want. So, do we still need zoos? Are they out of date and unnecessary, or do they still have an important role to play? There are different views on this subject.

[2] Many people think that zoos are a good thing. They say that zoos help to educate the public about animals and that children can see animals they wouldn't usually have the chance to see and learn about. In addition, zoos give animals a safe place to live and plenty of food. If we didn't have zoos, many animals would not exist at all.

[3] On the other hand, some people disagree. They believe we shouldn't put animals in cages for our entertainment and that people don't learn anything by looking at animals in zoos. In addition, they feel that many zoos don't look after the animals well and that animals in cages feel bored and stressed. As a result, some animals don't live long in zoos.

[4] In conclusion, people have different opinions about zoos. However, we will continue to have zoos as long as people visit them, so governments must make sure that they are looked after well.

2 Read the Focus box. Where does the writer's opinion usually appear in a for and against essay? Why?

Organising ideas

In a for and against essay, you give reasons and information to support different opinions about a topic. You want to help the reader understand the issues and decide for themselves who or what is right or wrong.
Introduction: In your introduction, state the topic for discussion.
Middle paragraphs: In one paragraph, give reasons and information **in support of** the topic. In another paragraph, give reasons and information **against** the topic.
It's important not to support one opinion or the other in the two main paragraphs. Use phrases like this:
Some/Many people say/think …
Other people disagree/believe …
Conclusion: In your conclusion, you can repeat the main points and say what you personally think or make a recommendation.

3 a Read the essay again and answer the questions.
   1 What topic is introduced in paragraph 1?
   2 In paragraph 2, underline the main reasons that the writer gives in favour of zoos.
   3 In paragraph 3, underline the main reasons that the writer gives against zoos.
   4 What phrases does the writer use in paragraphs 2 and 3 to introduce other people's opinions?
   5 What does the writer recommend in the conclusion in paragraph 4?

b Read the alternative conclusion. What does the writer recommend? Which conclusion do you agree with most?

In conclusion, people have different opinions about zoos. Personally, I would prefer to find different ways to protect animals. If people want to see wild animals, they can visit a safari park or a nature reserve. Alternatively, they can watch them in the wild.

Prepare

4 a You're going to write your own essay. Choose a question below or think of your own idea.
   • Should people have animals as pets?
   • Should we all become vegetarians?
   • Should we stop using plastic bags?

b Think of ideas for and against the topic. Then make notes about what to write in the introduction, the for and against paragraphs and the conclusion.

Write

5 Write your essay. Use your notes to help you.

7A Develop your writing

> **Goal:** write short notices
> **Focus:** engaging a reader

1 a A local action group is organising a 'Save the environment' day and has produced a leaflet to advertise it. What sort of information would you expect to see in it?

b Read the leaflet. Does it include your ideas?

Save the environment day

Come and join us this Saturday from 10 a.m. to 5 p.m. at the West Parade for our 3rd annual 'Save the environment' day!

Who are we?
Are you tired of seeing our streets full of rubbish? We are too! We are a local group who are passionate about the environment. We want to make our town clean and beautiful again.

What's happening at the event?
We're organising a special event to help save our local environment. There will be fun activities for all the family. Enter the competition to pick up the most litter and win an amazing prize!

Bring your ideas
Come along, bring your family, friends and your ideas! How can we reduce waste? How can we recycle the things we don't need? We'll share our ideas as a group and there will be prizes for the best ones.

Contact us
Interested? For more information and to contact us go to our website and get involved today!

2 Read the Focus box. How can we make a leaflet more interesting?

Engaging a reader
When we create a leaflet, we should think of how we can make people interested in what we are telling them and encourage them to take action. There are a few ways we can do this:

Ask questions
Do you want to get fit?
Are you tired of expensive phone bills?

Use imperatives
Click *on the link for your free seven-day trial.*
Come *and **see** our amazing range of models.*

Use positive adjectives
*It's a **great** opportunity to see an **exciting new** programme.*

---

3 Read the leaflet in Exercise 1a again and underline the following:
1 the questions
2 the imperatives
3 the positive adjectives

4 Complete the leaflet below with the words and phrases in the box.

> amazing   lovely   remember the day
> Spend some time in the garden.   Would you like a break?

Do nothing day!
Are you tired of always running around? ¹_____
We have an ²_____ idea – on 5th March we are organising our very first 'Do Nothing Day'!
What do I need to do?
Nothing! We'd like you to have a ³_____ relaxing day at home with a book. Listen to some cool music. ⁴_____
A relaxed community is a happy community.
So, ⁵_____ , 5th March is 'Do Nothing Day'!

Prepare

5 a You're going to write a leaflet about something you're organising in your town (e.g. a music event, courses to help people). Work in pairs and think of different things you could organise.

b Decide what you want to organise. Make notes about:
- why you want to do this
- if you are on your own or part of a group
- what kind of people you want to involve
- what events/activities there will be
- what you want people who read the leaflet to do
- how they can contact you

Write

6 Write your information leaflet. Use questions, imperatives and positive adjectives.

7B Develop your reading

> **Goal:** understand a magazine article
> **Focus:** understanding the sequence of events

1 a Discuss the questions.
1 What is a 'chance meeting'?
2 Have you ever had one? If so, who did you meet and what happened?

b Read the text and answer the questions.
1 How did the chance meeting happen?
2 What was the result of the chance meeting?

A chance meeting

Although we live in different parts of the world, my cousin Seb and I have always been close friends. Our mothers are sisters. They are both British, but his mother married an Australian and went to live in Melbourne, while my mother married an American and went to live in New York. Our families used to get together in England almost every summer.

My story starts eight years ago. At that time, Seb was still living in his home city of Melbourne and I was living and working in New York. Seb hadn't had a holiday for two years and so he decided to come and stay with me in New York. I started arranging things for him to do and thinking about the places we should visit. Around the same time, my old friend Ana from Barcelona contacted me and asked if she could come and stay with me — I was suddenly very popular! As my apartment was quite small for three people, I suggested that she should come on the day Seb left. I hadn't seen Ana for a few years, so I was excited about catching up with her.

When Seb arrived at the airport, I was waiting for him. I took him to all the places I really liked in my neighbourhood and to all the famous New York sights, too. We went to the Empire State Building on the first day and after that we walked in Central Park. We even went to the theatre on Broadway.

Seb left for the airport on his last day to catch his morning flight, and I picked up Ana in the afternoon. She was really excited and wanted to start sightseeing immediately! I took her to MOMA, the Museum of Modern Art, as I know she loves art. We were walking around when I saw a familiar face. I couldn't believe my eyes, it was Seb! His flight had been delayed until the evening and his phone had died, so he'd decided to spend a few hours doing some last-minute sight-seeing by himself and he'd come to MOMA. Ana and Seb had never met before, but they got on really well. After the holiday, they stayed in touch and Seb went to visit her in Barcelona. Two years later, Seb moved to Barcelona and, shortly after that, they got married. They've been married for six years now and next year they're planning an anniversary trip to the Museum of Modern Art!

2 Read the Focus box. How can we understand the order of events in a story?

Understanding the sequence of events

The tenses that a writer uses can help us understand the order of events in a story.

The past perfect emphasises which action came first and can often give us the background in a story.
*Seb **hadn't had** a holiday for two years and he decided to come and stay with me in New York.*

The past continuous shows an action that was not finished at a certain point in the past.
*I **was living** and **working** in New York.*

When we use the past continuous together with the past simple, the past simple action 'interrupts' the past continuous one.
*When Seb **arrived** at the airport, I **was waiting** for him.*

We can also understand the order of events by looking at words that describe time (e.g. *eight years ago, two days later*, etc.) and sequence (e.g. *after that, in the end*).

3 Find and underline examples of the following in the story.
1 the past perfect
2 the past continuous
3 time expressions

4 Find the two actions in each sentence. Write (1) next to the action that starts/happens first and (2) next to the action that starts/happens second.
1 I saw Juana while I was walking in the park.
2 Before she left the house, she'd checked that the windows were closed.
3 They met about six years ago and got married soon after.
4 After they'd finished work, they went to a local restaurant.
5 They went to bed early, as they'd had a long day.

5 Put the events in the story in the correct order. Use the language you underlined in Exercise 3 to help you.
a Seb didn't have a holiday for a long time. *1*
b Seb's flight was delayed.
c The writer took Seb to all the famous places in New York.
d Ana and the writer visited MOMA.
e The writer saw a familiar face.
f Seb visited Barcelona to see Ana.
g He decided to do some last-minute sight-seeing.
h Seb moved to Barcelona.

6 Work in pairs and discuss the questions.
1 Have you or anyone you know ever had a chance meeting that was important?
2 How important do you think chance is in our lives?

7C Develop your listening

Goal: understand a presentation
Focus: listening for specific information

Want to do something different?
How about climbing Mount Fuji or going hiking in the Pyrenees? Maybe you could walk the Great Wall of China? Even better, what if you could do these things and raise money for a charity, too?
Sounds like you need a charity challenge!

1 a Look at the advert and discuss the questions.
  1 Where are the people in the photo? What are they doing?
  2 What are charity challenges? Why do people do them?

2 Read the Focus box. When you make notes, what should you do? Why?

Listening for specific information
When listening for key information in a talk or presentation, be clear what you are listening for. Before you listen, think about the information you want to know. You could prepare by writing down some questions.
Then listen carefully for the information you want and make notes to help you remember it. Just write key words. You don't have time to write down every word or full sentences.

3 a You're going to listen to a talk explaining what a charity challenge is and how to do it. What do you want to know? Write at least three questions.
  b 🔊 7.9 Listen and make notes. Do you have answers to your questions?
  c Work in pairs and compare your notes. Have you written the same key words?

4 a Read the advert for a charity challenge below and think of some questions to ask the organisers. Think about the following:
  • the route you will take
  • things you will take with you
  • the total cost of the trip

PYRENEAN HIKE
Register for £250
Four days hiking through the Spanish Pyrenees.
Join us for an experience you'll never forget!

  b 🔊 7.10 Listen to the organisers' webinar and make notes. Do you have the answers to your questions?

5 a Compare the notes below with the notes you made. Are any of the questions the same as yours?

Pyrenean charity challenge
1 What route will we follow?
  • walk _____ kilometres in _____ days through Spanish Pyrenees
  • route goes along _____ , then through _____ and forest
2 How far will we walk every day?
  • walk approx _____ per day, should take _____ hours
  • start from _____ , finish at _____ on the route
3 What support will we have during the trip?
  • will have _____ – fully trained, knows the _____
4 Do I need to do any training to prepare for the trip?
  • depends on how _____ I am now
  • prepare by doing short walks of _____
  • increase to _____ per day
5 What things will I need to take?
  • most important: good _____
  • _____ to keep dry and warm
  • small _____ to carry lunch and water bottle
6 How much money do I need to raise?
  • £ _____
7 What's included in the cost?
  • _____ from and to the UK
  • _____ night's accommodation in _____ rooms
  • plus all _____

  b Try to complete the notes with one or two words in each gap.
  c Listen again and check. Add any missing information.

6 Work in pairs and discuss the questions.
  1 Would you like to do a charity challenge? Why/Why not?
  2 What sort of charity challenge would you like to do?

8A Develop your writing

> **Goal:** write a short email
> **Focus:** adding and contrasting ideas

1 **Discuss the questions.**
   1 What are the advantages of living alone/with other people?
   2 Which do you prefer? Why?

2 **Read the email. What is Sophie trying to decide?**

Hey Lisa,

How's it going? I'm really well. I'm enjoying the new job and everyone at work seems friendly and helpful. Plus, I'm getting the yearly bonus, even though I just joined!

I wanted to get your advice on something. I'm still living at home with my parents and I just can't decide if I should move out. I mean, my mum and dad are great and they like having me here, too. I also don't have to worry about money, which is a big thing.

However, I think moving out might be a good idea. A lot of my friends are already renting their own places and they seem to be having an amazing time. They've got much more freedom than I have – they can invite people over whenever they want, for example. I've started thinking I should do the same instead of living at home with my parents. Maybe I'm a bit old for living at home?

So what should I do? On the one hand, if I move out, I'll feel more like an 'adult' but I'll have lots of new problems to deal with. On the other hand, if I stay at home, I'll have an easy life, but I'll continue to feel like a little kid!

What do you think?

Sophie

3 **Read the Focus box. Which of the ways of adding and contrasting ideas do you use when you're writing?**

Adding and contrasting ideas

There are many useful words and phrases you can use when you're adding or contrasting ideas in a piece of writing.

Adding ideas
*If you stay here, you can live with your parents **and** be near your friends.*
***As well as** being near family and friends, you can find a job more easily.*
*There are activities during the day. You can **also** do a lot of different things in the evenings.*
*There are lots of opportunities to play a sport and to meet people, **too**.*
*It's nice living at home. **Plus**, it's cheap!*

Contrasting ideas
*There are a lot of sports clubs you can join, **but** you need to have time to practise.*
*I like living at home. **However**, I'd like to have more freedom.*
*I like the new place, **even though** it's expensive.*
***On the one hand**, joining a gym is expensive. **On the other hand**, it keeps you healthy.*

4 a **Find and underline four different ways of adding ideas in the email in Exercise 2.**

b **Find and underline three different ways of contrasting ideas in the email.**

5 **Choose the correct alternatives.**
   1 I'm working a lot but I'm *plus/also* having a lot of fun.
   2 It was nice for a short time. *However/Even though*, I'm happy that I don't live there now.
   3 *As well as/Also* getting a free meal, we got free drinks after dinner.
   4 It was expensive and really bad quality, *as well as/too*.
   5 *Even though/However* I was tired, I had a good time.
   6 The weather, was bad, *but/on the other hand* we had a good time.
   7 It's a nice gym. *Plus/Too*, they have a jacuzzi.
   8 On the one hand, the film looked amazing. *But/On the other hand*, the actors were poor.

Prepare

6 a **You're planning to make one of the major life decisions below. Decide what you're going to do and make a list of the advantages and disadvantages.**
   - moving to another country or staying where you are
   - getting a new job or staying in your present job
   - staying in your job or taking a career break

   b **Organise your ideas. Think about the words and phrases you can use to add to and contrast your ideas.**

Write

7 **Write an email to a friend. Ask what they think you should do. Use Sophie's email to help you.**

8 **Read your partner's email and write a reply.**

8B Develop your listening

> **Goal:** understand a radio phone-in programme
>
> **Focus:** guessing the meaning of unknown words

1 Discuss the questions.
1 What sports are popular in your country?
2 What sports do you enjoy watching/playing?
3 Do you enjoy watching the Olympics? Why/Why not?

2 Read the Focus box. What methods can you use to help you guess the meaning of an unknown word while listening?

Guessing the meaning of unknown words

You don't need to understand every word when you are listening, but sometimes we can make a guess about the meaning of words we don't know. Look at the words below in bold which might be new for you.

Guessing from general context

*The Olympics is a great way to **unite** people from all over the world.*

We know that 'unite' is connected to 'The Olympics' and 'people from all over the world'. From the context, we might guess that 'unite' means 'bring people together'.

Repetition of a word

*You have to be an amazing athlete to win a **medal** at the Olympics.*
***Medals** are given to the winner, second and third-placed athletes.*

From the two examples, we know that a 'medal' is something you can win, that you need to be good at your sport to do it and we know that they are given to the first three athletes in an Olympic event. This can help us guess the meaning of the word.

Examples

*I like **ball games** like football, rugby and basketball.*
The examples help us guess what 'ball games' are.

Explanations

*I'd like to try a **marathon**, which is a sport where you run a really long distance.*
The word 'marathon' is explained for us by the person speaking.

3 🔊 8.6 Listen to the first part of a radio phone-in programme. What is it about?
a How to become a top athlete.
b How to get people interested in sport.

4 a Listen again for the words and phrases in the box. Can you guess what they mean?

> facilities   funding   inspire

b Choose the correct definition for each word.
1 To *inspire* means …
 a to make someone excited about something and want to do it.
 b to force someone to do something they are not interested in.
2 *Facilities* are …
 a teachers and coaches.
 b football pitches, tennis courts and gyms.
3 *Funding* is …
 a money given by a government or organisation for an activity.
 b advice about the best way to do something.

c Work in pairs. What helped you choose the correct definition?

5 a 🔊 8.7 Listen to the second part of the programme. What's the best summary?
a We need to help young people find the sport that they enjoy.
b We need to find the best young people to become top athletes in the future.

b Listen again and guess the meaning of the words in the box.

> competitive (sport)   have a talent (for something)
> range (of sports/activities)

c Listen again and answer the questions.
1 What does Peter Jones say schools need to do?
2 What does he say is the benefit of this?
3 Does Susan Biggs agree with Peter Jones?
4 What kind of activities does she suggest schools should offer? Why?

6 Discuss the questions.
1 What do you think about this opinion?
 'Nowadays we have better sports facilities, but also better internet, better phones and better video games. It's hard to get young people interested in sport.'
2 What do you think is the best way to encourage young people to do more physical activity?

8c Develop your reading

> **Goal:** understand a brochure
> **Focus:** understanding reference

1. **Look at the photos and discuss the questions.**
   1. What's the wildest place you've visited? What did you do there?
   2. Would you like to visit any of the places in the photos? Which ones?

2. **Read the first paragraph of the brochure. What type of trip is it describing?**

3. **Read the Focus box. How do writers avoid repeating the same words?**

Understanding reference

When writers want to avoid repeating the same words and phrases in a text, they use words such as pronouns and adverbs to refer to the word or phrase.
Pronouns: *he, she, it, they*
Demonstratives: *this, that, these, those*
Adverbs: *here, there*
Wh- words: *what, which, where*
These words can be used to refer to something that comes before them.
The mountains are so high, they seem to touch the sky.
They refers to the word *mountains*.
You can visit one of the mountains which is near the village.
Which refers to *one of the mountains*.
They can also be used to refer to something that comes after them.
Here in Jamaica, you will receive a warm welcome.
Here refers to the word *Jamaica* that follows it.

4. **Complete the sentences with the words in the box.**

he	here	it	they	this	who

   1. I liked Denmark and Bob liked _____ , too.
   2. I love this area, I'm very happy _____ .
   3. Are Brian and Sophia OK? _____ look annoyed.
   4. _____ is the last time that I'm going to help you with money.
   5. Everyone always laughs at Mike, but _____ doesn't care.
   6. I like the guys _____ were at the table next to us.

5. **Look at the words in bold in the first two paragraphs of the brochure. What do they refer to?**

6. **Look at the last two paragraphs of the brochure and underline words that are used to refer to other words. Which words do they refer to?**

7. **Work in pairs and discuss. Which of the places in the brochure would you like to visit? Why?**

Looking for holiday ideas? Well, why not take a look at some of the amazing trips we offer to the world's most wonderful valleys. People don't often think of valleys when **they** think about their holidays, but **they** are often some of the most beautiful places on Earth. **Some** are deep, **others** have amazing waterfalls and so many of **them** are worth visiting!

The Grand Canyon, USA
It is probably the most well-known valley of all, but the Grand Canyon in the US will still surprise you with its size and great beauty. It's best viewed from the air, so you will fly along the Colorado River before hiking and camping in the national park, **where** you can see all kinds of wonderful wildlife.

The Verdon Gorge, France
This is often called the most beautiful valley in Europe. It is a deep river valley whose beautiful green water attracts water sports fans for activities such as sailing and water skiing. These aren't the only things you can do there. Its high walls also make it popular with people who like climbing. If you love adventure, you'll love it here.

The Antelope Canyons, USA
Here in the Antelope Canyon in Arizona, you will find a photographer's paradise. They come here for the amazing rock formations and the marvellous colours, which consist of brilliant oranges and purples. The canyon is actually two deep valleys, which have very narrow walls. People walking through them can touch both sides at the same time if they want to!

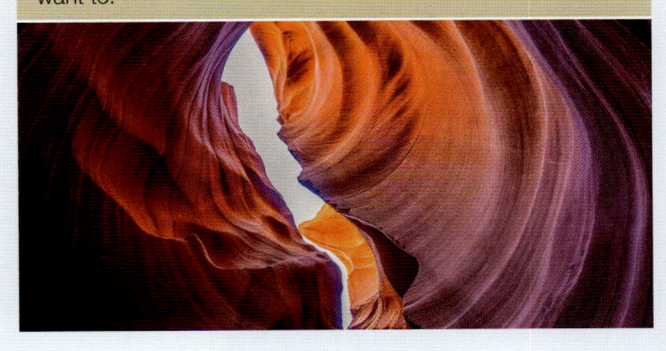

9A Develop your reading

> **Goal:** understand a short article
> **Focus:** recognising degrees of certainty

1 Read the comments. Which do you agree/disagree with? Why?

> Shopping is a huge waste of time.

> I only buy what I need when I need it.

> Shopping makes me feel good when I'm feeling down.

2 a You're going to read a short article. Look at the title. What do you think the article will be about?

b Read the article quickly and check your ideas.

Is shopping going out of fashion?

I've never understood it, but it's certainly true that a lot of people spend their free time giving money to stores. You'll probably find your local shopping centre full of people every weekend, families arguing with each other, teenagers hanging out with their friends and bored couples killing time. Almost everyone's there! It's also a fact that shopping helps our economy – when people stop spending, that's when we know there's trouble coming.

However, it looks like shopping may be becoming less popular than it was, certainly with young adults. Talking to lots of my friends these days, they tell me that they definitely shop less than their parents' generation. When I asked them why, I got a few different answers. Some said that they just don't have the money and need it for other things. Others said that it was probably because it felt like a waste – it's clear that we have more things than we need already, so why get more? One friend said that it was because he felt like he was always being pushed to buy new things by advertising on TV and social media and that he just didn't like that feeling. A few of these friends also expressed another idea – they felt that their generation is less interested in 'stuff' than the previous one and more interested in experiences.

I don't think shopping is going to disappear from our lives any time soon, but I hope that people are beginning to spend more time doing other things. My parents recently started going hiking at the weekends rather than going to the shops in town, so maybe there's hope!

3 Read the Focus box. What does using the word *possible* indicate?

Recognising degrees of certainty

Writers use various words and phrases to show how certain or uncertain they are about something they say.

To show they feel completely sure about something.
It is a fact that online shopping is very popular.
It is (certainly) true that online shopping is growing.
It's clear that online shopping is good for business.

To show they feel almost sure about something.
It is probably busy in the shopping centre today.
It is likely/unlikely to be busy in the shops today.
It looks like spending on food will go up.

To show they are not completely certain about something.
It is possible that our spending on gadgets will go down.
Maybe we will stop buying new things.

4 Read the article again and underline the words and phrases that show the writer is:
1 completely sure about the information.
2 almost sure the information is true.
3 not very sure the information is true.

5 Are the sentences true (T) or false (F) according to the article? Correct the false sentences.
The writer …
1 is sure most people spend a lot of time shopping.
2 is sure a lot of people go the shops at the weekend.
3 is almost sure that shopping is good for business.
4 isn't very sure that younger people do less shopping.
5 isn't very sure people will stop shopping.

6 Work in pairs and discuss. Do people shop too much?

9B Develop your writing

> **Goal:** write a story
> **Focus:** making comparisons

The mouse, the bird and the chilli

A mouse, a bird, and a chilli, three great friends, lived together in the same house. For a long time, they lived happily together in this house, each one using their own special skills. The bird, who was as quick as an arrow, flew every day to the forest to bring back wood. The mouse was the organised one, and he got the water, made the fire and got the table ready for dinner. The chilli did the cooking. He jumped in the pot and swam around like a strange sea animal, until the water was nice and spicy. It was a great life for the three friends. They never wanted their lovely life to change.

Then one day, the bird met another bird in the forest and told this second bird about his life and how he flew to the forest every day to get wood for the fire, while his friends did their jobs at home. This other bird, a crow with a bad personality, told the bird that he was doing too much work and that the mouse and the chilli had an easier life than the bird did.

The next day, because of the crow's words, the bird refused to go to the forest. He said that he was tired of working like a machine. The bird then said that they should all change roles. The chilli would get the wood, the mouse would become the cook and the bird would carry the water and set the table. The mouse and the chilli were not happy, but in the end, they agreed.

And what was the result, do you think?

Well, the chilli went out to the forest to get wood but on the way, he met a hungry dog, who ate him.

The mouse tried to copy the chilli and swam in the hot water. He soon realised it was too hot and he jumped out and ran away.

Now his friends were gone, the bird had to do everything. He had to fly and get wood, collect water, cook the food, set the table … He got so confused by everything he needed to do that he didn't notice that some of the wood from the fire had fallen onto the floor and the house was starting to burn. The house burned down and the bird was left with no home and no friends. If he'd listened to his friends, then none of this would have happened.

1 a Read the story. What mistake did the friends make?

b Complete the sentences to describe the story.
1 If the three friends hadn't decided to …
2 If the crow hadn't …

2 a Which of the friends did the writer compare to a sea creature/an arrow/a machine?

b Read the Focus box. Can you think of any other ways to make a comparison in English?

Making comparisons

We can use comparisons to make a piece of writing more interesting. There are different ways to do this.
We can use *as … as* to say that one thing is similar to something else, often using an adjective.
She was **as pale as** a ghost.
We can also use *like* to say that two things are similar.
He cried **like** a baby.
If we want to focus on appearance, we can use *look like*. We can use it with a noun or a clause.
The clouds **looked like** an ice cream dessert.
He **looked like** he was angry.

3 Choose the correct alternatives.
1 He looked *like/as* an angry bull.
2 She was as quiet *like/as* a mouse.
3 They looked like *tired/they were tired*.
4 She ran *like/as* the wind.
5 The sky was *as/like* a swimming pool.

4 Complete the sentences with your own ideas.
1 The moon looked like a …
2 She was so angry, she looked like she wanted to …
3 The forest was as dark as …
4 The man was always so calm, he was like a …
5 The bear was as big as …

Prepare

5 a You're going to write your own story. First, think about the questions below to help you with your ideas.
- Who were the people?
- Where were they?
- What happened?
- What were the consequences?

They were a successful couple called June and Hugo.
They were in New York.
They got married. Then they both met someone they preferred on their honeymoon.
They got married again, but to different people.

b Think of comparisons to make your story more interesting.
New York in winter looked like a Christmas cake.

Write

6 Write a short story using your ideas in Exercise 5a. Use the comparisons you made in Exercise 5b to make your story more interesting.

9c Develop your listening

> **Goal:** understand a radio discussion
> **Focus:** recognising a speaker's opinions

1 Look at the photos and discuss the questions.
  1 What's your reaction to the two pieces of public art?
  2 Which are the best/worst examples of public art in your country?

2 Read opinions 1–7 about public art. Which do you agree or disagree with?
  1 Public art is a waste of money.
  2 Public art is important and valuable.
  3 Modern public art should be creative and not just copy from life.
  4 Modern public art should be realistic, not abstract.
  5 The public should not have to pay for public art with their taxes.
  6 Public art should be chosen by experts.
  7 The public should be able to vote for new public art

3 🔊 9.8 Listen to the first part of a radio programme about public art. Which ideas in Exercise 2 do the speakers mention?

4 Read the Focus box. How might we know when someone is going to give you their opinion?

Recognising a speaker's opinions

The following words and phrases can help you recognise and understand speakers' attitudes.

Introducing your opinion
It seems to me (that), …
Actually, …
In my opinion, …
I believe/I think, …

Agreeing
That's true.
Right./You're right.
Exactly./Agreed.

Showing you partly agree but not completely
I see/know what you mean.
I take your point, but …

Disagreeing
But (think about …)
However, …/On the other hand …

5 a Listen to the first part of the programme again. Tick the phrases in the Focus box you hear.

  b Match opinions 1–4 with the speakers, Mark (M) or Angy (A). Then listen again and check your answers.
    1 People should value public art more.
    2 Public art has many benefits for people.
    3 A lot of modern public art is not very good.
    4 Lots of people will go to see good public art.

  c Which opinion in Exercise 2 do Mark and Angy both agree with?

6 🔊 9.9 Listen to the second part of the programme and complete the sentences.
  1 These experts usually prefer abstract art … _____ , most ordinary people prefer more realistic works.
  2 I _____ and I agree that a small group of people shouldn't make decisions for the rest of us.
  3 _____ , because the other question is money. Public art isn't free. _____ , it's paid for by the public with their taxes.
  4 Yes, _____ . I believe that we should all help to pay for public art.
  5 _____ the problem is the way public art is chosen.
  6 _____ the public should be able to vote for their favourite proposal.
  7 That's a very interesting idea, _____ will it work?

7 Read the sentences in Exercise 2 again. Has your opinion about any of them changed? Why/Why not?

10A Develop your writing

> **Goal:** write an email asking for information
>
> **Focus:** requesting information

1 Think of different reasons for sending emails. How many types of email have you written?

2 Read the advert and email. What extra information might the writer want?

HAMPTON EVENING UNIVERSITY
FULL-TIME AND PART-TIME COURSES

Our short courses are taught in the evenings in two central locations. They give you the opportunity to develop your interests and skills, boost your career or gain a qualification. Hampton also offers full-time courses to international students in a wide range of subject areas and at all levels of university study.

CONTACT US

To: Hampton University
Subject: How to enrol
Hello,
I am interested in enrolling on one of your short courses starting in September. I am writing to find out more about how to do this.
I would like to know if I can enrol for my course online and what information I need to provide. Could you also let me know when I have to register by and if there is a registration fee?
I look forward to hearing from you. Thank you in advance.
Many thanks,
John Smith

---

3 Read the Focus box. Do you think the style of the examples is formal or informal?

Requesting information

When we write an email to ask for information, we usually start by saying why we're writing and then ask questions/make requests. We often use the following phrases:

Saying why you are writing.
I am writing to ask for information about …
I am writing to find out more about …
I am writing to enquire about …

Asking detailed questions and make requests.
I would also like to know if …
Could you also let me know if/what/when …?
Could you advise me …?
Please could you send me details about …
I would be grateful if you could …

Ending your email.
I look forward to hearing from you.
Thank you in advance.

4 Read the email in Exercise 2 again and answer the questions.
What phrases does the writer use …
1 to say why he is writing?
2 to ask for information?
3 to end his email?

5 Complete the email. Use the phrases in the Focus box to help you.

Hello,
I am ¹_____ ask for more information about your English language courses. I am studying English at college in my country and I am at Intermediate level. However, I would like to improve my speaking skills and I am interested in doing one of your summer school courses.
I have looked at your website but I would be grateful if you ²_____ me some more detailed information. Could you ³_____ know what courses you will be offering in July and August? Also, I'd like ⁴_____ if your courses are already full, or if you are still taking bookings.
Finally, I have a question about accommodation. Does your school help students from abroad find accommodation? If so, please ⁵_____ send me further details about this? I look forward to ⁶_____ you. Thank you ⁷_____ .
Many thanks,
Joanna Lopez

Prepare

6 Read the advert below. If you were interested in this service, what questions would you want to ask about it?

Want a new direction?
Need some help?

Are you ready for a change in your life? Our team of experts offer a unique service which will help you decide what career options are best for your skills and life needs. We will:
• help you make a career action plan.
• recommend courses and training.
• review your CV.
• find you a job!
Your first appointment with us is free! To book it today, contact us at **info@movingon.netuk**

Write

7 Write your email asking for information. Organise your email into logical paragraphs.
• Say why you are writing.
• Ask for information. (You can use more than one paragraph to ask for information).
• End your email/letter and say thank you.

10B Develop your reading

> **Goal:** understand an article
> **Focus:** making inferences

1 a What are the good and bad effects of tourism?
  b Read the article. Are any of your ideas mentioned?

2 Read the Focus box. How can you find out the writer's opinion if it is not stated directly in the article?

Making inferences

Sometimes it's very clear what a writer wants to say, but sometimes we have to make guesses from the information that we are given - we need to 'infer' what they mean.
Read the extract:
People have more paid holidays. Travel has become cheaper. Many countries have built airports, roads and hotels so it is easier to find holiday accommodation.
From this information we can infer that tourism has increased because all the things that are mentioned would make it easier for people to go on holiday.
Read the comment:
'Where I live, we have about eight million tourists a year. Without them, we wouldn't have any jobs.'
From this we can infer that the person feels positive about tourism in their city. People having jobs is a good thing, so tourism must be a good thing.

3 a Read the extract. What can you infer about the effect of tourism from the information given?

In many places, tourism has replaced traditional jobs like farming or fishing. As a result, local people now depend on money from tourism for their living. Sometimes the number of tourists falls, for example, because of floods or fire.

  b Read the comment. How does the person feel about tourists?

It used to be wonderful. We used to have lots of workers with traditional skills in the city. Now, around 2,000 people leave each year. Soon there will be more tourists than residents.

4 Read the article again. Is this information stated (S) or not stated but can be inferred (NS)?
  1 Mass tourism can be bad for the environment.
  2 Many residents in Barcelona and Venice are angry because of the number of tourists.
  3 Many tourists behave well.
  4 The Peruvian government is worried about the negative effects of tourism on Machu Picchu.
  5 Peru controls the number of tourists visiting Machu Picchu.
  6 The writer is optimistic that tourism can continue without too many negative effects.

5 Discuss the questions.
  1 Does tourism affect your country/the place where you live? In what ways?
  2 How do people feel about it?

Tourism has become a huge industry. Tourists make millions of foreign trips a year, twice as many as 20 years ago. It's now the largest employer on Earth. Clearly, it can do great good, but it can also do great damage.

It is true that tourism has brought benefits to many areas of the world that were very poor. However, mass tourism also has negative effects. Local culture and customs change as more tourists arrive. Too much tourism damages the environment. And more and more tourists are behaving badly.

Complaints from local people are growing. In cities such as Barcelona or Venice, residents say that too many tourists arrive on cruise ships. As a result, town centres are overcrowded. They tell stories about noisy parties that keep people awake all night. In famous beauty spots, where tourist money was welcomed, people are now concerned about the damage tourists do to the environment.

Of course, many tourists enjoy the benefits of tourism in a responsible way. They choose holidays that support the local economy and they respect the local culture and the environment. Environmentally friendly tourism, or eco-tourism, is becoming more popular.

Responsible tourist behaviour is necessary, but it isn't enough to solve the problem. Many people now believe that governments should control how many visitors enter their country. They believe they should limit the number of cruise ships that use their ports and should not allow too many hotel developments.

Unfortunately, governments are in a difficult situation. Tourism brings in a lot of money and this helps them improve life for the local people. However, some governments are beginning to understand that too much tourism can be bad for the local population and the environment. For example, Peru has recently limited the number of tourists who can visit the ancient city of Machu Picchu, and countries such as Bhutan, Costa Rica and Kenya now promote environmentally friendly tourism. There may still be hope.

10c Develop your listening

> **Goal:** understand short conversations
>
> **Focus:** understanding meaning from context

2 Read the Focus box. What things can we focus on to help us guess someone's real meaning?

Understanding meaning from context

The words people use may have different meanings according to the context they are used in. To understand what someone wants to communicate, you can think about:

The situation
Who are the people involved, how do they know each other and why are they talking?
For example a boss says to her employee:
Would you mind writing the report by tomorrow?
The boss means:
I want you to write the report today.

Other things they say
Listening to what people say before and after a specific sentence can help us make guesses about what they mean.
A: Let's go out.
B: It's so hot!
A: Oh, come on!

It's so hot! may have lots of meanings, but if we look at what A says, we can guess that B means *I don't want to go out!*

How they say things
What tone of voice do they use? Do they sound angry, happy or disappointed?

3 a 🔊 10.8 Listen to the conversation. What does one of the people mean when they say 'He's usually early'? Choose the correct option.
  a I'm surprised and worried that he's not here.
  b I'm really angry that he's late.
  c I'm not surprised that he's not here.
 b What helped you guess the correct answer?

4 a 🔊 10.9 Listen to two people talking and answer the questions.
  1 What is the relationship between the people?
  2 What is the situation?
 b Listen again and answer the questions.
  1 Why does Lauren say 'What about it?'?
  2 Why does Lauren's mother say 'I know other students who are doing that'?
  3 Why does Lauren say 'You must be so disappointed'?
  4 Why does Lauren say 'I need to go out'?

5 Discuss the questions.
  1 Have you ever been/Were you ever in Lauren's situation at school?
  2 If so, what did your parents say?

1 a Look at the pictures and discuss the questions.
  1 What is happening?
  2 How does each person feel?
  3 Why are the people saying 'It's five o'clock'?
 b 🔊 10.7 Listen to the conversation and answer the questions.
  1 What is the relationship between the people?
  2 Where are they?
  3 Which picture best shows the situation?

Grammar bank

GRAMMAR

1A Present simple and present continuous

present simple

Use the present simple to talk about something we see as permanent and not changing. This could be:
- facts and general truths.
- permanent situations.
- habits and routines.

*The journey **takes** 30 minutes.*
*Does Sam **speak** Spanish?*
*I **walk** to school every day.*

When using the present simple to talk about habits and routines, a frequency expression is often used, e.g. *usually, sometimes, often, every day, once a month*.

*I **usually** cycle to school.*
*I watch TV **every evening**.*

present continuous

Form the present continuous with *am/are/is* +verb+*ing*.

Use the present continuous to talk about something in progress now or around now. The present continuous is also used to talk about something temporary.

***Is** it **raining**?*
*I'**m reading** a great book at the moment.*
*I'**m working** in Bristol this week.*

state verbs

State verbs express things such as likes, desires, attitude and feelings (e.g. *like, love, hate, need, want, agree, believe, feel, know*), appearance and characteristics (e.g. *look (like), appear, smell, sound, weigh, contain, consist of*) and possession (*belong (to), have (got), own*). We generally use state verbs in the simple form.

*I **need** some help.*
***Do** you **like** rock music?*
*This café **looks** nice.*
*I **don't have** any money.*

1B *be going to* and present continuous

be going to

Use *be going to* to talk about plans and intentions that were made before the time of speaking.

*I'**m going to look** for a new job.*
*We'**re going to meet** sometime soon.*
*What **are** you **going to say** to her?*

Note that when we use *be going to go*, we usually omit *to go*.

*I'**m going** ~~to go~~ *to bed*.

present continuous

The present continuous is used for something that is arranged, agreed or finalised. In other words, it is more than just a plan or intention. For example, it is often used

when we have an arrangement with another person. When the present continuous is used in this way, it is often with a time phrase, e.g. *this evening, in December, next year*.

*They'**re getting** married in December.*
*We'**re meeting** at 7.30.*
***Are** you **doing** anything this weekend?*

Note that *be going to* or the present continuous can sometimes both be used with little or no difference in meaning and use.

*I'**m going to stay** at home this evening.* or
*I'**m staying** at home this evening.*

1C *will* for prediction

Use *will*, or *'ll* with a verb to add a future meaning.

*I'**ll see** you later.*
*I **will come** to the party.*

In spoken English, *'ll* is more commonly used than *will*.

Use *will not* or *won't* to express a negative.

*We **won't** have a party like this again.*
*We **will not** see him today.*

Form a question by changing the position of the subject and *will*.

***Will** John be there tonight?*

Note that in speaking, the contracted form *'ll* is usually used.

Use *will* to predict things about the future. It is often used with verbs such as *think, believe, expect* and *hope* or with phrases such as *I'm (not) sure* or *I'm (not) certain*. *Will* can also be used with adverbs of (un)certainty such as *probably, possibly* and *definitely*.

*We'**ll have** regular flights to Mars in 50 years' time.*
*I'**ll definitely be** a millionaire by the time I'm 30!*
*In the future, I **think we'll spend** more and more of our time online.*
*I **don't think we'll arrive** before six.*
*I'**m sure she'll pass** the exam.*

When *will* is used in this way, it is often with a time phrase, e.g. *in the future, in ten years' time, by 2050*.

PRACTICE

1A

1 Complete the text with the correct form of the verbs in brackets.

I wake up early. It ¹_____ (not / matter) if my first lecture is at 9 a.m. or 3 p.m., I always ²_____ (get out) of bed before 8 o'clock. This year, I ³_____ (live) in a flat with two other students. They ⁴_____ usually _____ (not / get up) until I have left the flat and they often ⁵_____ (go out) in the evenings, so we ⁶_____ (not / see) each other very often. Anyway, each morning I first ⁷_____ (check) my social media and ⁸_____ (read) the latest news. I ⁹_____ (do) a degree in politics and business, so I ¹⁰_____ (need) to know what ¹¹_____ (happen) in the world.

2 Correct the conversations. There are two mistakes in each conversation.

1. **A:** How do you get to work?
   B: I'm usually getting the bus to work, but sometimes I'm driving.
2. **A:** Oh no! It rains. Get your umbrella.
   B: Yes, it's raining quite a lot at this time of year.
3. **A:** Why aren't you at work?
   B: They do some building work at the office, so I work at home this week.
4. **A:** How long is the film lasting?
   B: It's 100 minutes, I'm thinking.
5. **A:** How is your food being?
   B: I'm not normally liking Indian food, but I'm really enjoying this.
6. **A:** Who is this bag belonging to?
   B: I'm not knowing, sorry.

1B

1 Complete the New Years' resolutions with *be going to* and the verbs in the box.

| be | ~~do~~ | not/eat | learn (x2) | teach |
| travel | not/worry | | | |

1. I *'m going to do* more exercise and eat more healthily. I _____ so much junk food.
2. I _____ more sociable and meet more people.
3. A friend and I _____ a new language. She _____ French and me Spanish. And then we _____ each other!
4. I _____ about things so much. Life's too short!
5. My boyfriend and I _____ more and see more of the world.

2 Read the conversations. Does the present continuous refer to the present (P) or the future (F)?

1. **A:** I'm meeting Juan and Sara at 5 p.m. __F__
   B: Oh that sounds nice.
2. **A:** What are you doing?
   B: I'm just looking at places I'd like to go to on holiday in the future. ____
3. **A:** What are you doing, get your coat! The meeting is in five minutes!
   B: OK, relax, I'm coming! ____
4. **A:** I'm meeting Debbie's parents. ____
   B: Oh wow, when? Are you nervous?
5. **A:** I can't go tonight. I'm working, sorry. ____
   B: Ah, that's a shame.
6. **A:** When's the food coming? I'm so hungry! ____
   B: Five minutes.

1C

1 Put the words in the correct order.

1. **A:** think / what time / 'll / do you / you / here / be / ?
   B: Maybe around 9.30 if the traffic isn't too bad / .
2. **A:** 'll / think / do you / later / it / rain / ?
   B: I'm not sure. Let's take our umbrellas just in case / .
3. **A:** Is the new James Bond film good / ?
   B: 'll / it / you / love / !
4. **A:** think / who / the game / you / will / do / win / ?
   B: think / I / it / be / 'll / pretty close / .
5. **A:** will / do / what / I / if / can't find / I / my passport / ?
   B: I / it / find / sure / 'm / we / 'll / .

2 Complete the text with *will* and the verbs in the box. Which of the predictions do you agree with?

| be | go back | happen | not / live | use | walk |

Four predictions about space travel

- I'm certain that humans ¹_____ to the moon. But people ²_____ there. We ³_____ the moon as a base for exploring further into space.
- I'm sure a human ⁴_____ on Mars before the end of the century. It ⁵_____ a great achievement, but I'm not sure what ⁶_____ after that.

Want more practice? Go to your Workbook or app.

GRAMMAR

2A Past simple and past continuous

past simple
Use the past simple to talk about completed past actions and events.

I played football yesterday.

For most verbs, add *-ed* to the infinitive (e.g. *worked, watched, played*) to form the past simple. Some verbs have an irregular past simple form (e.g. *went, saw, knew*).

I met some nice guys at the party.

To form the negative, use *didn't* + infinitive and to form questions, use *did* + subject + infinitive.

Did you **see** Jenny last night?
I didn't have any lunch today.

For the verb *be*, the past simple is *was* or *were*. To form the negative, add *-n't* and to form a question, put *was* or *were* before the subject.

We **were** all quite tired last night.
He **was** there when I called.
We **weren't** very happy with her.

past continuous
To form the past continuous, use *was/were* + *-ing* form.

+	He was working. We were living in Rome in 2017.
-	He wasn't working. We weren't living in Rome in 2017.
?	Was he working? Were you living in Rome in 2017?

Use the past continuous to talk about an action or situation in progress at or around a time in the past. We often use the past continuous to give the background to a story.

It **wasn't raining** when we left.
How long **were** you **waiting** for the bus?

The past continuous is often used with the past simple when one action interrupts another. Use *when* and *while* to link the actions. *While* is usually used with longer actions (e.g. with the past continuous) and *when* for shorter action (e.g. with the past simple).

I **saw** Dasha **while** I **was driving** to work.
We **were living** in Rome **when** we **met**.

2B used to

Use *used to* + infinitive. Note that there is no final *-d* in negatives and questions.

I used to play the guitar.
When I was a child, we **used to** go skiing every year
I **didn't use to** play the guitar.
We **didn't use to** go skiing every year.
Did you **use to** play the guitar?
How often did you **use to** go skiing when you were younger?

Use *used to* to talk about actions, such as habits and routines, that happened regularly in the past, but don't happen now. Don't use *used to* for single events or actions in the past.

We **used to visit** my grandparents every weekend, but now we live too far away.

Also use *used to* to talk about past states and permanent situations.

I **used to love** watching cartoons when I was a kid.

Use *never used to* as a negative form.

I **never used to play** computer games much.

Note that *used to* and the past simple can have similar meaning, but *used to* emphasises that the situation no longer exists.

2C so/such ... that; too ... to; not enough ... to

so/such ... that
Use *so* and *such* to give emphasis to something. Use *so* before an adjective and *such* before an adjective + noun. We can also use *such* + noun. Note that the article *a* goes after *such*.

I was **so** tired!
It was **such** a lovely day.
It was **such** a waste of time!

Also use *so much / many* + noun.

There were **so many** people.
We spent **so much** money!

Use *so ... that* and *such ... that* to link a situation with its consequence or result. Note that using *that* is optional.

I was **so tired that** I went to bed at 8 o'clock.
It was **such a lovely day that** we didn't want it to end.

too/(not) enough ... to
Use *too* to say something is more than we want or need. Use *too* + adjective or *too much/many* + noun.

The pizza is **too hot**.
There was **too much noise**.

Use (*not*) *enough ...* to say we have or don't have as much as we want or need. Use adjective + *enough* and *enough* + noun.

This coat isn't **warm enough**.
Do we have **enough time**?

Use an infinitive clause (*to* ...) to explain why there is more than we want or need or that we have or don't have as much as we want or need.

There's not enough pasta **to make lunch**.

PRACTICE

2A

1 Complete the sentences with the pairs of verbs in the box. Use one in the past simple and the other in the past continuous.

> not answer/drive   meet/do   you queue/get
> rain/not go   see/wait   walk/start

1 I _____ you this morning while I _____ for the bus.
2 I _____ the dog when it _____ snowing.
3 We first _____ at university. We _____ the same degree.
4 Sorry I _____ the phone earlier. I _____ .
5 It _____ this morning, so we _____ for a walk.
6 How long _____ before you _____ into the exhibition?

2 Complete the stories with the correct form of the verb in brackets.

While she ¹_____ (celebrate) her grandparents' golden wedding in Stafford, UK, ten-year-old Laura Buxton ²_____ (release) a balloon with a note attached. The note asked the person who found the balloon to write back. Ten days later she ³_____ (receive) a reply. The girl, who ⁴_____ (find) the balloon while she ⁵_____ (play) in her garden 140 miles away, was also called Laura Buxton and was ten years old.

A couple ⁶_____ (have) an argument in a restaurant when the woman ⁷_____ (throw) a drink over the man. A few seconds later she ⁸_____ (slip) on the drink and ⁹_____ (hurt) her back. She later ¹⁰_____ (receive) over $100,000 in compensation because the restaurant ¹¹_____ (not / clean up) the liquid quickly enough. The manager said that the staff ¹²_____ (try) to stop the argument at the time.

2B

1 Rewrite the sentences with the correct form of *used to* so that they mean the same.
1 I played the guitar when I was younger, but I don't play it now.
2 We went skiing every year, but we hardly ever go these days.
3 Did you play computer games when you were younger?
4 I didn't like Chinese food in the past, but I love it now.
5 There was a park here but now it's an office block.

2 Make sentences about the past using the prompts and *used to*. Then write three similar sentences of your own.
1 there / be / more languages in the world .
2 people / think / the world / flat .
3 people / not / live so long .
4 we / not / buy / so many things online .
5 there / not / be so much pollution .
6 life / be / much simpler .

2C

1 Choose the correct alternative.
1 I was *too/so* tired to go out last night.
2 It's not warm *too/enough* to swim.
3 We don't have enough money *to/for* buy both of them.
4 We were *so/too* cold that we put the heating on.
5 It was *so/such* a lovely place that we decided to go back there next year.
6 Your parents are *such/so* nice!
7 There were so many people *that/to* we couldn't all sit down.
8 I wanted to go, but I didn't have *money enough/enough money*.

2 Rewrite the sentences using the word in brackets so that they mean the same.
1 I'm too young to vote. (enough)
   I'm _____ vote.
2 It was such a boring film that I fell asleep. (so)
   The film _____ asleep.
3 The room isn't big enough to fit everyone. (too)
   The room _____ everyone.
4 The food was so cold that we couldn't eat it. (too)
   The _____ eat.
5 The traffic was so bad that it took us five hours to get there. (such)
   It _____ to get there.
6 It was too dark to see anything. (so)
   It _____ see anything.

Want more practice?
Go to your
Workbook or app.

GRAMMAR

3A Present perfect and past simple

present perfect

+	I	've	been	to India.
-	She	hasn't	finished	the report.
?	Have	you	seen	that film?

Use the present perfect to connect the past and the present. This could be:

- to talk about actions or events in the recent past that have a result in or an impact on the present. Use *just* to emphasise that the action or event is very recent. *Already*, *yet* and *still* can also be used with the present perfect.

I**'ve lost** my passport.
Jake**'s** just **bought** a new phone.
We**'ve** already **eaten**.
Have you **finished** your homework yet?

- to talk about experiences in our lives up to now. This is often with time expressions such as *never, twice, several times, a few times*, etc. or with the question *Have you ever …?*

Jenny**'s been** to the US.
I**'ve** never **been** skiing.

- or situations that started in the past and continue to the present. To do this, use *since* or *for*. Note that *since* + a point in time (e.g. *since 2016, since last May, since my birthday, since I left university*) and *for* + a period of time (e.g. *five years, a few weeks, ages*).

He**'s been** vegetarian since he was about twelve.
I **haven't been** to the UK since 2015.

past simple

Use the past simple to talk about completed past actions and events. Whereas the present perfect connects the past and the present, the past simple tells us only about the past.

We **saw** a very good film last night.

3B Present perfect continuous and present perfect simple

present perfect continuous

Use *have/has* + *been* + verb+*ing* to form the present perfect continuous. Use the contracted form of have (*'s/'ve*) in more informal contexts, especially in speaking.

I**'ve been going** to the gym a lot these days.

To form the negative, use *haven't/hasn't* + *been* + *-ing* and to form questions, put *have/has* before the subject.

I **haven't been studying** a lot.
Have you been waiting long?

Use the present perfect continuous for actions that are ongoing or only just finished. It is often used to focus on the length of time of an action.

I**'ve been having** driving lessons for two months.
We**'ve been going** out a lot recently.
How long **have** you **been living** here?

present perfect simple

Use the present perfect simple to focus on the present result of a completed action. See 3A for more detailed information.

We**'ve finished** all our work.

3C Articles

a/an (indefinite article)

Use *a* before a consonant sound (e.g. *a car, a tree, a euro*) and use *an* before a vowel sound (e.g. *an apple, an idea, an umbrella*). Use *a/an* to talk about one example of something, often when it is mentioned for the first time.

I've got **a new phone**.
We're going to see **a film**.

a/an can be used in a number of other ways. These include job titles and illnesses, e.g. *a cold, a teacher*.

the (definite article)

Use *the* to talk about something that both the speaker and listener knows. This could be because the thing has already been mentioned or is obvious from the situation or there is only one of something.

What time is **the lecture**?
The Earth goes round **the Sun**.

the can be used in a number of other ways. These include:

- countries with a plural element, e.g. *the Netherlands* or *the UK*

- mountain ranges, rivers, canals, seas, oceans, deserts, e.g. *the Alps, the Thames, the Gobi*.
- hotels, theatres, museums, e.g. *the Hilton, the British Library*.
- peoples, e.g. *the Chinese, the French*.

No article (zero article)

Don't use an article when you're talking about something in a general sense:

We have **lectures** every day.
I love visiting **museums**.
Sugar is bad for you.

We also don't need an article when we talk about these things:

- countries (without a plural element), continents, cities, e.g. *Belarus* or *Russia*.
- mountains, lakes, e.g. *Everest, Lake Geneva*.
- streets, parks, squares, stations, airports, e.g. *Central Park, Heathrow Airport*.
- nationalities and languages, e.g. *French, Spanish*.

PRACTICE

3A

1 Look at the list of eight actions. For each one, write a sentence saying if you have or haven't done it.

1 leave home
   I haven't left home yet.
2 read some Shakespeare
3 visit a different continent
4 learn a musical instrument
5 do a bungee jump
6 fall in love
7 meet a famous person
8 write a book

2 Complete the sentences with the past simple or the present perfect form of the verb in brackets.

1 **A:** How long _____ (Alex / work) here?
   B: She _____ (be) here for about ten years now. She _____ (started) here just after I _____ (do), I think.
3 **A:** I _____ (be) in Russia last week for work. _____ you _____ (ever / be)?
   B: Yes, I _____ (be) a couple of times.
4 **A:** _____ you _____ (email) me those photos yesterday? I _____ (just / check) and I _____ (not / receive) them.
   B: I _____ (just / send) them a few minutes ago. Sorry, but I _____ (be) really busy for the last couple of days.

3B

1 Choose the correct alternatives.
1 **A:** Reading anything interesting?
   B: Not really. I've *been reading/read* a book about the war, but I don't think I'll finish it.
2 **A:** Sorry I'm late.
   B: Hey, no problem. We *haven't waited/haven't been waiting* long.
3 **A:** How's it going?
   B: Busy. I've *studied/been studying* a lot. I've got exams all next week. In fact, I*'ve had/'ve been having* one already.
4 **A:** Hi Silvia. I *haven't seen/haven't been seeing* you for ages. What *have you done/have you been doing*?
   B: I*'ve just got/'ve just been getting* a new job actually.

2 Find three mistakes in 1–6 and correct them.

It's been a while since my last blog. This is basically because **¹I've been travelling** for the last few weeks, mainly speaking at conferences. **²I've been giving** six workshops so far. **³I've already been going** to Italy, Poland, Peru and Cyprus. **⁴I've met** lots of wonderful people. **⁵I've also learned** a lot both professionally and personally. While in the different countries, **⁶I've been visiting** such wonderful places as Machu Picchu in Peru, and the cities of Krakow in Poland and Nicosia in Cyprus.

3C

1 Correct the mistakes in each conversation There are two mistakes in each conversation.
1 **A:** Have you got car?
   B: Yes, I've got the old sports car, actually.
2 **A:** Is there the ATM near here?
   B: Yes, there's one next to a supermarket over there. Can you see it?
3 **A:** Do you listen to the music when you work?
   B: No, I usually prefer to work in the silence.
4 **A:** Is there much to see and do in your town?
   B: Yes, there's museum and an art gallery. Gallery has a great exhibition at the moment.
5 **A:** Where I live, the cars are banned in the city centre. Only bus and taxis can drive there.
   B: That's good. I think cars should be banned in all cities.

2 Complete the email with *a/an*, *the* or no article (-).

Hi Dina,
We've been here in ¹_____ US for two weeks now and we're having ²_____ great time. We're in ³_____ New York at the moment and we've been visiting the famous New York sights such as ⁴_____ Empire State Building, ⁵_____ Central Park and ⁶_____ Museum of Modern Art. Yesterday, we had afternoon tea at ⁷_____ Plaza Hotel and tomorrow we're going to take ⁸_____ boat trip on ⁹_____ Hudson River and to ¹⁰_____ Statue of Liberty. Anyway, see you soon and hope all's good.
Jim and Suzy x

Want more practice?
Go to your
Workbook or app.

GRAMMAR

4A Comparatives

type of adjective	example	comparative	example
short adjectives (one-syllable and some two-syllable adjectives)	old quiet	add -er	old**er** quiet**er**
short adjectives ending in -e	nice	add -r	nice**r**
short adjectives ending in -y	noisy	delete -y and add -ier	nois**ier**
short adjectives ending in one consonant, one vowel and one consonant	big	double the final consonant and add -er	big**ger**
long adjectives (most two syllable adjectives and all with three or more syllables)	modern beautiful	use more/less + adjective	**more** modern **less** beautiful
irregular adjectives	good bad far	no rules	better worse further

Use *than* to make a direct comparison with something else.
*France is **bigger than** Spain.*
*Today's lecture was **more interesting than** yesterday's.*
Use *(not) as … as* to say things are (not) the same.
*Today is **as nice as** yesterday.*
*The US is **not as big as** Canada.*

4B Superlatives

type of adjective	example	superlative	example
short adjectives (one-syllable and some two-syllable adjectives)	small quiet	add -est	small**est** quiet**est**
short adjectives ending in -e	nice	add -st	nice**st**
short adjectives ending in -y	busy	delete -y and add -iest	bus**iest**
short adjectives ending in one consonant, one vowel and one consonant	big	double the final consonant and add -est	big**gest**
long adjectives (most two syllable adjectives and all with three or more syllables)	interesting popular	use most/least + adjective	the **most** interesting the **least** popular
irregular adjectives	good bad far	no rules	best worst furthest

Use 'most' to make most adverbs superlative:
She eats the most healthily.

4C Defining relative clauses

Use a defining relative clause to give information about something. This is to identify, classify or to define the thing. A defining relative clause begins with a relative pronoun or relative adverb: *who, whom, which, that, whose, where, when*.
Use *who* or *that* for people. However, using *that* for a person can sometimes seem a little informal and impersonal.
*The film is about a child **who** loses his memory.*
Use *which* or *that* for things.
*This is the book **that** I was telling you about.*
*A camel is an animal **which** lives in the desert.*
Use *whose* to show possession or relationship.
*There's the man **whose** keys we found.*

Use *when* for a time and *where* for a place
*Christmas is a time **when** families get together.*
*Is this the hotel **where** we stayed last year?*
Note that the relative pronouns *who, which* and *that* can be omitted when they describe the object of the sentence. In other words, the relative pronoun can be omitted when it comes before a noun or a pronoun.
This is the book ~~that~~ I was telling you about.
Are they the people ~~who~~ we met last weekend?
The relative pronoun cannot be omitted when it comes directly before a verb.
*Are they your friends **who** live in Scotland?*

PRACTICE

4A

1 Correct the mistake in each sentence.
1. China isn't big as the US.
2. Silver is less expensive as gold.
3. People are less happier than they used to be.
4. People today live more longer than in the past.
5. Less people are going to the cinema as 20 years ago.
6. There are more millionaires in France as in Germany.
7. News spreads around the world more quick than it used to.
8. The global population is twice bigger as it was about 50 years ago.

2 Complete the sentences with words from the box.

| taller | better | hard | good | harder |
| difficult |

1. I don't work as _____ as I used to.
2. This show isn't as _____ as it used to be.
3. You can do it, you just need to work _____ .
4. I think the food here was _____ in the past.
5. Exams are definitely more _____ these days.
6. My sister is _____ than me by 5 cm.

4B

1 Complete the sentences with the superlative form of the words in the box.

big borders commonly expensive small sunny

1. Jupiter is _____ planet in the solar system. And Mercury is _____ .
2. The countries with _____ are China and Russia. They both have 14 neighbouring countries.
3. One of _____ misspelled words in English is 'accommodation'.
4. Yuma in Arizona in the US is _____ city on earth. It gets an average of 11 hours of sunlight a day.
5. Caviar is _____ food in the world. It can cost up to $50 per gram.

2 Complete the sentences with the superlative form of the words in brackets.
1. Chinese is probably _____ (popular) kind of foreign food in my country.
2. _____ (expensive) thing I have ever bought is my car.
3. _____ (good) present I have ever received is a picture.
4. _____ (far) I have travelled to buy something is about 100 kilometres.
5. I live near _____ (old) café in my country. It sells _____ (amazing) coffee and cakes.
6. The clothes I buy _____ (often) are probably socks and shirts.

4C

1 Join sentences 1–5 with sentences a–e to make new sentences using a relative clause.

1 Shrek is a fairytale about an ogre who rescues and falls in love with a princess.

1. *Shrek* is a fairytale about an ogre.
2. *The Lord of the Rings* is about the search for a ring.
3. *Planet of the Apes* is set on a future Earth.
4. *La La Land* is about an actress and musician.
5. The *Harry Potter* films are about a school.

a It is ruled by intelligent apes.
b It has magic powers and must be destroyed.
c Students go to the school to learn about magic and wizardry.
d He rescues and falls in love with a princess.
e They want to make it big in Hollywood.

2 Complete the conversations with the ideas in the box and a relative pronoun. Omit the relative pronoun if possible.

I lent it you last week.   She works as a journalist.
We stayed in it last time we were here.
~~You wanted to borrow it.~~

1. **A:** Here's the DVD.
   B: Which DVD?
   A: The DVD *you wanted to borrow* .
2. **A:** Have you got that £10?
   B: Which £10?
   A: The £10 _____ .
3. **A:** I'm going to visit my friend Simona next week.
   B: Simona?
   A: You know, my friend _____ .
4. **A:** Is that the hotel?
   B: Which hotel?
   A: The one _____ .

Want more practice?
Go to your
Workbook or app.

GRAMMAR

5A Modal verbs: possibility and deduction

A modal verb always has the same form and we don't change the ending after *he*, *she* or *it* in the present, or to form the past tense. After a modal verb, use the infinitive. To form a negative, use a modal verb + *not/n't*. To form a question, put the modal verb before the subject.

possibility

Use *may (not)*, *might (not)* and *could* to talk about what is possible or likely in the present or future.

*This **could be** Roberto's house.*
*It **might rain** tomorrow.*
*We **may not arrive** on time.*

deduction

Use *must* to make a deduction and to say we are sure something is true.

You haven't eaten all day.
*You **must be** hungry.*

The opposite of *must* is *can't*. Use *can't* to make a deduction and to say we are sure something isn't true.

*You've just had lunch. You **can't be** hungry.*

5B Zero and first conditional

zero conditional

Use the zero conditional for things that are always true or when one thing is the result of another. The zero conditional is *if/when* + present tense + present tense.

***When** the power **is** low, the red light **flashes**.*
***If** you **win** the game, you **get** three points.*

first conditional

Use the first conditional to talk about the possible future result of another action. The first conditional is *if* + present tense + *will*. *Might/could/can* can be used instead of *will*.

*If they **increase** the rent, I'**ll find** another apartment.*
*If I'**m feeling** better, I'**ll go** out this evening.*

unless

Use *unless* in conditional sentences with similar meaning to *if not*.

***Unless I phone you**, we'll be there at 6.30. = **If I don't phone you**, we'll be there at 6.30.*

5C Quantifiers

A quantifier comes before a noun and it tells us about the quantity of that noun.

*There are **several cafés** near here.*
*I haven't got **much time**.*

some, any, no

- Use *some*, *any* and *no* with both countable and uncountable nouns.
- Use *some* in affirmative sentences and *any* in negative sentences and questions. However, *some* can be used in questions which are requests or offers and when we expect the answer 'yes'.

   *There's **some** milk in the fridge.*
   *There aren't **any** chairs in the room.*
   *Have you got **any** bread?*

- *no* can be used instead of *not any*.

   There are no chairs in the room.

much, many, a lot of/lots of, plenty of, several

- Use *much* with uncountable nouns and *many* and *several* with countable nouns. Use *a lot of/lots of* and *plenty of* with both countable and uncountable nouns. *Lots of* is generally used in more informal contexts, especially in speaking.
- Use *much* and *many* in negative sentences and questions and *a lot of/lots of* and *plenty of* in positive sentences. Note the questions *How much* and *How many* and the short answer *Not much* and *Not many*.

   *I eat **lots of** fruit.*
   *I don't eat **much** fruit.*
   *I don't eat **many** vegetables.*

much and *many* can also be used in positive sentences, although this can sometimes sound quite formal.

(a) few, (a) little, a bit of

- Use *a little* and *a bit of* with uncountable nouns and use *a few* with countable nouns. *A bit of* is used in more informal contexts, especially in speaking. Use the short answers *a little*, *a bit* and *a few* and use *just* to emphasise the small number of amount.

   *There's **a bit of** pasta left. You want some more? – Just **a little**, please.*

- Use *little* and *few* (without *a*) to mean less than expected or hoped for, although this can sometimes sound quite formal. We can use *very* to emphasise the small amount.

   *Unfortunately, **few** people came to the meeting.*
   *There's been very **little** snow this year.*

too much, too many, (not) enough

- Use *too much/too many* + noun to mean more then we want or need.

   *I've eaten **too much** ice cream.*
   *There were **too many** people in the shops.*

- Use *not enough* + noun to mean less than we want or need. Use *enough* to say we have the correct number or amount.

   *There's **not enough** rice to make a risotto.*
   *More coffee? – No, I've had **enough**, thanks.*

PRACTICE

5A

1 Correct the mistake in each conversation.
1. **A:** There's a lot of traffic. We can be a little late.
   B: OK, see you later
2. **A:** Have you found your keys?
   B: Not yet. But they must to be somewhere here.
3. **A:** Sofia isn't here? I wonder why.
   B: Well, it's possible she mustn't know about the meeting.
4. **A:** I don't might be able to go to the party.
   B: Oh, that's a shame. It'll be fun!
5. **A:** Is this Alice's phone?
   B: I'm not sure, but it must be.
6. **A:** He isn't answering his phone.
   B: Well, it's still before nine. He could not be in the office yet.

2 Rewrite the sentences using *might*, *may*, *could*, *must* or *can't*, so that they mean the same.
1. It's possible we'll be a few minutes late.
   We _might be a few minutes late_ .
2. Perhaps this is David's house, but I'm not sure.
   This _____ , but I'm not sure.
3. I'm totally sure the café is near here.
   The _____ .
4. It's possible Diana won't come to the meeting.
   Diana _____ .
5. Take an umbrella. Maybe it'll rain later.
   Take an umbrella. It _____ .
6. I'm sure this isn't her coat. It's too small.
   This _____ . It's too small.
7. The bill is £25. I'm sure there's a mistake.
   The bill is £25. There _____ .

5B

1 Choose the correct alternatives.
1. If it's nice at the weekend, I *might/can/do* go to the beach.
2. If I need to know something immediately, I *checking/check/checked* online.
3. If we don't do our homework, the teacher *maybe/will/can* get angry.
4. If ever I have nothing to do, I usually *could watch/might watch/watch* TV.
5. I'll be so angry if he *'s/'ll be* late again.
6. When I *'m/will be* stressed, I take a walk in the park.

2 Complete the conversations with the correct form of the verbs in brackets.
1. **A:** If you _____ (have) a free moment, _____ (you / email) me those photos?
   B: Sure. I'll do it later.
2. **A:** Would you say food shopping _____ (be) generally more expensive if you _____ (live) on your own?
   B: Yes, I think so.
3. **A:** I _____ (be) so pleased if I _____ (pass) my driving test.
   B: Yes, good luck.
4. **A:** I _____ (help) you with the decorating at the weekend if you _____ (like).
   B: Great, thanks. And if you _____ (do), I _____ (buy) us dinner in the evening.

5C

1 Choose the correct alternatives.
1. **A:** Would you like *some/a few* more ice cream?
   B: Yes, please. But not *many/much*. Just *little/a little*.
2. **A:** We've got *any/no* milk.
   B: OK, I'll go to the shop and get *some/any*. Do we need *any/a few bread* while I'm there?
3. **A:** What kind of music do you listen to?
   B: All kinds. But I'm listening to *much/a lot of* jazz at the moment. My brother's recently bought *a little/a few* old records and I've been listening to those.
4. **A:** How *much/many* countries have you been to?
   B: Just *few/a few*. Five or six, I think.

2 Complete the sentences with an appropriate quantifier.
1. I eat _____ fast food. I should eat less.
2. I don't eat _____ fruit. I should eat more.
3. I listen to _____ rock music. I love it.
4. I don't listen to _____ pop music. Most of it is boring.
5. I read _____ science fiction books. They're my favourite kind of book.
6. I don't own _____ pairs of shoes. Just two or three.
7. I've visited _____ countries. Eight or nine, I think.
8. I haven't visited _____ countries. Just two.

Want more practice?
Go to your Workbook or app.

GRAMMAR

6A Second conditional

Use the second conditional for things that are imaginary in the present or future and for future actions and situations that are unlikely, but possible.
If I had more free time, **I'd read** more books.
The second conditional is formed with *if* + past tense + *would*. In informal contexts, especially in speaking, *would* is usually contracted to *'d*.
If I lived nearer to work, **I'd go** there by bike.
Other modal verbs such as *could* and *might* can be used instead of *would*. The past continuous can be used in the *if*-clause.
If I had more money, **I could get** a new phone.
If it **wasn't raining**, we **could go** for a walk.
would is not usually used in the *if*-clause.
If I ~~would~~ had more money, I could get a new phone.

After *I/he/she/it*, use either *was* or *were*. Some people may think that *were* is more correct, but it usually depends on the person who is speaking.
If I **was/were** richer, I'd get a bigger apartment.
If she **was/were** here, I'd talk to her.
If I were you, I'd … is a useful phrase for giving advice. You may hear *If I was you, I'd …*, but this is considered incorrect by many people.
If I were you, I'd get a new computer.
I'd talk to your boss **if I were you**.
The *if*-clause can come first or second in the sentence. When the *if*-clause comes first, it is followed by a comma. When the *if*-clause is at the end, there is no comma.
If I had a signal, I'd call her.
I'd call her if I had a signal.

6B Structures for giving advice

Use *should* to give and ask for advice. Use it to say what you think is the correct or best thing to do.
You **should use** your car less and walk more.
You **shouldn't waste** so much food.
What **should** I **do** about my job?
Use *ought to* as an alternative to *should*, but not in questions.
You **ought to use** your car less and walk more.
You **ought to be** more careful.
Use *really* to make the advice stronger.
You **really should complain** to the hotel.
You **really ought to do** more exercise.

Use *If I were you, I'd …* to give advice.
If I were you, I'd get a new computer.
I'd leave now **if I were you**.
Use *could* to make suggestions and to give advice. Use it to suggest options and possible solutions rather than to say what is the best thing to do. *could always* is also used.
You **could stay** with us for a few days.
She **could always look** for a new job.
Use *had better* and *had better not* to give strong advice or to give a warning. Use *had better* for particular situations rather than to give advice in general. In informal contexts, especially in speaking, *had* is usually contracted to *'d*.
You**'d better** apologise to him.

6C Question tags

Use a question tag after a statement.
It's a nice day, **isn't it**?
There's an ATM on Green Road, **isn't there**?
Form a question tag with an auxiliary verb (*be, do, have, can*, etc.) + pronoun. Use the same subject/pronoun and the same auxiliary verb as in the statement. Use *do* for the present and past simple.
You haven't been to Brazil, **have you**?
Jane works at the university, **doesn't she**?
You used to live in the UK, **didn't you**?
Peter can drive, **can't he**?
Use a negative question tag after a positive statement.
He**'s** a teacher, **isn't** he?
Anna **can** speak German, **can't** she?
They **arrived** late, **didn't** they?
Use a positive question tag after a negative statement.
You **haven't** been to Russia, **have** you?
Andrew **isn't** here yet, **is** he?

Note the following question tag forms:
- After *I'm …*, use *aren't I*?
I'm going to get the tickets, **aren't I?**
- After *Let's …*, use *shall we*?
Let's go for lunch, **shall we**?

Use question tags to check a piece of information and/or to prompt the listener to respond.
When we are almost sure something is true and we expect the listener to agree with us, our voice goes down at the end.
When we are not sure about something and we ask a real question, there is a very short pause between the statement and the question tag and our voice goes up at the end.

PRACTICE

6A

1 Correct the mistake in each sentence. Then write your own sentences using the *if*-clauses.
1. If I would have more time, I'd cook a lot more.
2. If I was younger, I'll learn to snowboard.
3. If we don't have social media, we'd go out a lot more.
4. I'd prefer living here if it wouldn't rain so much.
5. If I am you, I'd eat less junk food.
6. I'd get a new phone if I have more money.

2 Rewrite the sentences using *If ..., would/ could ...* so that they mean the same.
1. I'm so busy and I don't have time to relax.
   If I wasn't so busy, I'd have time to relax.
2. We can't go for a walk because it's raining.
3. I haven't got a signal on my phone, so I can't call them.
4. She wants to get a new laptop, but she can't afford it.
5. I have to leave but I want to stay here longer.
6. I can't find an ATM and I want to get some money out.

6B

1 Write responses to the advice. Use the ideas in the box and the word in brackets to help you.

> buy a new one   ~~get something to eat~~   go to the Coliseum   look for a new one   set off now

1. **A:** I'm hungry. (should)
   B: ___You should get something to eat___ , then.
2. **A:** I'm fed up with my job. (could)
   B: Well, _____ .
3. **A:** My computer keeps crashing. (ought to)
   B: It sounds to me like _____ .
4. **A:** We're going to Rome next month. (should)
   B: Nice! _____ .
5. **A:** I need to be at the station in 30 minutes. (better)
   B: 30 minutes? _____ .

2 Complete the responses to the forum questions with the words in the box. Then, write your own responses to the questions.

> could   had   should   were

A
Dina99: Some classmates have offered to give me money so they can copy my homework. What should I do?
Reply: You really [1]_____ tell the teacher. If you let them copy, you are as bad as they are. And you [2]_____ better tell your classmates the same thing.

B
StevieH: We can't decide where to go for a long weekend.
Reply: You [3]_____ go to Moscow. It's perfect for a long weekend. There are lots of things to see and do.
Reply: If I [4]_____ you, I'd go to Istanbul. It's fascinating with great food and great weather at this time of year.

6C

1 Complete the conversations with a question tag.
1. **A:** Fernando's from Colombia, _____ ?
   B: Yes, he is. Bogotá, I think.
2. **A:** Do you know anyone who lives in Paris?
   B: Yeah, Sophie lives there, _____ ?
3. **A:** You've been to Australia, _____ ?
   B: Yes, a couple of years ago.
4. **A:** Let's go for lunch, _____ ?
   B: Good idea. I'm hungry.
5. **A:** Which university did Lucy go to?
   B: She went to Sheffield, _____ ?

2 Write sentences with question tags for each situation.
1. You're almost sure Carla is from Argentina.
   Carla's from Argentina, isn't she?
2. You're almost sure the meeting is at 3.30.
3. You're almost sure your friend will agree that the lesson was interesting.
4. You think John plays the guitar, but you're not sure.
5. You're almost sure your friends will agree that the film was not very good.

Want more practice?
Go to your
Workbook or app.

GRAMMAR

7A Modal verbs: ability

can/can't
Use *can* and *can't* to talk about general abilities.
*I **can speak** Swedish.*
***Can** you **play** a musical instrument?*
Also use *can* and *can't* to talk about ability at a particular time.
*I **can't open** the window.*
*I think I **can fix** the problem.*

could/couldn't
Use *could* and *couldn't* to talk about general abilities in the past.
*I **could swim** when I was very young.*
*I **couldn't drive** until I was in my twenties.*
Use *couldn't* to talk about ability at a particular time in the past. However, do not use *could* to talk about ability at a particular time in the past (instead, use *was/were able to*).
*I **couldn't open** the window.*

be able to
Use *be able to* as an alternative to *can/can't/could/couldn't*. This is usually in more formal contexts.
*Some children **are able to speak** at a very early age.*
*I **wasn't able to open** the window.*
Use *was/were able to* instead of *could* to talk about ability at a particular time in the past.
*I **was able to fix** the problem after several hours.*
Use *be able to* with other tenses and structures (e.g. with *will*, in a perfect tense and when we need the infinitive or the *-ing* form).
*I**'ll be able to** help you later.*
*I've never **been able to** learn languages easily.*
*I'd love **to be able to** play the piano.*
*Do you **need to be able to** speak a foreign language for your job?*
*Do you enjoy **being able to** speak six languages?*

7B Past perfect

To form past perfect, use *had* + past participle. Use the contracted form *'d* in informal contexts, especially in speaking.
*I**'d** finished.*
*We**'d** met a few times.*
Form a question by changing the order of had and the subject:
***Had** you **been** there before?*
Use the past perfect to show that one event happened before another event or before a specific time in the past. Use the past perfect for the action or situation that happened first. Use the past simple for the action or situation that happened second.
*The meeting **had finished** when James arrived.*
*I found some keys that someone **had dropped**.*

Actions or situations can be connected with sequence words and expressions such as *when, before, after, by the time, by this time*.
*We**'d lived** in the flat for weeks **before** we **met** the neighbours.*
*William **had left** the party **by the time** we **arrived**.*
Use the past perfect with *already* and *just*. *Already* emphasises the action is completed and *just* tells us that it was just a short time before. Also use the past perfect with *always*.
*The meeting had **already** finished when James arrived.*
*I had **always** wanted to be a teacher.*
Note that in a sequence, the second, third, etc. *had* is sometimes not used.
*After she **had visited** South America and (had) **gone** to Hawaii, she then went to ...*

7C Expressing purpose

Expressing purpose, or saying why we do something, can be done in a number of ways:

- Use *to* + infinitive.
  *I'm going to the shop **to get** some milk.*
  *Save some money **to get** a taxi.*
  *Why do you want to speak to Jack? – **To tell** him about the meeting.*

- Use *in order to* as a more formal alternative to *to* + infinitive.
  *We recommend that you book early **in order to** get the best seats.*

- Use *so* or *so that* + clause (subject + verb).
  *We set off early **so that** we would miss the rush-hour traffic.*
  *Download the map **so** you don't get lost.*

- Use *so* to express result or consequence. *so that* is not used in this way.
  *I was tired, **so** I went to bed.*

- Use *for* + *-ing* to express the purpose or function of something. The *to* infinitive can be used in a similar way.
  *This cloth's **for cleaning** the floor.*
  *What's this for? – It's **to make** holes in things.*

PRACTICE

7A

1 Complete the sentences with *can*, *can't*, *could* or *couldn't* and the verbs in the box.

play	ski	speak	swim

1 I _____ English quite well. I've been learning it for a few years.
2 **A:** _____ you _____ a musical instrument?
   B: Yes, the guitar, but I _____ it very well.
3 I _____ until I was a teenager. As a child I used to be quite afraid of water, actually.
4 I _____ when I was three. We have a lot of snow and hills and most people here learn almost as soon as they learn to walk.

2 Complete the conversations with *can*, *can't*, *could*, *couldn't* or a form of *be able to*.

1 I forgot my house key, so I _____ get in the house.
2 **A:** Did you fix your computer?
   B: Yes, it took me a long time, but I _____ fix it in the end.
3 **A:** _____ you surf?
   B: Yes, I _____ surf since I was about five.
4 **A:** How was the exam?
   B: Not bad, but I _____ answer all the questions.
5 **A:** _____ you drive?
   B: No, I _____ . But I'm going to start lessons soon. So, hopefully I _____ drive by the summer.

7B

1 Complete the conversations with the words in the box. Use one verb in the past simple and one in the past perfect.

already start/arrive	book/look
not join/already eat	work/become

1 **A:** Where did you two meet?
   B: At work. But we _____ together for years before we _____ friends.
2 **A:** Did you get to the meeting in time?
   B: No, they _____ by the time I _____ .
3 **A:** _____ you _____ tickets for the concert?
   B: Yes, after I _____ on about 20 websites.
4 **A:** Why _____ you _____ us for lunch earlier?
   B: I _____ . I wasn't hungry

2 Complete the text with the correct form of the verbs in brackets.

The best year of my life

I ¹_____ (start) university when I was 20, by which time I ²_____ (already / spend) a year travelling. I ³_____ (think) it would be good to have a gap year and get away from studying for a while and it was also a chance to go travelling. I ⁴_____ (always / want) to go to the US, so I ⁵_____ (decide) to work for six months and then spend a few months in the US. I ⁶_____ (previously / work) part-time in a shop when I was at school, so I ⁷_____ (get) a full-time job there and ⁸_____ (start) to earn the money for my trip. After I ⁹_____ (save up) enough money, I bought my ticket and finally set off.

7C

1 Write responses to the questions using *to* plus on of the verbs in the box.

celebrate	change	get	tell	visit

1 **A:** Why are you going to Manchester?
   B: _____ my grandparents.
2 **A:** Why did Oksana want to see you?
   B: _____ me about the meeting on Friday.
3 **A:** Where are you going?
   B: _____ some milk.
4 **A:** What's the party for next weekend?
   B: _____ the end of exams.
5 **A:** Why do you need the password?
   B: _____ the profile settings.

2 Rewrite the sentence using the words in brackets so that they mean the same.

1 We arrived early to get good seats. (so)
   _____
2 This cloth is to clean the computer screen. (for)
   _____
3 We took the sat nav in order not to get lost. (so)
   _____
4 Tick the box so that you receive our special offers. (order)
   _____
5 Can I borrow your phone so I can call my friend? (to)
   _____
6 I use this drive to save all my work. (for)
   _____

Want more practice?
Go to your
Workbook or app.

129

GRAMMAR

8A Modal verbs: obligation and necessity

must and mustn't
Use *must* to express what is necessary, required or what we are obliged to do. Use *mustn't* or *must not* to express what we are obliged not to do.
*You **must wear** a seat belt at all times.*
*We **mustn't be** late.*

have to and have got to
Have to has a similar meaning to *must* and either can usually be used.
*You **have to wear** a seat belt at all times.*
***Do** we **have to** wear a tie?*
In more informal contexts, use *have got to*.
*We**'ve got to win** this game.*
*I**'ve got to work** late.*

had to
Had to is the past tense of both *must* and *have to/have got to*.
*We **had to** leave because they were closing.*

don't have to
Use *don't have to* (past tense: *didn't have to*) to say that something is not necessary, but we can do it if we want to.
*We **don't have to wear** a suit at work.*
*I **didn't have to go** into the office today.*

need
Use *need* (past tense: *needed*) to express what is necessary or required. Use *need to* + infinitive and *need* + noun.
*We **need to leave** in a few minutes.*
*We **needed to go** shopping.*
Use *don't need* or *didn't need* to say it is not necessary to do something, but often we can do it if we want to.
*We **don't need to leave** just yet.*
*We **didn't need to book** tickets in advance.*

be (not) allowed to
Use *be not allowed to* to express permission or prohibition.
*We**'re not allowed to** use our phones in class.*

8B Passives: present and past

Form the passive by using the appropriate tense of *be* + past participle.
Note the form of the passive in these different tenses:
- present simple:
  *The rooms **are cleaned** every day.*
- present continuous:
  *My computer **is being repaired** at the moment.*
  *The offices **are being decorated** this week.*
- past simple:
  *We **were invited** to the party.*
- past continuous:
  *The road **was being repaired** last week.*

Use the passive to focus on the action and not on who or what does the action ('the agent'). This is usually because:
- the agent is unknown.
  My bike was stolen.
- the agent is obvious.
  Billions of emails are sent every day.
- the agent is not important.
  The museum was opened in 1970.
- we don't want to name the agent.
  I was asked to apologise.

Use the passive with *by* + agent when we want to focus on the agent.
*The research **was carried out by** a team from Oxford.*

8C Non-defining relative clauses

The non-defining relative clause comes immediately after the person, thing or place. Always separate a non-defining relative clause from the main clause with a comma.
Use *which* for things, *who* for people and *whose* for possession.
*He was born in Maltby, **which** is a small town near Sheffield.*
*It's a wonderful college, **whose** buildings are some of the oldest university buildings in the world.*
Use *where* for places and *when* for times.
*The hotel, **where** many famous people have stayed, is in the heart of the city.*
*The best time to visit Dubai is November to March, **when** it isn't so hot.*

Don't use *that* in a non-defining relative clause.
Don't omit the relative pronoun or relative adverb in a non-defining relative clause.
Use a non-defining relative clause to give extra information about a person, thing or place.
*The mountain, **which is over 4000 metres high**, is climbed by thousands of people every year.*
Use a non-defining relative clause to comment on the whole of the previous clause. This is common in speaking.
*The park was closed to the public, **which was a real shame**.*

PRACTICE

8A

1 Correct the mistake in each sentence.
1. I need tidy my desk.
2. Yesterday, I must work late.
3. You must to work hard at school.
4. You don't must send private emails at work.
5. I need to a new computer at work.
6. We haven't to wear a suit at work, but we must dress smartly.
7. Do you must work today?
8. I haven't to wear a suit in the office, but I think it looks nice.

2 Look at the first sentence. Then choose the correct sentence to follow it.
1. You don't have to wear a uniform.
   a You can wear what you want.
   b It's important to look smart.
2. I mustn't forget to take my food home.
   a I'll leave it here, I think.
   b I forgot yesterday and I had nothing for dinner.
3. You're allowed to arrive late ...
   a so please be on time!
   b so don't worry if the traffic is heavy.
4. Have you got to go?
   a I need to go, too.
   b I had to go, too.

8B

1 Complete the sentences with the nouns and the verbs in the boxes. Use the correct passive form of the verbs.

> ~~The White House~~   Facebook   The Olympics
> The novel *1984*   X-rays   The Mini

> ~~build~~   discover   hold   launch   make
> publish

1. The *White House was built in* the 1790s.
2. _____ was _____ in 2004.
3. _____ were _____ in 1895.
4. _____ was _____ in 1949.
5. _____ are _____ every four years.
6. _____ is _____ in Oxford in the UK.

2 Complete the messages with the correct passive form of the verb in brackets. Add *by* where it is needed.
1. Sorry I haven't sent you those photos, but my computer _____ (repair) at the moment. I'll hopefully get it back in a couple of days.
2. Fifty people _____ (arrest) during an anti-government protest in New York yesterday.
3. Did you hear? Val's apartment _____ (break into) yesterday. They stole her laptop and television.
4. Is Christmas a big thing in your country? It _____ (not / celebrate) here, apart from by a few people.

8C

1 Complete the sentences with the correct relative pronoun and the phrases in the box.

> is an industrial city   is full of history   is the capital city of Peru   the weather starts to get warmer
> was the first European to cross   you have great views

1. My favourite city is Rome, _____ and interesting things to see and do.
2. I was born in Sheffield, _____ in the north of England.
3. I know a great place near here called Brill Hill, _____ of the countryside.
4. I used to work in Lima, _____ .
5. I recently read about the Portuguese explorer Magellan, _____ the Pacific Ocean.
6. My favourite time of year is spring, _____ and the trees grow leaves.

2 Combine the sentences using a non-defining relative clause.
1. The Great Barrier Reef is the world's largest living thing.
   It stretches for 2,300 kilometres off the coast of Australia.
   The Great Barrier Reef, which stretches for 2,300 kilometres off the coast of Australia, is the world's largest living thing.
2. The best time to go trekking in Nepal is September to November.
   Temperatures are at their best at this time.
3. Angel Falls in Venezuela is named after the US pilot Jimmie Angel.
   He was the first person to fly over the waterfall in 1933.
4. Istanbul is the biggest city of Turkey.
   Asia meets Europe here.

Want more practice?
Go to your
Workbook or app.

GRAMMAR

9A The passive all tenses

We can use the passive in a range of tenses.

Present and past tenses
Use *be* + past participle.
*Millions of items **are bought** online every day.*
*My laptop **is being repaired** at the moment.*
*Google **was started** in 1998.*
*The computers at work **were being fixed**.*

Perfect tenses
Use the appropriate perfect tense of *be* (*has been, have been, had been*) + past participle.
*The website **has been updated**.*
*The house **had been broken into**.*

will and other modal verbs
Use *will*/modal verb + *be* + past participle.
*The programme **will be repeated** on Sunday.*
*Many films **can be downloaded** for free.*
*The flight **might be delayed** by an hour or so.*
Form the passive with *be going to, have to, need to* in the same way.
*The website **is going to be launched** next month.*
See 8B Grammar bank for more detail on how to form the passive and why we use it.

9B Third conditional

Use the third conditional to talk about imaginary results of imaginary actions in the past. It is often used to express regret or a complaint. Form the third conditional with *if* + past perfect + *would/ wouldn't have* + past participle.
***If** we **had left** earlier, we **wouldn't have been** late.*
*I **would have helped** you if you **had asked** me.*
Other modal verbs such as *could* (for ability or possibility) and *might* (for possibility) can be used instead of *would*.
*I **could've** helped you if you'd asked me.*
*If he'd worked harder, he **might** not have failed his exam.*

The *if*-clause can come first or second in the sentence. When the *if*-clause comes first, it is followed by a comma. When the *if*-clause is at the end, there is no comma.
*If I'd known**,** I'd have told you.*
I'd have told you if I'd known.

9C Short responses with *so, neither, too/either*

Short responses can be used to agree or disagree in a number of ways.

so do I, neither do I
Use *so* + auxiliary verb + subject to agree with a positive statement. Use the same auxiliary verb as in the statement. Use the auxiliary verb *do* if the statement is in the present or past simple.
*I **love** modern art. - **So do I**.*
*I **can** speak French. - **So can I**.*
Use *neither* + auxiliary verb + subject to agree with a negative statement.
*I **don't like** modern art. - **Neither do I**.*
*My parents **can't** speak any foreign languages. - **Neither can mine**.*

me too, me neither
Use *me too* to agree with a positive statement and *me neither* to agree with a negative statement.
*I love modern art. - **Me too**.*
*I didn't enjoy the exhibition. - **Me neither**.*

I do too, I don't either, etc.
Use subject + auxiliary verb + *too /either* to agree with a statement. Use the same auxiliary verb as in the statement. Use *too* with a positive statement and *either* with a negative one.
*I **love** modern art. - **I do too**.*
*I **haven't** been to the UK. - **I haven't either**.*

I do, I don't, etc.
Use subject + auxiliary verb to disagree with a statement.
*I **love** modern art. - **I don't**.*
*I'm going to the party. - **I'm not**.*
*I **haven't** seen the exhibition. - **I have**.*
*I **can't** speak French. - **I can**.*

PRACTICE

9A

1 Complete the signs and notices with the passive form of the verbs in the box.

> can/purchase   must/accompany
> must/report   need/submit   will/destroy
> will/refuse

1 Bags left unattended _____ .
2 Anyone dressed in jeans or trainers _____ entry to the club.
3 Any accidents _____ to the manager.
4 All children _____ by an adult.
5 Tickets _____ in advance on our website.
6 End-of-term essays _____ by 15th December.

2 Complete the extracts with correct form of the verbs in brackets.

Long before there was money, cattle and spices ¹_____ (use) as currency. In fact, cattle are the world's oldest 'currency'. Today, animals, food and other items ²_____ (replace) by coins and bank notes. Coins first appeared over 2,000 years ago and the first bank note ³_____ (introduce) in the late 1300s in China.
Today, in some shops and cafés around the world, items ⁴_____ (can / purchase) in exchange for a simple tweet using the hashtag of the shop or café.
About $46 billion ⁵_____ (spend) every day in the US. This means that over $200 million ⁶_____ (may / spend) while you are doing this grammar exercise.

9B

1 Correct the mistake in each sentence.

1 If I would have known about the meeting, I would've told you about it.
2 He wouldn't have missed the bus if he got up earlier this morning.
3 If she'd worked harder, she might passed the exam.
4 If it didn't rain so much earlier today, we could've gone for a walk.
5 If I wouldn't already see the film, I'd have come to the cinema with you last night.
6 We'd have arrived in time if we set off a bit earlier before the rush hour.

2 Complete the sentences with the third conditional.

1 I didn't buy it because I didn't like it. But if _____ , _____ it.
2 I didn't go to the party because I didn't know about it. But _____ if _____ it, though.
3 We didn't like the restaurant, so we never went there again. But I'm sure that if _____ , _____ again.
4 My friend had a spare ticket, so I was able to go to the concert. But I _____ _____ a spare ticket.
5 Tom didn't get into university because he failed the entrance exam. But I think that if _____ , _____ in.

9C

1 Write two short responses to A's sentences, one to agree and one to disagree. Write a different response each time.

1 **A:** I love going to galleries.
   B: _____ . I love them.
   C: _____ . They're boring.
2 **A:** I've never been to Paris.
   B: _____ . I went there two years ago.
   C: _____ . But I'd love to one day.
3 **A:** I can't play a musical instrument.
   B: _____ . I'm just not at all musical.
   C: _____ . I play the guitar and a bit of drums.
4 **A:** I'd love to go to Australia.
   B: _____ . I hate long flights.
   C: _____ . I've always wanted to go there.

2 Complete the short responses with the phrases in the box.

> I can't either   I have   Neither am I
> Me too.   So did I.

1 I can't sing very well.
   _____ . In fact, I've got a terrible voice.
2 I'm not very artistic.
   _____ . I can't draw or paint.
3 I haven't been to the US.
   _____ . A couple of times.
4 I love rock music.
   _____ . As long as it's not too loud.
5 I went to the beach yesterday.
   _____ . It was busy, wasn't it?

Want more practice?
Go to your Workbook or app.

GRAMMAR

10A Reported statements

Direct speech uses the exact words that are spoken and these words are put between speech marks.
Jane said, 'I really enjoyed this book.'
Reported (or indirect) speech is when the words are reported, i.e. we don't use exactly the same words and we don't use speech marks.
Jane said that she had really enjoyed that book.
Use *say* or *tell* to report what someone says. Use an object (e.g. *me, us*) after *tell*.
*She **said** that she loved teaching.*
*She **told me** that she really enjoyed his job.*
That can sometimes be omitted.
She said she loved teaching.
When we report with *said* and *told*, the tense of the verb changes, e.g. present tense → past tense, past tense and present perfect → past perfect, *will* → *would*, *can* → *could* etc.
'I'm an engineer.' → *She said she **was** an engineer.*
*'I **play** the piano.'* → *He said he **played** the piano.*
'I'm feeling tired.' → *She said she **was feeling** tired.*
*'I **saw** Jim earlier.'* → *He told me he**'d seen** Jim earlier.*
'He's left the office.' → *She said he**'d left** the office.*
'We'll be there at 6.30.' → *I told them we**'d be** there at 6.30.*

Note that sometimes the tense doesn't change. This is usually to show or emphasise that something is still true, relevant or important.
'I'm in the café.' → *He said he's in the café.*
'We'll be about an hour late.' → *She said they'll be about an hour late.*

The tense also isn't changed with the present tense of *say* and *tell*.
*'Alex **plays** the drums.'* → *Oliver **says** Alex **plays** the drums.*
'I'll meet you in 20 minutes.' → *She **says** she**'ll meet** us in 20 minutes.*

In reported statements, change the pronouns, e.g.
I → *he, we* → *they, me* → *her, you* → *me*, etc.
*'I saw **you** yesterday.'* → *He said **he**'d seen **me** yesterday.*

10B Verb patterns

Different reporting verbs are followed by different verb patterns. Note that some verbs can be followed by more than one pattern.

Verb + -ing
Some common verbs that are followed by -ing are: *admit, consider, deny, discuss, look forward to, recommend, suggest*.
*He **denied breaking** the window.*
*She **admitted taking** the money.*

Verb + to infinitive
Some common verbs that are followed by the *to* infinitive are: *agree, arrange, ask, decide, demand, expect, hope, offer, pretend, promise, refuse, remember, threaten, want*.
*They are **hoping to arrive** at about 8.30.*
*She **promised to be** on time.*

Verb + object + to infinitive
Some common verbs that are followed by object + *to* infinitive include: *advise, allow, ask, convince, encourage, invite, persuade, remind, tell, want, warn*.
*She **encouraged me to say** something.*
*I **warned him not to do** it.*

Negative forms
Note that to make a *to* infinitive or -ing negative, we put *not* in front of it.
*I promise **not to be** late.*
*He suggested **not going** by bus.*

Verb + that + subject + infinitive
Some common verbs that are followed by *that* + subject + infinitive include: *recommend, request, suggest*.
*Simon **suggests that we wait** a few minutes.*

10C Reported questions

For reported questions, requests and orders, use the same tense, pronoun and time and place rules as in reported statements. See 10B above.

reporting questions
Use *asked* + object (e.g. *me, us*) or *wanted/ wants to know*.
*She **asked me** where I lived.*
*He **wanted to know** how much it cost.*
The word order is different from in a direct question. The word order is the same as in a statement:
*'Where **do you live**?'* – *She asked me where **I lived**.*
*'What **are you doing**?'* – *He wanted to know what **I was doing**.*

For *yes/no questions* that don't have a question word, use *if*.
'Are you going to the meeting?' – *Yuki asked me **if** I was going to the meeting.*

reporting requests, imperatives and orders
To report requests, use *ask* or *want* + object + *to* infinitive.
'Can you help me?' – *He asked me **to help** him.*
'Could you give me a lift?' – *Lana wants me **to give** her a lift.*
To report imperatives, commands and orders, use *ask* or *tell* + object + *to* infinitive.
'Wait a moment, please.' – *He asked us **to wait** a moment.*

PRACTICE

10A

1 Read what Dasha says about her job and then complete the reported version.

'I'm a teacher and I work in a language school in Cambridge. I've been a teacher for over ten years and I really love it. What I like most about my job is meeting people from different countries. I'm also really interested in languages and I speak French and Spanish.

> She said she ¹_____ a teacher and that she ²_____ in a language school in Cambridge. She ³_____ us that she ⁴_____ been a teacher for over ten years and that she really ⁵_____ it. She then said that what she ⁶_____ most about ⁷_____ job ⁸_____ meeting people from different countries. She said she ⁹_____ really interested in languages and that she ¹⁰_____ French and Spanish.

2 Report the statements.
1. 'I'm a student.'
   He said he *was a student*
2. 'I don't enjoy school.'
   She told us _____ .
3. 'I hope to go to university.'
   Diana said _____ .
4. 'I've never liked maths.'
   He said _____ .
5. 'I'm really enjoying the course.'
   Tom told me _____ .
6. 'Everything will be OK.'
   She said _____ .

10B

1 Correct the mistakes in each sentence.
1. Sam suggested to go to the cinema this evening.
2. Olivia refused telling me what happened.
3. He's looking not forward to start his new job.
4. Harry promised not telling anyone about the party.
5. Erica persuaded me go to the concert with her.
6. She suggested that we to wait here for a few minutes.
7. Paula's considering to quit her job.
8. They've offered me to help with my homework.

2 Report the statements.
1. 'I didn't break the mirror.'
   He denies _____ .
2. 'Let's go for lunch.'
   Emily suggested _____ .
3. 'OK, it was me. I made the mess.'
   Alex admitted _____ .
4. 'I'll cook dinner if you like.'
   Danny offered _____ .
5. 'You really should talk to him.'
   She encouraged _____ .
6. 'Can you help me?'
   He wanted _____ .

10C

1 Choose the correct alternative to complete the sentences.
1. Why do you want to work in a clothes shop?
   He asked me why *I did want/ wanted* to work in a clothes shop.
2. Have you worked in a shop before?
   She asked *if I had/ had I* worked in a shop before.
3. How many days can you work per week?
   He wanted *to know/ that I tell* how many days I could work per week.
4. Is this your first interview?
   She asked if this *had been/ was* my first interview.
5. What did you before?
   He wanted to know what *did I do/ I did* before.

2 Report the requests, imperatives and orders.
1. 'Can you help me?'
   He asked _____ .
2. 'Please, take a seat?'
   She asked _____ .
3. 'Can you give me a lift?'
   Jack wants _____ .
4. 'Don't sit there.'
   Irina told _____ .
5. 'I'd like you to go to the conference?'
   My boss wants _____ .
6. 'Can you email me the report?'
   He asked _____ .

Want more practice? Go to your Workbook or app.

Vocabulary bank

1A Jobs and qualifications

1 a Complete the sentences with the words in the box.

> architecture   economics   engineering   journalism
> law   medicine   politics   science

1 I studied _____ at university. I've always loved writing so it's the perfect career for me.
2 I was really bad at _____ at school, except biology. I hated physics and chemistry.
3 I have a friend who did _____ at university – he works in banking now.
4 My sister's studying _____ . She's going to Rome next month to study the design of all the amazing buildings there. I'm so jealous!
5 I'd like to do _____ at uni. I want to work in healthcare one day – I love helping people.
6 Why are you studying _____ ? Do you want to work in the government one day?
7 My brother teaches _____ at university. He's always been good at maths and problem solving. He 's actually worked on the construction of a number of big bridges!
8 I don't want to be a lawyer or work in the legal profession, but it would be interesting to study _____ .

b Complete the table with a job for each subject.

subject	job
science	
journalism	
medicine	doctor
engineering	
economics	
architecture	
politics	politician

2 Complete the jobs by adding -er, -ian or -ist.
1 dent___
2 electric___
3 paint___
4 driv___
5 art___
6 reception___
7 farm___
8 music___

1B Personal characteristics

1 a Complete the sentences with the words in the box.

> bossy   disorganised   easy-going   kind
> moody   negative   sociable   stubborn

1 A _____ person is always telling people what to do.
2 A _____ person does nice things for other people.
3 A _____ person likes spending time with other people.
4 A _____ person doesn't change their mind easily.
5 A _____ person changes how they're feeling very quickly.
6 A _____ person never knows what they're doing next.
7 A _____ person often thinks things will be bad.
8 An _____ person is usually relaxed and doesn't worry too much.

b Match words 1–5 with their opposites a–e.

1 flexible   a easy-going
2 organised   b disorganised
3 unsociable   c stubborn
4 positive   d negative
5 strict   e sociable

2 a Which characteristics are good for the jobs below? Use the adjectives in Exercise 1 to help you.
1 a nurse
2 an economist
3 a manager
4 a journalist
5 a teacher

b Work in pairs and discuss your answers in Exercise 2a.

To be a nurse you need to be kind, because you look after patients all day.

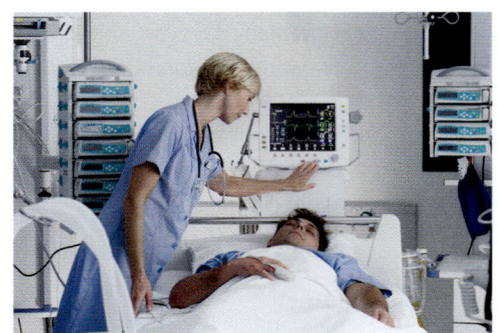

2B The senses

1 a Complete the table with the verbs in the box.

| feel | hold | listen to | look at | see | watch |

sense	verb
sight	_____ / _____ / _____
sound	hear / _____
touch	touch _____ / _____
smell	smell
taste	taste

b Look at the sentences. What are the differences in meaning between the words in bold?
1. a I **heard** a car outside.
   b I relaxed for a while and **listened** to some music.
2. a I **saw** Fiona in the street earlier.
   b I sat in the park and **watched** the people have their lunch.
3. a I **watched** TV till about 1 a.m.
   b I **looked** at myself in the mirror.

c Choose the correct alternatives.
1. This doesn't *taste/sound* very good. How long did you cook it for?
2. I can't *taste/hold* these bags much longer – they are very heavy!
3. *Look at/Watch* that woman over there – she's wearing the same dress as you!
4. Can we *hear/listen to* something else? I'm not a fan of rock music.
5. My jacket *touches/feels* wet. Did you leave it out in the rain again?
6. Did you *see/watch* Jim yesterday? He wanted to ask you something.
7. These roses *taste/smell* amazing! Where did you buy them?
8. Please don't *touch/feel* the computer screen. I've just cleaned it.
9. A: Why didn't you come out last night?
   B: Sorry, I was *seeing/watching* the match on TV.
10. Shhh! I can't *listen to/hear* what they are saying!
11. He *sounds/looks* terrible! Even I can sing better than that!

2C Adjectives

1 a Complete the adjectives with a suffix in the box.

| -able | -ant | -ed | -ful | -ial | -ing | -ious |
| -ive | -ous | | | | | |

1. It's so quiet and peace____ here, I love it.
2. The holiday was very relax____, I didn't do much!
3. The show wasn't so enjoy____, I was pretty bored.
4. He was crazy, I was actually quite frighten____.
5. The cake was delic____, thank you!
6. The journey was really unpleas____. It was hot and took ten hours!
7. Don't be so negat____, things will be OK in the end.
8. That's really danger____, don't touch it!
9. It's a spec____ day for me today – it's my birthday!

b Complete the table with the adjectives. Use the suffixes in Exercise 1a to help you.

noun	verb	adjectives
drink	drink	*drinkable*
finance	finance	
stress	stress	
creation	create	
anxiety	-	
disappointment	disappoint	/
poison	poison	
attraction	attract	
help	help	
importance	-	

c Complete the sentences with the adjectives in Exercise 1b.
1. Are you sure the water is ___*drinkable*___? I don't want to get sick.
2. He's very _____. Why doesn't he have a girlfriend?
3. I never give my _____ details over the telephone.
4. I like to work with _____ people who have lots of ideas.
5. I feel a little _____ when I meet new people. I'm shy, you see.
6. The staff are not very _____ here. They just ignore me!
7. I think it's _____ to be honest with people.
8. We were _____ with the service. They forgot our drinks and the meal was cold!
9. I don't think we have any _____ snakes in this country, do we?
10. Living in a big city can be _____. Everything happens so fast!
11. The film was quite _____. It was easy to guess the ending.

3A *get*

1 a Choose the correct meaning of the phrases in bold.
1. I hope he **gets in touch** soon. He hasn't answered my calls all week.
   - a makes contact
   - b becomes fit
2. I don't **get what she's saying**. Does she want to do it or not?
   - a believe what she's saying
   - b understand what she's saying
3. I **got a bonus** yesterday. I'm so pleased!
   - a received a bonus
   - b gave a bonus
4. Can you **get me a sandwich** while you're out?
   - a buy me a sandwich
   - b give me a sandwich
5. I'm **getting tired** of all these lies.
   - a becoming tired
   - b feeling tired
6. I think we all **get on** quite **well**. We hardly ever argue.
   - a have a good relationship
   - b communicate our ideas
7. What time did you **get here**?
   - a leave
   - b arrive

b Match the sentence halves.
1. It was a long day, I didn't get
2. I'm afraid Giulia and I don't get
3. After ten years here, I'm starting to get
4. If you're going to the supermarket, can you get
5. That's nice, I got
6. Remember the girl I met on the app? She never got
7. Some people loved the film, but I didn't get

a in touch with me again after our first date.
b a birthday card from my boss.
c it at all.
d me a cold drink?
e on well. She doesn't like me for some reason.
f bored of this city.
g home til after midnight.

c Rewrite the sentences using a phrase with *get*.
1. We don't have a good relationship.
   We don't get on well.
2. I don't understand what he's saying.
   _____
3. Do you think he'll contact you?
   _____
4. I arrived about half an hour ago.
   _____
5. If you're going to the shops, can you buy me a drink?
   _____

3C Prepositions of place

1 a Match directions 1–3 with pictures A–C. Where are the people going in each picture?
1. Cross the road, then go **through** the square with the fountain **on your right**. It's **next to** the post office
2. Go **over** the bridge, then cross the road. Go **around** the lake, and it's **on the right**.
3. Walk **along** this road for about 50 metres. After the supermarket, turn left and walk **across** the car park. It's on the other side of the road, **between** the bank and the cinema.

4B Products

1 a Match words 1–9 with photos A–I.
1 a fitness tracker
2 a laptop
3 a tablet
4 make-up
5 perfume/aftershave
6 a console
7 an e-reader
8 luggage
9 jewellery

b Work in pairs and discuss your favourite brands for some of the products in Exercise 1a.

4C Word building: nouns

1 a Complete the table with the correct adjectives and nouns.

adjective	noun
popular	popularity
	action
	reliability
animated	
environmental	
	romance
	tiredness

b Complete the groups of nouns with a suffix in the box.

| -ance | -ation | -ence | -ion | -ity | -ment | -ness |

1 educ*ation*
2 reponsibil_____
3 govern_____
4 excell_____
5 happi_____
6 instruct_____
7 appear_____

relax*ation*
electric_____
advertise_____
differ_____
late_____
fash_____
import_____

applic*ation*
creativ_____
excite_____
conveni_____
dark_____
complet_____
dist_____

c Choose the correct alternatives.
1 I think life is very *different/ difference* these days.
2 I don't think you need money to be *happy/ happiness*.
3 I hate *late/ lateness*. I really don't like waiting for people to arrive.
4 I shop online as I like the *convenient/ convenience*.
5 Last week we had no *electrical/ electricity*. We had to eat dinner in the dark!
6 Working with *creative/ creativity* people is great.
7 A lot of people go on holiday for sun, sand and *relaxed/ relaxation*.
8 I think a healthy diet is very *important/ importance*.

d Complete the sentences with the correct words in Exercise 1b.
1 I think it'd be very hard to live without running water or _____ity.
2 The show is good but there are too many _____ments.
3 He changed his _____ance by growing a beard.
4 Some people get angry about _____ness, but I think it's OK to arrive at any time you want.
5 What's the _____ence between *say* and *tell*?
6 I like living in the centre of town because of the _____ence, everything is so close.
7 I don't care about _____ion, I wear what I want.
8 I can't understand these _____ions for the washing machine. Which one is the cold wash?

5A Clothes and accessories

1 a Match words 1–10 with photos A–J.

1. earrings
2. scarf
3. trainers
4. belt
5. sandals
6. high heels
7. bracelet
8. tie
9. tracksuit
10. sweatshirt

b Work in pairs and discuss. Do you have many of the items in Exercise 1a? Which ones do you enjoy wearing?

2 Complete the sentences with words from Exercise 1a.

1. I like _____ because they make me a little taller.
2. I'm going running today, but I can't find my _____ or my _____ .
3. These trousers are loose, I'll need to wear a _____ .
4. It's cold today, so put your _____ on to keep your neck warm.
5. It's a formal meeting, so please wear a suit and _____ .

5C Food preparation

1 Match verbs 1–10 with photos A–J.

1. grate
2. fry
3. boil
4. bake
5. chop
6. grill
7. peel
8. stir
9. pour
10. roast

2 Work in pairs and discuss. What can you do with the following foods? Use the verbs in Exercise 1 to help you.

| cheese | chicken | egg | pasta |
| potatoes | soup | | |

140

6B Crime

1 a Complete the sentences with the words in the box.

| a criminal | a judge | a motive | prison |
| a suspect | a thief | a victim | a witness |

1 _____ is a person who the police think may be responsible for a crime.
2 In UK law, _____ decides how long a criminal stays in prison.
3 _____ is a person who saw a crime happen.
4 _____ is the place where criminals are sent.
5 The reason why people commit a crime is _____ .
6 _____ is a person who has broken the law.
7 _____ is a person that a crime happens to.
8 _____ is a person who steals things.

b Choose the correct alternatives.

1 The *witness/judge* saw the criminals running away with the money.
2 The *suspect/judge* decided that the criminal should stay in prison for ten years.
3 The *prison/victim* was a scary place to visit.
4 They decided that she was responsible for the crime because she had a good *motive/criminal*.
5 The police followed the *witnesses/suspects* to see what they would do.
6 The *criminals/victims* stole more than 20,000 euros.
7 The *victim/motive* was very anxious about describing the crime.
8 The police caught the *thief/victim* while she was trying to escape with the jewellery.

c Work in pairs. What connections can you make between the words in Exercise 1a?

A criminal may go to prison if he or she has done something very bad.

6C The environment

1 a Complete the table with the correct nouns and verbs.

noun	verb
destruction	
protection	
	pollute
damage	
waste	

b Complete the sentences with words in Exercise 1a.

1 The _____ of the rainforest leads to an increase in the amount of carbon dioxide in the atmosphere.
2 Scientists worry that permanent _____ to the environment has already been done.
3 We must do more to _____ endangered animals in this country.
4 If we continue to _____ our rivers and seas, many more animals will die.
5 How much food do you _____ each week?

6C Confusing words

1 a Choose the correct alternatives.

1 You *injure/damage* an object, but you *injure/damage* a person or part of your body.
2 You *lose/miss* objects that you have, for example, your wallet. You *lose/miss* things like appointments and transport.
3 When you move away from somewhere, you *take/bring* your things with you. When you move towards somewhere, you *take/bring* your things with you.
4 If you *lend/borrow* something from someone, you take it from them for a period of time. If you *lend/borrow* something to someone you give it to them for a period of time.
5 *Journey/Travel* is countable, but *journey/travel* is uncountable.
6 *Actually/At the moment* means 'in fact'. *Actually/At the moment* means 'at this time'.

b Choose the correct alternatives.

1 That driver *injured/damaged* my car.
2 She *injured/damaged* her foot last week and she's finding it hard to walk.
3 I was late today because I *lost/missed* the bus.
4 I *lost/missed* my umbrella today. I have no idea where I put it.
5 When you come tonight, can you *bring/take* my jacket?
6 When you go home today, remember to *bring/take* your phone. You left it here yesterday.
7 Can you ask before you *lend/borrow* my clothes, please?
8 Can you *lend/borrow* me your suitcase? I'm going away for the weekend.
9 I think *journey/travel* is really good for people.
10 I went on an interesting *journey/travel* last year.
11 I thought it would be terrible, but *actually/at the moment* it was pretty good.
12 Are you doing anything exciting *actually/at the moment*?

7C Compound nouns

A B C D E F G H I J

1 a Match compound nouns 1–10 with photos A–J.
   1 headphones
   2 a passport
   3 a tennis racket
   4 a swimsuit
   5 a can opener
   6 a basketball
   7 running shoes
   8 a guidebook
   9 sunscreen
   10 a toothbrush

b Which of these things do you usually take on holiday with you?

2 a Complete the pairs of sentences using the same word.
   1 a She went on holiday and got a good _____ tan.
     b I might need my _____ hat if it gets hotter than this!
   2 a Have you seen my _____ pack? I need it for my hiking trip.
     b I've got bad _____ ache this morning. Maybe I slept in a strange position.
   3 a Did you get her a birthday _____ this year, or did you forget?
     b I left my credit _____ at home today, so can you pay for lunch?
   4 a I have a note _____ but I never write anything in it.
     b I'm going to need more _____ shelves soon, there's no more space for them all!
   5 a You don't have _____ conditioning in your flat? But it's so hot!
     b I bought all my presents at the _____ port, just before flying home.
   6 a Do you have a sofa _____ in your place? If so, can I stay this weekend?
     b It's an amazing place, with three _____ rooms.
   7 a My flat _____ is really annoying. He never cleans up.
     b My office is very sociable. I often go out with my work _____ s on Fridays.
   8 a I put your books in the _____ board, so you don't lose them again.
     b Can you pass me my coffee _____ ? It's the blue one.

b Are compound nouns always one word, always two words, or can they be either?

142

8A Multi-word verbs

1 a Choose the correct alternatives.
1. If you **look after** someone, you *care for/try to find* him or her.
2. If you are **looking forward to** something, you are *excited/worried* about it.
3. If you **take after** someone in your family, you *are similar to/don't like* him or her.
4. If you **take up** golf, you *start/stop* doing it.
5. If you **get over** an illness or bad event, you feel *better/worse*.
6. If you **get in** a car, you *enter/leave* it.
7. If you **put** something **back**, you *take/return* it.
8. If you **put off** doing something, you decide to do it *earlier/later* than you planned.

b Complete the sentences with words in Exercise 1a.
1. I take _____ my father. We are so similar!
2. Can you please put your clothes _____ in the wardrobe?
3. I'm looking _____ to my holiday.
4. I'm not getting _____ that ugly car.
5. I look _____ my nephew every weekend.
6. I think I'll put _____ going to the dentist til next month.
7. I love taking _____ new sports.
8. I'll never get _____ this cold.

c Match sentences 1–8 in Exercise 1b with pictures A–H.

2 a Write one more thing that you use with each multi-word verb.
1. put back: a book, _____*a pen*_____
2. get over: a cold, _____
3. put off: visiting your family, _____
4. take up: painting, _____
5. look forward to: travelling, _____
6. look after: my friend's cat, _____
7. take after: your father, _____

b Complete the sentences with your own ideas.
1. I'm really looking forward to …
2. I'd like to take up …
3. I don't think you should get in a car with …
4. I always put off doing …
5. It's hard for people to get over …
6. I take after …
7. I don't like looking after …
8. I always forget to put back …

c Work in pairs and compare your answers.

143

9B Extremes

1 a Match sentences 1–8 with photos A–H.
1. It's **freezing** outside today.
2. When the sun is out, it's absolutely **boiling**.
3. When he heard I was leaving the company, he was **shocked**.
4. Wow, those buildings are **enormous**!
5. This place is so **ancient**. Imagine the people who used to sit here.
6. The news today was **awful**, I was really upset.
7. They found the presentation **fascinating**.
8. She was **delighted** with her gift.

b Complete the table with the adjectives in the box.

ancient	awful	big	boiling	cold
happy	interesting	surprised		

strong	weak
freezing	
	hot
shocked	
enormous	
	old
	bad
fascinating	
delighted	

2 Complete the sentences with the strong adjectives in Exercise 1b.
1. I'm not going to eat there again. The food was _____ and it was expensive.
2. She was _____ with her present. It was exactly what she wanted.
3. The book is _____. I couldn't put it down. You must read it.
4. The house is _____. There are more than five bedrooms.
5. It's _____ in here, let's put the heating on.
6. That dress is _____! I bought it so long ago but I love it.

10A *say, tell* and *speak*

1 Complete the word webs with the words in the box.

about something goodbye a language nothing on the phone ~~quietly~~ someone a secret someone something a story ~~the truth~~ what you think with someone ~~yes~~

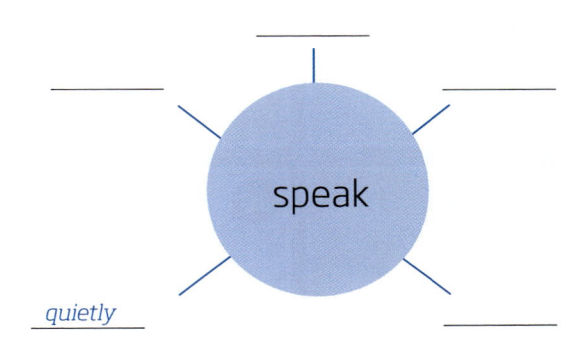

say: yes, ___, ___, ___

tell: the truth, ___, ___, ___

speak: ___, ___, quietly, ___, ___, ___

2 a Complete the sentences with the words and phrases in Exercise 1.
1 I was surprised when she said _____ to my plan! I thought she'd hate it.
2 I'd love to speak another _____. One day I might learn Japanese.
3 The presenter was speaking _____ changes to the environment.
4 Why can't you tell us _____? We know you took it.
5 I don't like complaining. I prefer to say _____.
6 I spoke _____ John this morning and we agreed it was a bad idea.
7 Jessica told me a great _____ about how her parents met.
8 Could you tell _____ which buses go to Toledo?
9 Just be honest, say _____. I promise I won't cry!
10 I hate it when people speak loudly _____. It drives me crazy!

b Complete the sentences with your own ideas.
1 I would say yes if someone offered me _____.
2 I would love to speak with _____. That would be so interesting.
3 _____ is a person who I always tell my secrets to.
4 I'd rather say nothing than _____.
5 I'd love to hear _____ speaking about _____.
6 I _____ tell the truth.
7 If I could speak another language, it would be _____.
8 It would be difficult to say goodbye to _____.

c Work in pairs and compare your ideas in Exercise 2b.

Communication games

First to finish! (Units 1–2 review)

Work in groups. Write numbers 1-6 on pieces of paper and put them in a bag. Take turns to take a number and move along the squares. Follow the instructions in the square. The first person to reach FINISH wins.

15 If someone makes a suggestion that you don't agree with, what can you say?

14 Make a suggestion for someone who wants to eat more healthily.

13 Give two verbs that mean 'go down'.

12 Tell the group one way in which your life will change in the future.

11 Share a prediction for the future of work with the group.

10 Would you like to work *part time* or *full time*? Why?

16 What's an adjective that describes how you feel after a long day?

27 Tell the group about a time you felt *homesick*.

26 What's the missing word? *It reminds me _____ home.*

25 Tell the group about a positive experience you've had.

24 Tell the group about a place you visited where you had a happy experience.

9 What's the opposite of *shy*?

17 Tell the group what you were doing at 4 p.m. yesterday.

28 Tell the group about a time when someone helped you.

29 What's the missing word? *What _____ next?*

30 FINISH

23 Tell the group about something you didn't use to like when you were a child.

8 Tell the group something that you're going to do next weekend.

18 Tell the group about a time when you felt disappointed.

19 Tell the group three things you did last weekend.

20 Tell the group about your earliest memory.

21 What sound makes you feel happy?

22 Tell the group about a game you used to play when you were a child.

7 Tell the group three adjectives to describe your personality.

1 START

2 Tell the group why you're studying English.

3 What's the missing word? *graduate _____ university.*

4 Tell the group three things you like doing in your spare time.

5 What's the opposite of *paid work*?

6 Tell the group two of your goals in life.

True or False (Unit 3–4 review)

1 Write answers to the questions in the boxes. In eight of your answers you should tell the truth, and in seven of your answers tell a lie.

Have you taken up a new sport in the last two years?	What's your favourite season?	When was the last time you ate in a restaurant?
What type of film was the last one you watched?	What's your job?	What did you think of the last meal you had?
How far is your home from the school?	Which company do you think provides excellent customer service?	Have you ever performed in a play?
How many messages have you sent today?	What's your favourite museum?	What type of films do you like? Use adjectives (*I like films which/that are …*)
Who do you like to spend time with at the weekend?	Which place to eat where you live offers the best value?	What's your favourite brand? Why? (Use a superlative.)

2 Work in pairs. Take turns to ask each other the questions. Ask follow up questions and decide if your partner is lying or telling the truth. You get one point if you're correct. The person with the most points wins!

A: What's your job?
B: I'm an engineer.
A: Do you like it?
B: Yes, it's really interesting!
A: What company do you work for?

Cross the lake (Units 5–6 review)

- Work in pairs. You both need to cross the lake one square at a time, either horizontally, diagonally or vertically.
- Student A starts at the top of the lake, Student B starts at the bottom.
- Choose a square and follow the instructions. If you are successful, you win that square. If the other person has already won a square, you can't use it. The winner is the person who reaches the other side first.

START A

Complete the sentence: *Unless it rains at the weekend,…*	Give two pieces of advice for someone going to a job interview.	Complete the sentence: *If I had a helicopter, …*	Describe your diet. (Use quantifiers)	What type of clothes do you wear to work/school?
What's the opposite of *innocent*?	Think of a sentence with this question tag: *… , can't we?*	Someone asks you to help with their work, but you're very busy. What do you say?	Describe the type of clothes you usually like to wear.	Correct this sentence: *I eat lot of fruit.*
What are your three favourite foods and what adjectives can you use to describe them?	Respond negatively to the request: *Could you put these away for me?*	What's the opposite of *polite*?	What do you need to do to your mobile phone when the battery is empty?	What do we call a system which makes a house warm?
Correct the mistake in this sentence: *They seem be very upset.*	Your friend is stressed at work and can't sleep. Give them three pieces of advice.	Complete the sentence: *I wouldn't do my homework if, …*	Complete the sentence: *When I'm late for work/school, …*	Say three ways our lives would be different if we didn't have the internet.
How long does it take you to get dressed in the morning? Why?	Ask someone to help you with your homework: a) politely, b) very politely.	Say three things you can do to help the environment.	What's the opposite of *switch on*?	Correct the mistake in this sentence: *You ought say sorry to her.*

START B

Roadmap race (Units 7-8 review)

Work in groups. Write numbers 1–6 on pieces of paper and put them in a bag. Take turns to take a number and move along the squares. If you answer the question correctly, stay on the square. If your answer is incorrect move back to the square you were on before. The first person to reach FINISH wins.

START

1. Complete the sentence: *Thankfully, _____*
2. Complete the sentence: *When I go camping, I sleep in a sleeping _____*
3. What's the missing word? *I've never been _____ to swim well.*
4. Correct this mistake: *When I arrived, she already went out.*
5. Say two multi-word verbs with *away*.
6. What can you describe as *sandy*?
7. Say three things you need to take with you when you go camping.
8. You're late for class. Apologise.
9. Say two positive adverbs and two negative adverbs.
10. What's the missing word? *You'll need a waterproof jacket in _____ to stay dry.*
11. What's the missing word? *They met at university and _____ in love.*
12. Say three life events you've experienced.
13. Which verb goes with *confidence* and *experience*?
14. Say three things you'd done before you went to bed last night.
15. What's the missing word? *Look at this mess! _____ it up immediately!*
16. Name something you'll be able to do in the future.
17. Say three reasons why you're learning English. Use the infinitive.
18. What's the missing word? *The forest, where you can see very tall trees, is very old. It's _____*
19. Which verb goes with *photos* and *your work*?
20. Say something you couldn't do when you were younger, which you can now.
21. Which verb goes with *an award*?
22. Combine the sentences: *The mountain has steep sides. It's the tallest mountain in the country.*
23. Say three rules you had at school.
24. What's the missing word? *Do you _____ part-time classes at your school?*
25. What's the missing word? *You need to hand _____ your homework tomorrow.*
26. You made a mess in the kitchen. Explain why.
27. Make this sentence passive: *Teachers didn't use computers when I was at school.*
28. Are these sentences the same or different. Why?: *You mustn't wear jeans. You don't have to wear jeans.*
29. Call a hotel to find out if they have any free rooms next weekend.
30. Make this sentence passive: *They are giving young people new opportunities.*

FINISH

Keep talking (Units 9–10 review)

- Play in two teams. Each team chooses a topic from the table. You have two minutes to plan what to say.
- Try to talk about your topic for 30 seconds to win one or two points.
- Repeat four more times, choosing different topics.
- The team with the most points wins!

- Describe your school days (1 point)
- Use at least two reported statements. (2 points)

- Describe what we can do to make cities 'greener' (1 point)
- Use the verbs *recommend* and *encourage* correctly. (2 points)

- Describe your favourite shop (1 point)
- Use at least two passive sentences. (2 points)

- Give some advice on learning English (1 point)
- Use 'suggest' and 'recommend' (2 points)

- Describe how you feel about modern art (1 point)
- Use at least four adjectives. (2 points)

- Describe how to use a website you know about (1 point)
- Use at least two passive sentences. (2 points)

- Describe the last time someone gave you useful advice (1 point)
- Use the verbs *warn* and *avoid*. (2 points)

- Describe your last day at work or school (1 point)
- Use at least two reported questions. (2 points)

- Report a question that you were asked in an interview. (2 points)

- Describe the last film you saw with someone else (1 point)
- Use *so* and *neither*. (2 points)

- Describe the last time you had to complain (1 point)
- Use at least two phrases for complaining politely. (2 points)

- Describe something you regret (1 point)
- Use at least two third conditional sentences. (2 points)

- Explain the difference between a *bargain* and a *special* offer. (2 points)

- Describe a time you had to ask for a refund (1 point)
- Use at least two shopping phrases. (2 points)

- Describe your ideal job (1 point)
- Use at least four work phrases. (2 points)

- Describe some good news you've had (1 point)
- Use at least four adjectives. (2 points)

Communication bank

Lesson 3D

5

Student A

1. Look at the map. You are at 📍. Ask your partner for directions to Edinburgh Castle
2. Give your partner directions. Your partner is at 📍.

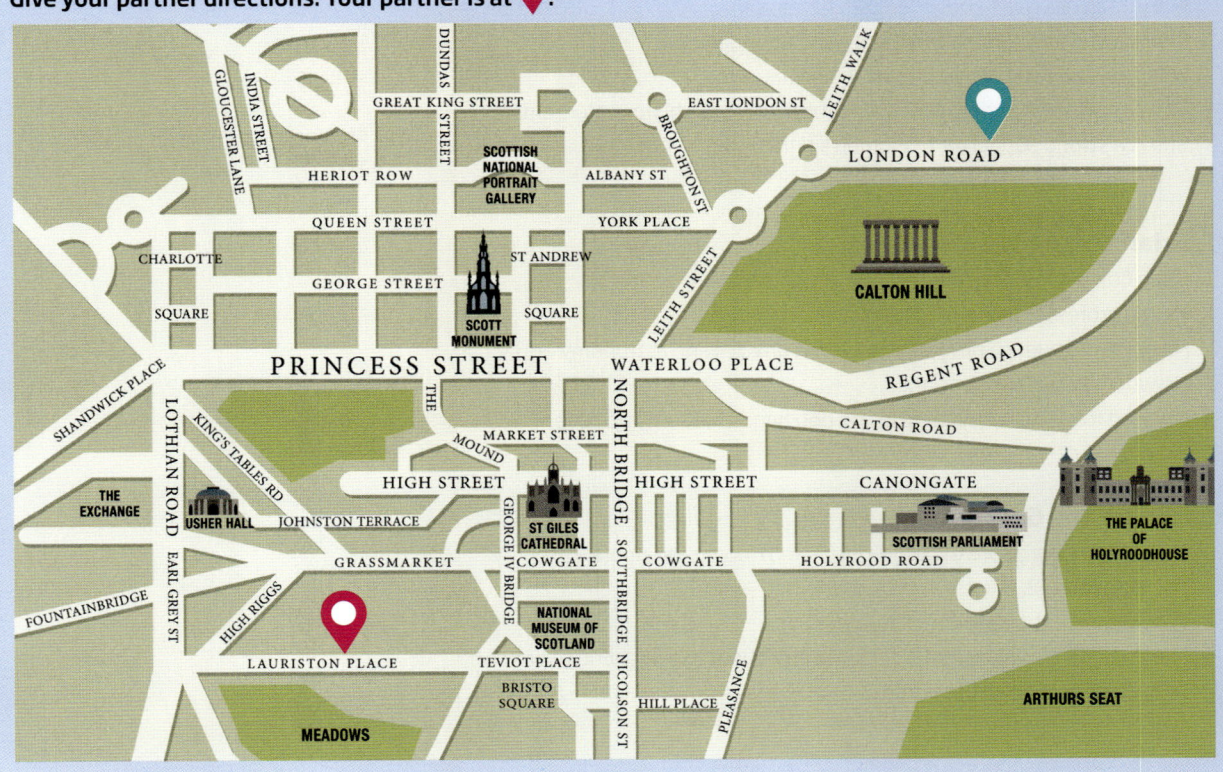

Lesson 5B

11

Student A

1. You're looking for somewhere new to live. Listen to Student B and ask questions about the two types of accommodation they show you. Then decide which place you prefer.
2. You're an estate agent. Student B is looking for somewhere new to live. Ask them what things are important to them. Then talk about the two places in the adverts. Use the Useful phrases to help you.

A Detached house on the edge of the town. Big kitchen and living room. Three bedrooms. No cupboards. One bathroom – needs some repairs. Near shops and underground station. Twenty minutes from town centre.
Rent: 600 euros per month.

B Large studio apartment. Very modern. Close to city centre. Separate large kitchen and bathroom. No pets.
Rent: 450 euros per week.

Useful phrases
This house/apartment has got …
If you want a … , you will …
If you're a … person, you need …
This place is perfect for you because …

Lesson 5A
13a

Mary Beard
Mary Beard is a well-known English historian.
She is a professor at the University of Cambridge.
She is a writer and active on social media.
She has often appeared on TV presenting her own history programme.
She is a strong supporter of women's rights.

Brian Cox
Brian Cox is an English physicist.
He is a professor at Manchester University.
He presents science programmes about physics and astronomy on TV.
He writes books about science.
He used to play the keyboard in the pop bands D:Ream and Dare.

Gilbert and George
Gilbert and George are Gilbert Proesch and George Passmore.
They are famous artists.
They produce their artworks together.
Their work is usually brightly coloured and about the East End of London.
They live and work in London.

Lesson 5B
11

Student B

1 You're an estate agent. Student A is looking for somewhere new to live. Ask them what things are important to them. Then talk about the two places in the adverts. Use the Useful phrases to help you.

A Two-bedroomed flat in beautiful block of flats in the old town. Quiet neighbourhood. Near shops and bus stops. No central heating or lift. Staircase only.
Rent: 400 euros per month.

B Small terraced house near the town centre. Two bedrooms, kitchen and living room. Small patio at the back. No garage. Suitable for couple with no children.
Rent 500 euros per week.

Useful phrases
This house/apartment has got …
If you want a … , you will …
If you're a … person, you need …
This place is perfect for you because …

2 You're looking for somewhere new to live. Listen to Student A and ask questions about the two types of accommodation they show you. Then decide which place you prefer.

Lesson 3D

5

Student B

1 Look at the map. Give your partner directions. Your partner is at 📍.
2 You are at 📍. Ask your partner for directions to the Scottish National Portrait Gallery.

Lesson 7D

6

Student A

1 Listen to Student B. Use the information to answer Student B's questions.

   You are the manager of a restaurant. You offer:
   - a room for special events evenings and weekends.
   - rooms for children's parties.
   - special party menus and birthday cakes.
   - a promotional price of £10 per person.

   Entertainment can be provided at customer's own cost.

2 You're at the train station in Pemberley. You want to go to Liverpool. Ask the person at the Information desk for help. You want to know about:
   - train times – how often trains run when the next train leaves.
   - how much a return ticket costs.
   - how long the journey takes.
   - if it is a direct train or if you have to change.
   - what platform the train leaves from.

Lesson 7D

4b

Student B

1. You're organising a birthday party for a child. You'd like to have it at a local restaurant. Call the restaurant to find out:
   - if you can book the restaurant for a children's birthday party.
   - if they can make a special menu for the party.
   - if they can make a birthday cake.
   - if they can book an entertainer like a clown or a magician.
   - if you can have the party on a Sunday afternoon.
   - how much it will cost.

2. Listen to Student A. Use the information on the train timetable to answer Student A's questions.

Train times
Direct trains to Liverpool:

Depart Pemberley	Arrive Liverpool
09.32	10.42
(10.32) Next train	11.42
11.32	12.42
12.32	13.42
13.32	14.42
14.32	15.42
15.32	16.42
16.32	17.42
17.32	18.42
18.32	19.42
19.32	20.42
20.32	21.42
21.32	22.42
22.32	23.42

*Usual platform of departure: Platform 1.

Fares
Single: £34
Return: £44

Lesson 5A

13a

Look at the people and make guesses about them. Think about:
- their personalities
- their ages
- their jobs
- their interests

Mary Beard

Brian Cox

Gilbert and George

Lesson 6B

11

You're going to ask your partner for advice about a problem. Read about the problem in the text below and think about how you can explain it in your own words to your partner.

> **Student A**
> You have a friend who has been shoplifting regularly. You went shopping with her recently, and you saw her take a T-shirt and go to the dressing room to try it on. She came out without the T-shirt, but you thought she left it in the dressing room. When you went out of the shop together, she told you that she was wearing the T-shirt under her sweater. She thought it was funny. You told her shoplifting is a crime but she laughed at you. What should you do?

Lesson 5D

4a

Student A

Making a tomato salad

Ingredients

4 large tomatoes
– ready to eat.
1 onion
1 cucumber
Olive oil
Cheese

1. Cut the tomatoes into big pieces.
2. Cut the onion and the cucumber into small pieces.
3. Add olive oil and mix everything together.
4. Grate some cheese.
5. Put cheese on top of the salad.
6. Serve and eat.

Lesson 5D
4b

Student B

Making a cup of tea the British way

Ingredients

Tea (1 bag for each person)
Water
Milk
Sugar (optional)

1. Boil the water.
2. Add tea to the teapot.
3. Pour water into the teapot.
4. Leave it for a few minutes.
5. Pour tea into a cup.
6. Add milk and sugar.

Lesson 6B
11

You're going to give your partner for advice, and also ask them for advice about a problem. Read about your problem in the text below and think about how you can explain it in your own words to your partner.

Student B
You work near a school and several times when the children are leaving school you have seen three older children push or hit a younger child and take their school bag. You are sure it is the same three older children each time. What should you do?

Lesson 8B
10

Student A
Read the information about the artist Frida Kahlo and answer the questions. Then use your answers to tell her story in your own words.
1. Who was Frida Kahlo?
2. Why is she famous?
3. What happened to her when she was a child?
4. What happened when she was 18? What were the results?
5. When did she start painting?
6. What kind of pictures did she paint?

Frida Kahlo
- twentieth-century Mexican artist
- very successful – her work is known around the world and is bought by international museums
- caught the disease polio at six years old – walking was difficult for her
- did different sports, including boxing
- badly injured in a bus accident at 18 years old – had to use a wheelchair
- started painting while recovering from the accident
- often in terrible pain
- most paintings are pictures of herself – they show her pain and sadness

Lesson 10D
5

Student A

1. You're going to interview Student B for the job below. Read the advert and decide what questions to ask.

Waiting staff
Are you looking for fun and well-paid work that can fit around your studies?
We are looking for intelligent and reliable people to join our team, with or without previous experience.
Work opportunities include:
- waiting at tables in top restaurants.
- answering customers' questions.
- serving customers from all over the world.

You need to have good spoken English, excellent communication skills and be available evenings and weekends.
Education level: Secondary school or above.
If you are interested and can start work immediately, please contact us.

2. It's time for the interview! Ask Student B questions.

3. You're going to have an interview for the job below. Read the advert and think of questions you might be asked and how to answer them.

Web designer
We're looking for enthusiastic and creative web designers to join a small, friendly and creative team in an exciting new software company.
We're looking for someone:
- who is excited about technology.
- who wants to create new and interesting products.
- who has excellent communication skills.
- who has relevant qualifications.

Excellent salary for the right person.
If you'd like to learn more, register on our website and give us a call as we'd love to hear from you.

4. It's time for your interview! Answer Student A's questions. Use the Useful phrases on page 84 to help you.

Lesson 9C

9

1 The town council want to commission a new piece of public art for your town centre. Look at the photos and information about possible pieces of art A–D, and think about questions 1–4 below.

1. Will it look good in the town centre?
2. Will the general public feel proud of it? Or will they think it's a waste of money?
3. Will it make visitors want to come to the town to see it?
4. Will it cost a lot of money to look after?

Useful phrases
What do you think about this one?
I'm not sure I agree with you.
That's a good point.
Let's vote.
So, we've decided on this one, right? Do we all agree?

A The sculpture will be made of recycled metal so it will be good for the environment.
B This piece was made by local children. It will help people remember their connection with the natural world.
C This piece has attractive bright colours, and will be made from steel which is produced in our local factory.
D This piece of artwork will make interesting noises when the wind blows through it. It will be created by the most famous artist this town has ever had.

2 Discuss which of the pieces of art your town should choose. Use the Useful phrases to help you.

Lesson 10D

5

Student B

1 You're going to have an interview for the job below. Read the advert and think of questions you might be asked and how to answer them.

> **Waiting staff**
> Are you looking for fun and well-paid work that can fit around your studies?
> We are looking for intelligent and reliable people to join our team, with or without previous experience.
> Work opportunities include:
> - waiting at tables in top restaurants.
> - answering customers' questions.
> - serving customers from all over the world.
>
> You need to have good spoken English, excellent communication skills and be available evenings and weekends.
> Education level: Secondary school or above.
> If you are interested and can start work immediately, please contact us.

2 It's time for your interview! Answer Student A's questions. Use the Useful phrases on page 84 to help you.

3 Now you're going to interview Student A for the job below. Read the advert and decide what questions to ask.

> **Web designer**
> We're looking for enthusiastic and creative web designers to join a small, friendly and creative team in an exciting new software company.
> We're looking for someone:
> - who is excited about technology.
> - who wants to create new and interesting products.
> - who has excellent communication skills.
> - who has relevant qualifications.
>
> Excellent salary for the right person.
> If you'd like to learn more, register on our website and give us a call as we'd love to hear from you.

4 It's time for the interview! Ask Student A questions.

Lesson 8B

10

Student B
Read the information about Iqbal Masih and answer the questions. Then use your answers to tell his story in your own words.

1 Where was Iqbal born?
2 What happened to him when he was a child?
3 What happened when he was 10?
4 What did he do then?
5 What happened to him when he was 12?
6 Was he successful?

Iqbal Masih
- born in Pakistan – had a terrible childhood
- sent to work in a carpet factory by his father at age 4
- was not looked after well by the owner – worked 12 hours a day, not enough to eat, couldn't leave the factory
- in 1993 at the age of 10, Iqbal escaped
- decided to help other children – went to other factories and told the children about their human rights; gave speeches in public
- went to school – wanted to be a lawyer
- killed when he was 12
- thousands of children became free because of him.
- today more than 20 *Iqbal Masih Shaheed Children's Foundation* schools around Pakistan

Irregular verbs

Verb	Past simple	Past participle
be	was	been
become	became	become
begin	began	begun
bite	bit	bitten
blow	blew	blown
break	broke	broken
bring	brought	brought
build	built	built
buy	bought	bought
catch	caught	caught
choose	chose	chosen
come	came	come
cost	cost	cost
cut	cut	cut
do	did	done
draw	drew	drawn
drink	drank	drunk
drive	drove	driven
eat	ate	eaten
fall	fell	fallen
feel	felt	felt
find	found	found
fly	flew	flown
forget	forgot	forgotten
freeze	froze	frozen
get	got	got
give	gave	given
go	went	gone
grow	grew	grown
have	had	had
hear	heard	heard
hide	hid	hidden
hit	hit	hit
hold	held	held
hurt	hurt	hurt
keep	kept	kept
know	knew	known
learn	learned/learnt	learned/learnt
leave	left	left

Verb	Past simple	Past participle
lend	lent	lent
let	let	let
lie	lay	lain
lose	lost	lost
make	made	made
mean	meant	meant
meet	met	met
pay	paid	paid
put	put	put
read	read	read
ride	rode	ridden
ring	rang	rung
run	ran	run
say	said	said
see	saw	seen
sell	sold	sold
send	sent	sent
shine	shone	shone
show	showed	shown
shut	shut	shut
sing	sang	sung
sit	sat	sat
sleep	slept	slept
smell	smelled/smelt	smelled/smelt
speak	spoke	spoken
spend	spent	spent
spill	spilled/spilt	spilled/spilt
stand	stood	stood
swim	swam	swum
take	took	taken
teach	taught	taught
tell	told	told
think	thought	thought
throw	threw	thrown
understand	understood	understood
wake	woke	woken
wear	wore	worn
win	won	won
write	wrote	written